IMAGES
*of America*

# TELFAIR COUNTY

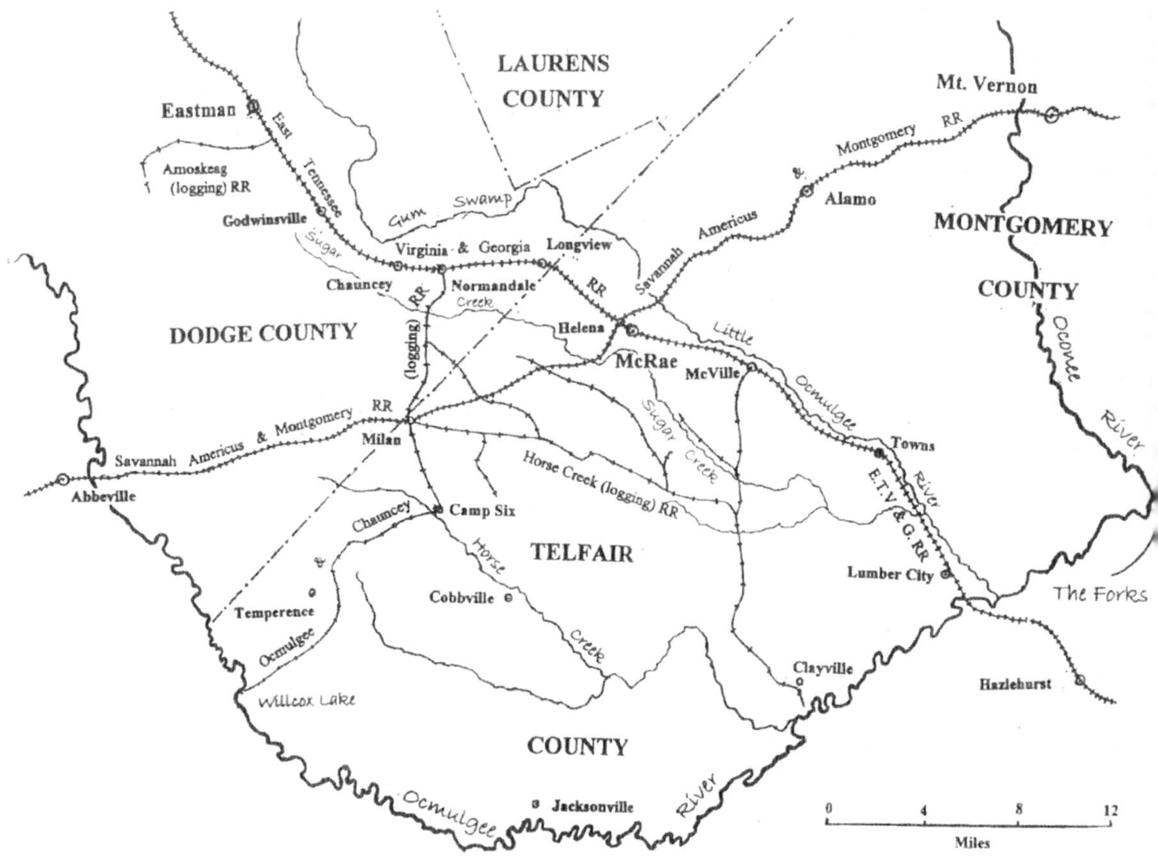


Telfair County, Georgia, lies between the Ocmulgee River and the Little Ocmulgee River. These two rivers meet at a place called the Forks, forming the mighty Altamaha River. Much of Telfair's history is involved with these legendary waterways. For years, giant longleaf yellow pines were formed into rafts and floated down to Darien and St. Simons, where they were then sold. Due to the steady harvesting of these majestic trees, they have been depleted and may never make a comeback. (Courtesy of Chris Trowell.)

**On the Cover:** In this 1936 photograph, a crowd of supporters of Gene Talmadge gathers in front of the old McRae's Pharmacy under a banner that refers to the colorful and controversial candidate as the "Sage of Sugar Creek." He also was often referred to as "the wild man from Sugar Creek" because of his unorthodox manner of communicating and his legendary red suspenders, which his almost gaunt frame certainly did not require. This campaign photograph was taken during his heated race against Sen. Richard Russell for the US Senate. (Courtesy of the Kenan Research Center at the Atlanta History Center.)

IMAGES
*of America*

# TELFAIR COUNTY

Jane H. Walker and Robert E. Herndon
Foreword by Jim Wooten

ARCADIA
PUBLISHING

ISBN 978-1-4671-1376-2

Published by Arcadia Publishing
Charleston, South Carolina

Printed in the United States of America

Library of Congress Control Number: 2014950860

For all general information, please contact Arcadia Publishing:
Telephone 843-853-2070
Fax 843-853-0044
E-mail sales@arcadiapublishing.com
For customer service and orders:
Toll-Free 1-888-313-2665

Visit us on the Internet at www.arcadiapublishing.com

*With love and appreciation, we dedicate this book to the people of Telfair County, who constantly strive to make our county a better place to live.*

# Contents

# Foreword

In a noteworthy 1946 election, some Telfair County residents had the foresight to switch their allegiance from famous father to soon-to-be famous son. Their write-in decision spawned one of America's most chaotic political transitions, the so-called "Three Governors Controversy." The episode was noteworthy for two primary reasons. One is that it extended the Talmadge political dynasty that rose from Telfair County to dominate Georgia for half a century. Eugene, dubbed "the wild man from Sugar Creek," was one of only two governors in the state's history to be elected to four terms. His son Herman followed with six years as governor and 24 as a US senator. That write-in effort also established Telfair voters as unusually dedicated. An *Atlanta Journal* reporter won a Pulitzer Prize for discovering that some in the Helena precinct had risen from the grave, and others had stood in line in alphabetical order to vote.

Not entirely in jest, I note that there was a certain basis for believing that the living might know the political preferences of the dead. Walk into any church cemetery outside the county seat and you will likely discover that virtually everybody interred there is related by blood or marriage. Such were the bonds of early settlers, many of Scotch descent, who migrated from the Carolinas, attracted by the availability of the area's rich, fertile land. Generations later, those who moved to larger cities were guided in the same way: word-of-mouth, family-connected networks. One's toehold was another's opening to a more prosperous future.

For this book, Jane Walker, one of Georgia's premiere writers, is joined by another historian intimately familiar with this community, Robert Herndon. Their combined talents tell the story of those who have lived in and built Telfair County. Walker has additionally written, with coauthor Chris Trowell, a splendid account of the most consequential story affecting this county since its 1807 founding. The book *The Dodge Land Troubles: 1868–1923* and a companion novel she wrote, *Widow of Sighing Pines*, are must-reads.

—Jim Wooten

# Acknowledgments

For their photographic loans and other special assistance, we wish to thank the following individuals: Paula R. Anderson, Thomas Wayne Anderson, Bill Babb, H.B. Barnes, John Bartlett, Mary Margaret McRae Batcha, Dr. Dennis Blanton, LaJoy Boney, Sarah Bowen, Brian Brown, Marjorie Burch, Melissa Carroll, Patricia Cravey, Norwood Davidson, Janet Fields, Elizabeth Garrett, Margaret Hall, Danny Harbin, Eunice Harris, Judy Harris, Robert Herndon, Connie Huddleston, Bill Hunt Jr., Kenneth Jackson, Harriett McClung, Edison McDonald, Virgeline McDonald, Jane McRae, Mickey Nelson, Thomas Ross, Billy Ryals, LoAnn Ryals, Sue Sammons, Frankie Snow, Don Stone, Lynda Talmadge, Eddie Taylor, Chris Trowell, Mike Varnadoe, Billy Ware Walker Jr., Jane Walker, Ruby White, and Rita Williams.

We also want to thank the following organizations for their help: the Five Stars of Harmony, McRae First Baptist Church, Merchants and Citizens Bank, McRae Coca-Cola Bottling Company, the McRae Presbyterian Church, the McRae United Methodist Church, the Telfair County Library, the Telfair Museum of History, the Rotary Club of McRae, and the *Telfair Enterprise*. If we have omitted any names and organizations, we are deeply sorry.

# INTRODUCTION

Hundreds of years ago, the land that became Telfair County, Georgia, was covered with longleaf pine as far as the eye could see. It teemed with Native Americans, who used the giant trees for firewood and to make their bows, arrows, and canoes, and it was home to many species of wild animals, even the buffalo and the panther.

During the spring and summer of 1540, Hernando de Soto and his entourage of 600 men and horses explored land in Georgia, intermingling with the local Indians and leaving traces of their presence in the area. Recent archaeological excavations point to the possible sojourn of de Soto in Telfair County. Photographs of the archaeological digs and the artifacts discovered from nearly 475 years ago pique the interest of those who call Telfair County home.

Named for Edward Telfair, governor of Georgia, Telfair County was incorporated in 1807. It is theorized that when Sherman burned Atlanta, any existing images of Governor Telfair were destroyed.

At the time of its incorporation, Telfair County was still covered with longleaf pine. When the wind stirred the limbs and the needles of these majestic trees, it caused a moaning or soughing that rippled through the trees. The early Scottish settlers of Telfair used these trees for firewood and constructing their houses. Little did they know what was about to descend upon them on account of this resource.

Northern capitalists heard of the vast growth of longleaf pine in central Georgia and the great wealth it promised to anyone with the know-how and skill necessary to fell the giant trees and send them to the coast. At first, merchants built sawmills at Lumber City, but this venture soon failed. The Civil War intervened between 1860 and 1865, and the timber harvesting was suspended. The late Julian Williams, regional historian and a former resident of Telfair County, wrote *The Confederacy and Old Jacksonville, Ga.*, an intriguing book about the men from our area who fought and died in the War between the States.

In 1868, while the South lay devastated from the war, Northern mercantile capitalists, headed by the William E. Dodge family of New York, came to central Georgia with questionable deeds to 300,000 acres of land in the counties of Telfair, Dodge, Laurens, Pulaski, and Montgomery. The local people held their own deeds to these lands and had paid taxes, some for 50 years and longer. A land war ensued and continued for 40 years between the Northerners and Southerners. They battled it out in court cases, which always seemed to favor the Northerners, and in gun battles, which left people dead on both sides.

If the law of adverse possession had been applied in the court cases, Southerners would certainly have prevailed, for Georgia law decreed that 20 years of possession, even without title, gave a man absolute claim to the land. This is still Georgia law today. Northerners called the residents squatters, claiming Southerners were illegally squatting on their land. The land war was a continuation of the War between the States, for state laws were ignored, and the carpetbaggers from the North were favored by the Republican courts. The last court case was heard and finalized in regard to the land litigations in 1923, some 40 years later, after many people died trying to defend their land.

Though the first county seat of Telfair was in Jacksonville, on the banks of the Ocmulgee River, it was moved to McRae in 1871 after the railroad was built, and depots sprang up in the towns of Helena and McRae. The Ocmulgee River, which runs by the town of Jacksonville, was the scene of Indian raids, and forts were built along the river to protect the local people. This river was also the scene of many rafting trips to the sawmills of Darien and St. Simons. Residents cut their trees and fashioned them into rafts, which they floated down the Ocmulgee and Altamaha Rivers. The river headquarters of the Dodge Land and Lumber Company, headed by William

E. Dodge of New York, was at Willcox Lake on the Ocmulgee River. The main headquarters of the Dodge Land and Lumber Company was at Normandale in Dodge County. On December 13, 1883, an *Eastman Times* article quoted a Clayville man who claimed that he counted over 100 rafts drifting down the river in one day, many of which belonged to the Dodge Land and Lumber Company.

In spite of the chaos of the times, South Georgia College was chartered in McRae and opened its doors to students in 1893. According to a 1907 article in the *Telfair Enterprise*, "The college buildings, five in number, including three dormitories, were erected at a cost of about $40,000 and arrangements are about complete to build another dormitory to take the place of one of the buildings, at a cost of $15,000." Though its enrollment was 65 in 1896, by 1907 the enrollment was around 550 pupils from over 35 counties in Georgia and four from other states and Cuba.

The local college took the rough diamonds of the area and strove to transform them into refined and educated young ladies and gentlemen. It prohibited intoxicating drinks, dancing, gambling, and other wild conduct while inculcating in its students the same Christian values their parents had instilled in them. An intriguing paragraph in the *History of Telfair County Georgia* describes the weekly Sunday morning walk of the college girls to the churches of their choice in McRae—Methodist, Baptist, and Presbyterian—all on College Street. Escorted by dormitory matrons of strict and unquestionable character, the long line of girls, dressed in the school uniform of navy blue serge skirts with lawn waists and navy blue Oxford caps, walked six blocks to their Sunday school and church services.

In 1898, the college offered Latin and Greek, higher algebra, geometry, trigonometry, calculus, English rhetoric, composition, literature, physics, chemistry, civil government, psychology, and moral philosophy. In later years, the school added music, art, and elocution. During the 1914–1915 term, a 10-piece orchestra was organized, which by the next year had increased to 25 instruments. Piano, violin, and voice were also taught. The art department offered courses in oil, watercolor, and china painting.

South Georgia College closed its doors in 1928, right before the Great Depression. Today, only the administration building remains. Its 600-seat auditorium with its renowned acoustics is used for the community's cultural activities. When the Atlanta Symphony performed in the auditorium in 1978, Louis Lane, co-conductor of the Atlanta Symphony, wrote to the Georgia Department of Natural Resources, recommending preserving the old South Georgia College building: "We were delighted to find that the acoustical properties of this auditorium for music are outstandingly fine . . . in richness and resonance of sound it reminded me of the celebrated Troy Music Hall in Troy, New York."

The 1930s saw the rise of Civilian Conservation Corps camps in the United States. These were programs Pres. Franklin Delano Roosevelt initiated as part of his New Deal during the Great Depression. The CCC camp in McRae began its work in the mid-1930s. It was made up of World War I veterans who built Little Ocmulgee State Park near McRae. Chester A. Ryals of McRae was the park superintendent who oversaw the building of the park. Though most of the park is in Wheeler County, it is used by Telfair residents for meetings, recreational activities, and dining in its park restaurant.

Two powerful political families arose in the 1930s, headed by Eugene "Gene" Talmadge and John B. Walker. Both Gene Talmadge and his son Herman E. Talmadge were governors of Georgia. Herman also served as a US senator. Gene was elected governor of Georgia four times, but he died before taking office for his fourth term on December 21, 1946. The John B. Walker family produced three sheriffs of Telfair County, along with Wimbric Walker, who was chairman of the Georgia Department of Natural Resources.

Telfair County has produced other citizens who attained national prominence. These include Marion B. Folsom, who developed one of the nation's first private-industry social security plans while being employed at Eastman Kodak Company. In 1934, Folsom was appointed by Pres. Franklin D. Roosevelt to an advisory council on economic security, which laid the groundwork for the present Social Security program. Marion Folsom also served as secretary of health, education, and welfare from 1955 to 1958. Also, James E. Livingston is a recipient of our nation's highest military award, the Medal of Honor, for his heroism in the Vietnam War.

Spending his early years in the China Hill area of Telfair County, George Frank Boney became the chief justice of the Alaska Supreme Court in 1968. He was the youngest chief justice of any state supreme court at the time and served until his untimely death in 1972. The state courthouse in Anchorage, Alaska, is named after him. The memorial plaque proclaims: "This building is dedicated to the memory of the Honorable George Frank Boney, second Chief Justice of the Supreme Court of Alaska, who died in office on August 30, 1972, and who served the people of the state with great distinction." He was 42 years old when he died.

During the wars and conflicts of the 20th century, Telfair lost a number of residents who died defending our great country. These included the following men: Walter C. Anderson, John W. Ashley, William E. Batchelor, Alpheus W. Brewer, Leroy Brown, B. Burkhalter, William C. Cannon, O.C. Cook, Henry D. Cravey, Marion A. Davis, Paul Douglas, John Dowdy, Claxton L. Evans, Charlie B. Fennell, James M. Flannagan, John W. Foster, Herman Gillis, Foster P. Harbin, Joseph T. Heard, Bennie Horton, David E. Hulett, William E. Love, Thomas R. Lowery, Grooms K. Maloy, William H. Mimbs, Fred Peavy, Adrain Powell, Arthur K. Powell, Warren W. Powell, Calvin Oliver Smith, Roland Sutton, Oscar Warren, Earl Webb, Mongue Wells, Olin L. White, James C. Williams, Joe B. "Jack" Williams, and William A. Yancey Jr.

Three men, John Dominey, Russell Rawlins, and Sanders Walker, were prisoners of war during World War II. Jack McGinty, an accountant in McRae for many years, lost all of his toes to frostbite at the Battle of the Bulge during the war. D.J. Burch saw action in England, France, Belgium, Luxembourg, and Germany, not returning home for four years of the war. He belonged to the 832nd Engineer Aviation Battalion, which had its accomplishments documented in a booklet about the battalion. In the booklet, Gen. H.H. Arnold wrote the following tribute to the men in this battalion: "Often as not, our men slept in slit trenches, lived off field rations, and worked in shifts that shattered all preconceived notions of human endurance. The Engineer Battalion, which went ashore on the morning of D-Day was at the Maginot Line on D-plus 120, having built seven airfields en route. . . . Jungle clearings in New Guinea, inaccessible by land, were put into operating condition in a matter of days through use of airborne equipment." This description gives us some insight into the largest seaborne invasion in history, and a Telfair resident was present.

Telfair County has produced many firsts in the nation and the world. The first Protestant baptism was conducted in the Ocmulgee River in Telfair County, around 1540. A world-record bass was caught in Montgomery Lake in 1932. The buck with the largest antlers in the state was harvested in 1998. The largest dewberry farm in the United States was right here in Telfair County. Two Olympic medalists were residents of Telfair County. In 1960, Martha Bell Hudson's relay team won a gold medal at the Summer Olympics in Rome, Italy. Kim Batten won an Olympic silver medal for the 400-meter hurdle in 1996. Mark Cartwright, a musical prodigy, was inducted into the Country Music Hall of Fame in 2013. Matt Walker won national titles in dirt bike competitions. Jackie Ryals's foxhound won two national titles. The game of beano, or bingo, has its origin in Jacksonville.

Only this past year, the adjoining towns of McRae and Helena in Telfair County were officially merged, creating the new town of McRae-Helena. The first mayor of McRae-Helena, Mike Young, was elected in November 2014. Mayor June D. Bradfield of McRae, who served with distinction for two mayoral terms, did not seek reelection. She brought about many improvements in McRae.

From humble beginnings in a schoolhouse in 1891, and later in a brush arbor, Midway Church has had enormous influence for the good in Telfair County. Though church membership and attendance remain small, the prayer breakfast that is faithfully held the second and fourth Saturdays of each month observed its 20th year of existence on February 28, 2015. Jack Lowery, a member of Midway Church for many years, is the spark who began the prayer breakfast in 1995, and he continues to play a major role in its continuance. Ninety-four-year-old Ruby White plays the piano, and different speakers address the group and lead those in attendance in prayer for our community and nation.

Though all of Telfair County's churches are bastions of the Christian faith, the coming together of different denominations for a simple prayer breakfast for a period of 20 years is a testament to the influence of the historical, yet small, Midway Church. It may have had a bearing on McRae's recent nomination as one of the safest towns in the state of Georgia, in addition to being touted also as a town of distinction. The people of Telfair County continue to strive for the best.

# One

# Hernando De Soto in Telfair County

When Hernando de Soto crossed the Ocmulgee River in April 1540 and camped in a Native American village, it was the first recorded European presence in Telfair County, Georgia, but this event remained unknown until 2006. De Soto had looted the gold of the Incas in Peru with Francisco Pizarro. He was appointed governor of Cuba, where he raised an army and sailed to Florida. He landed at Tampa Bay in 1539. He soon moved to a site at Tallahassee, Florida, and spent the winter. In the spring of 1540, de Soto marched north with an army of 600 soldiers—some on horses, some on foot—accompanied by hundreds of pigs and a number of war dogs.

De Soto was in search of gold, reported to be in the Southeast. The path of his army across southern Georgia has remained controversial for over a century. Several routes have been proposed based on Spanish documents, but no Spanish artifacts that could be associated with his army were found until 2006–2007.

Dr. Dennis Blanton of the Fernbank Museum of Natural History, with the help of Frankie Snow of South Georgia College, found Spanish artifacts and Native American artifacts at a site on Glass Land and Timber Company lands in Telfair County. Blanton was seeking the site of the Spanish mission Santa Isabel de Utinahica that was established in the 1600s; instead, he found Spanish artifacts at the Glass site dating to the early 1500s.

Blanton returned to the Glass site in 2007, 2009, 2010, 2012, and 2014 to survey and excavate the site. Several archaeologists and many volunteers assisted with the excavations. Fernbank Museum of Natural History supported the project, as did the National Geographic Society.

Blanton and Snow felt that the artifacts were associated with the Hernando de Soto expedition. This is the only place where de Soto–period artifacts have been found in southern Georgia. The artifacts provide evidence that de Soto followed a route through Telfair County on his march across Georgia. The study also opens a new window into the life of the Indians in this area and the life of the Spanish soldiers on the expedition. It also provides a beginning point in the Telfair County story.

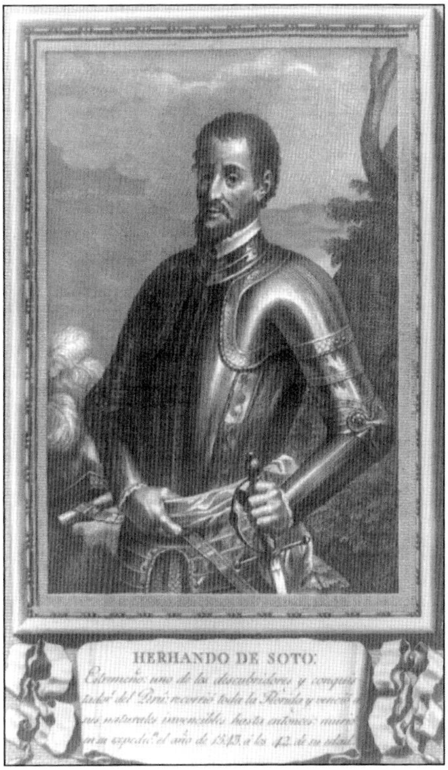


Hernando de Soto was the leader of the 1539–1542 Spanish expedition through the southeastern United States. This 19th-century portrait is in the collection of the Library of Congress. (Courtesy of the Library of Congress.)

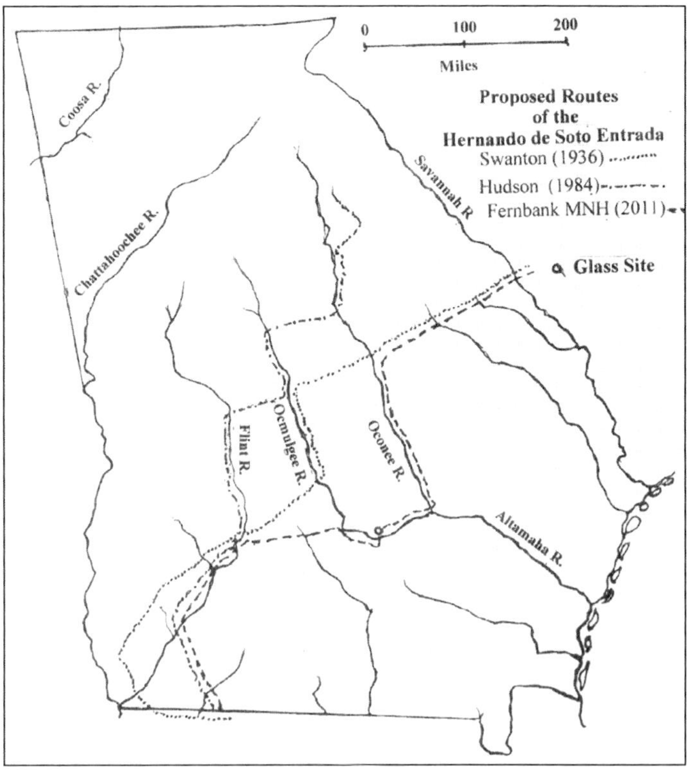


This map of Georgia depicts the proposed routes of Hernando de Soto's expedition through the state. The Glass site in Telfair County is now believed to be a part of the discoverer's travels. (Courtesy of Chris Trowell.)

Locations for large-scale excavation are identified from the results of shovel tests. These tests are being dug in areas suggested by the presence of artifacts on the surface. (Courtesy of Dr. Dennis Blanton and the Fernbank Museum of Natural History.)

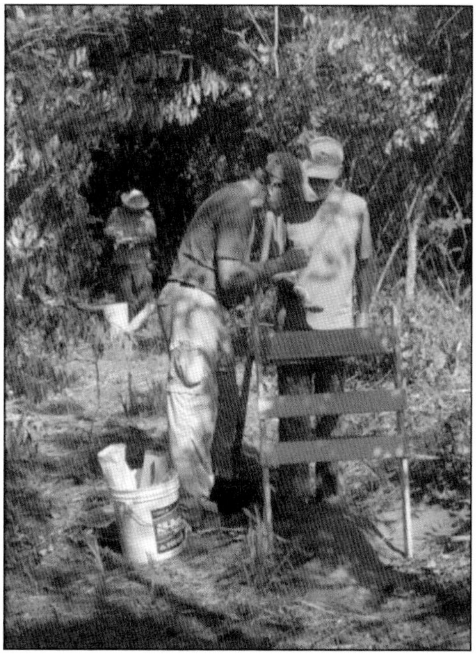

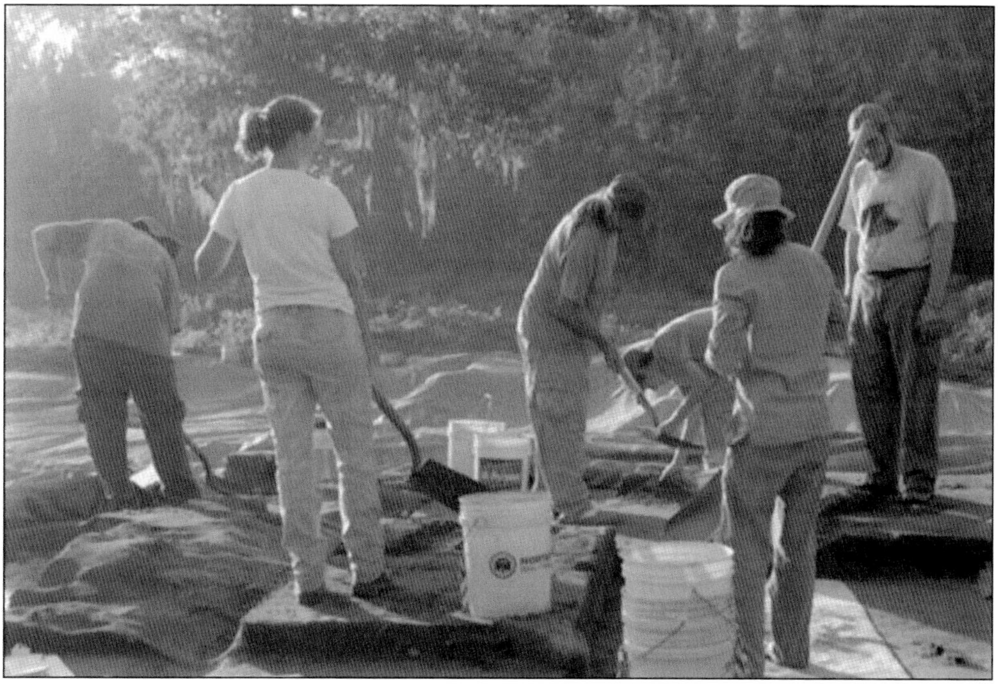

Archaeological excavation is a labor-intensive activity that requires the coordination of trained professionals, students, and volunteers. The trained professionals employed at the Glass site excavation were funded by grants from the Fernbank Museum in Atlanta, Georgia, and the National Geographic Society. Students from Georgia State University and James Madison University excavated the site. Local volunteers also contributed their time and sweat in an effort to uncover the story buried at this place. (Courtesy of Dr. Dennis Blanton and the Fernbank Museum of Natural History.)

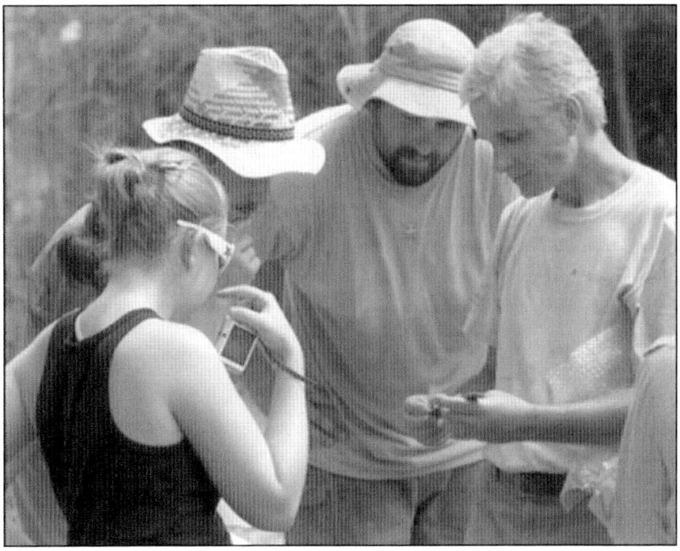

Discoveries of 16th-century artifacts are rare events that generate much excitement, not to mention opportunities for learning. Dr. Dennis Blanton (right) found Spanish and Indian artifacts at the Glass site. Dr. Blanton launched an archaeological project supported by Fernbank Museum and returned in 2007, 2009, 2010, 2012, and 2014. (Courtesy of Dr. Dennis Blanton and the Fernbank Museum of Natural History.)

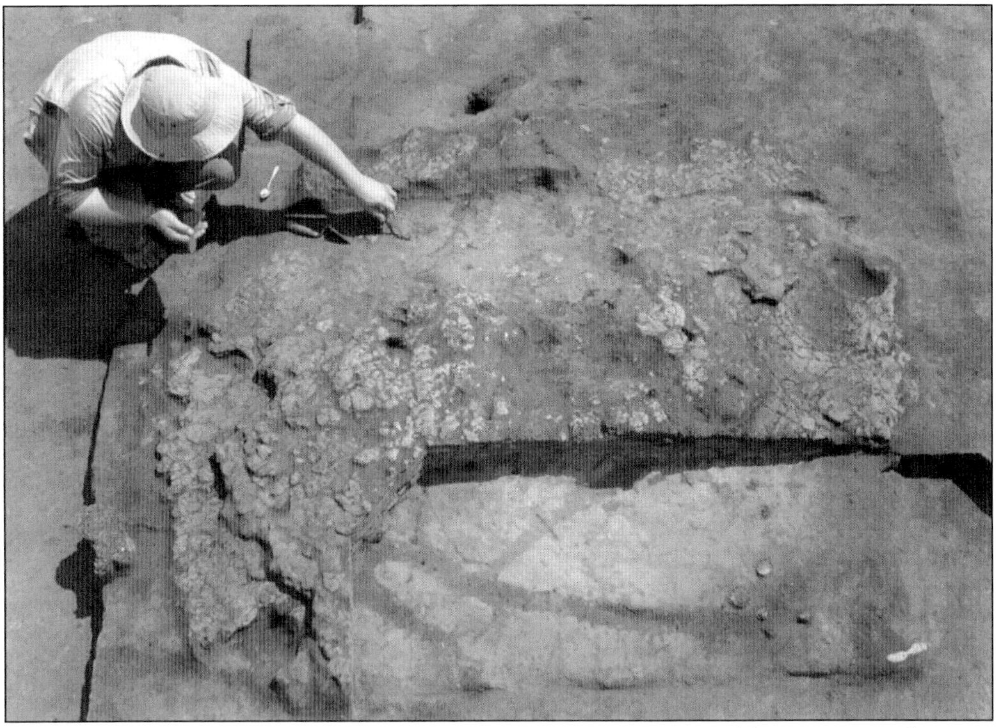

A fully exposed hearth at the center of a Native American council house or temple was a focal point for important activities at the Glass site five centuries ago. The red-stained soil indicated the location of the fire. (Courtesy of Dr. Dennis Blanton and the Fernbank Museum of Natural History.)

An archaeological project succeeds only if detailed permanent records are made of all findings. Usually one member of the excavation crew is assigned to maintain the logbook. Here, a student notes the type of artifact found and its location. (Courtesy of Dr. Dennis Blanton and the Fernbank Museum of Natural History.)

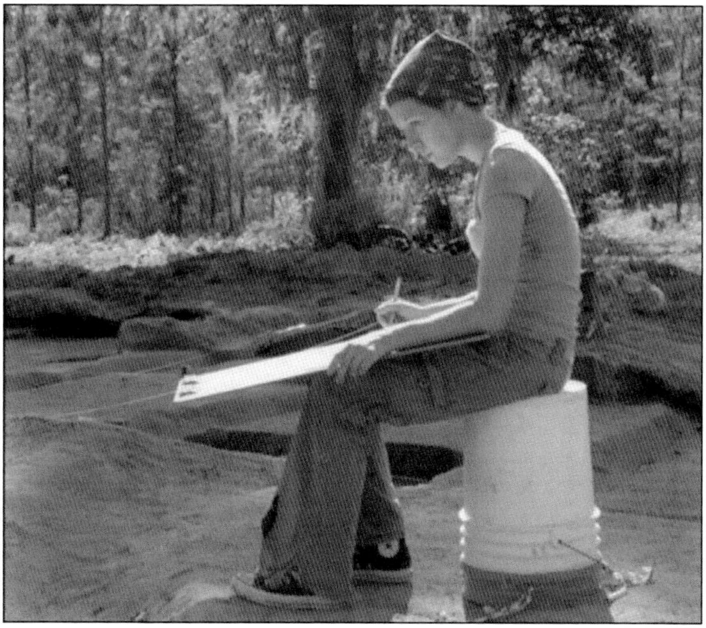

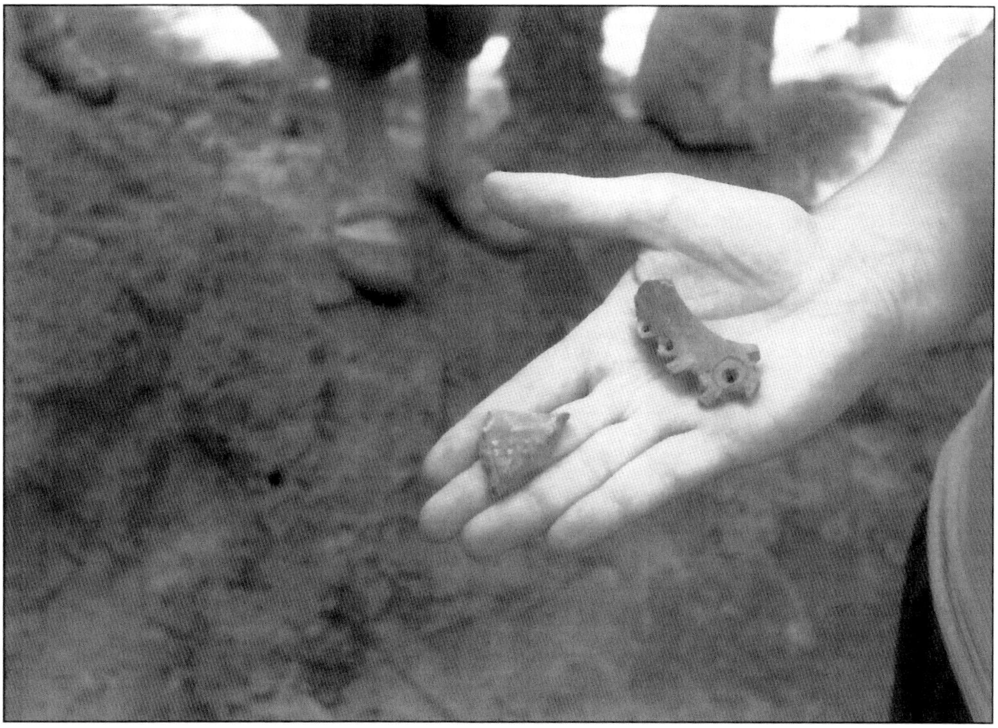

The Glass site is believed to have been an important town for local Indians. Fragments of elaborate smoking pipes, like this bird's head adorning the side of a pipe, were indications of the special activities that occurred here. Hundreds of pipe fragments were recovered. (Courtesy of Robert Herndon.)

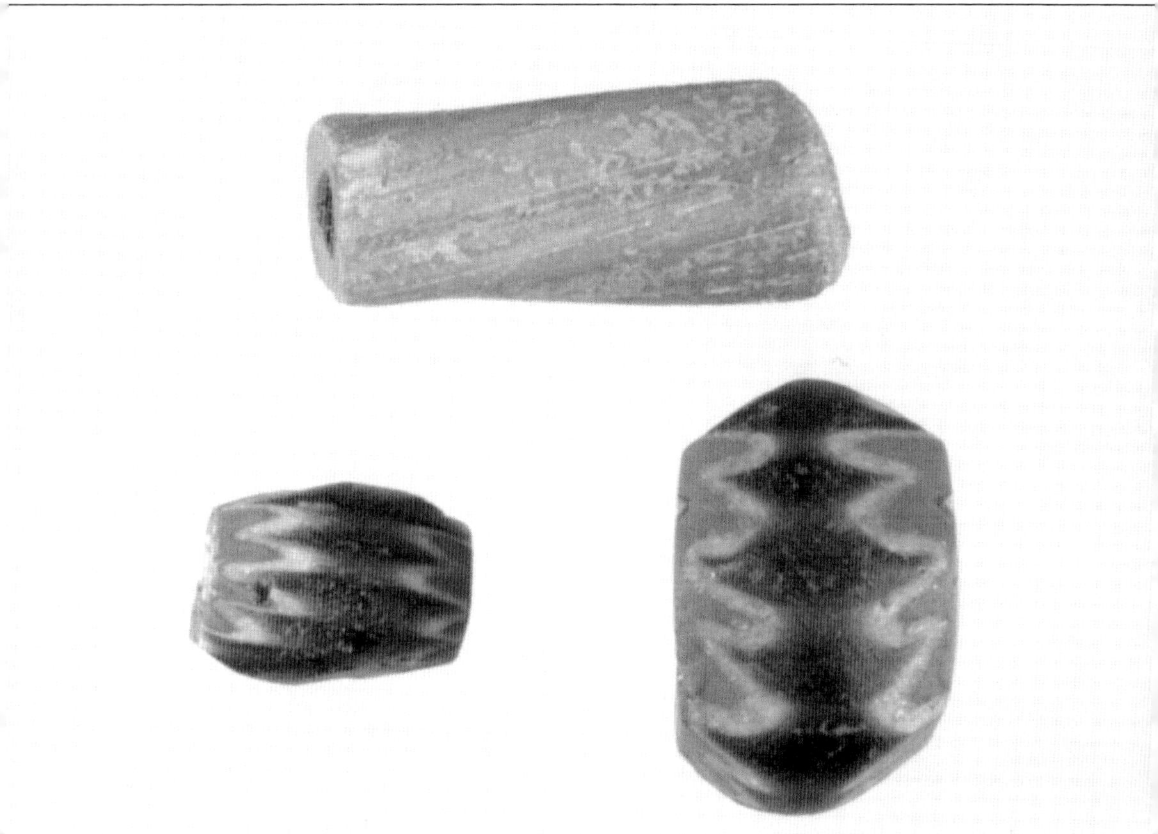

Glass beads probably made near Venice, Italy, are among the telltale clues of de Soto's presence in Telfair County. They were carried by the Spanish explorer to exchange for Indian food and assistance. (Courtesy of Dr. Dennis Blanton and the Fernbank Museum of Natural History.)

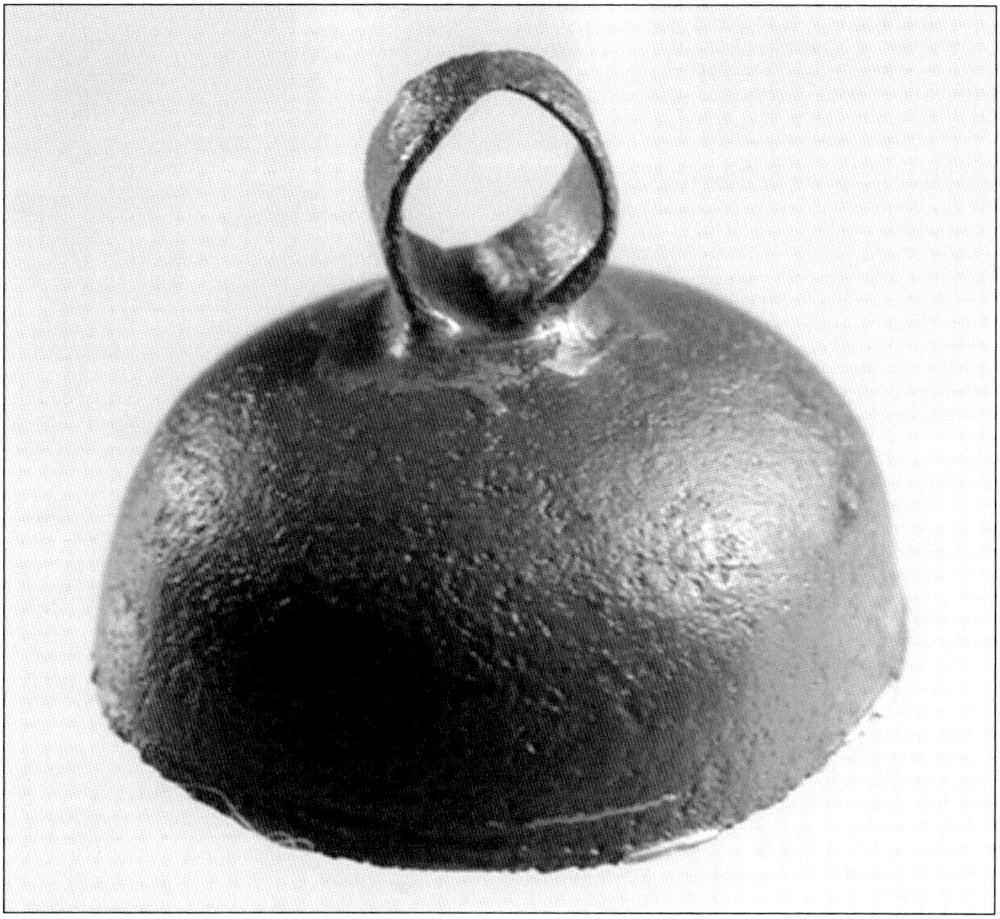

The upper portion of a brass Clarksdale bell also signifies interaction between Indians and the Spanish in the early 16th century. They were used as trade items with the Native Americans. Since the Indians were terrified of the Spanish horses, Clarksdale bells were sometimes hung from the horses' harnesses to increase the fears of the Indians. (Courtesy of Dr. Dennis Blanton and the Fernbank Museum of Natural History.)

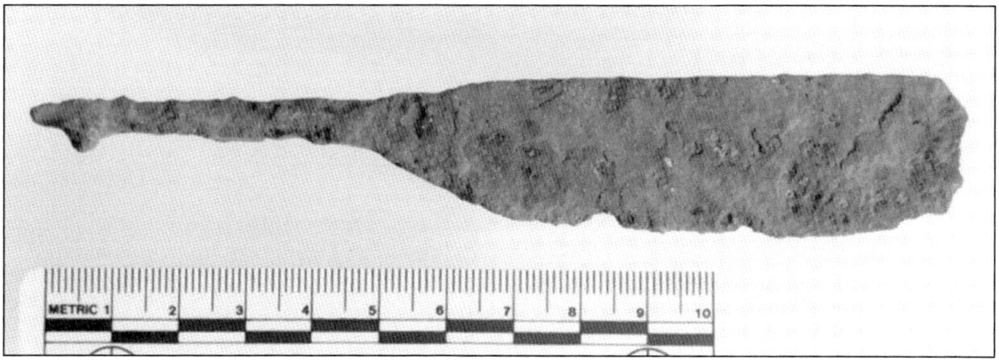


Iron artifacts like this knife blade are the most common evidence of the de Soto party in Telfair County. Tools, chain links, and other iron objects were also found at the site. They were widely scattered over the village area. (Courtesy of Dr. Dennis Blanton and the Fernbank Museum of Natural History.)

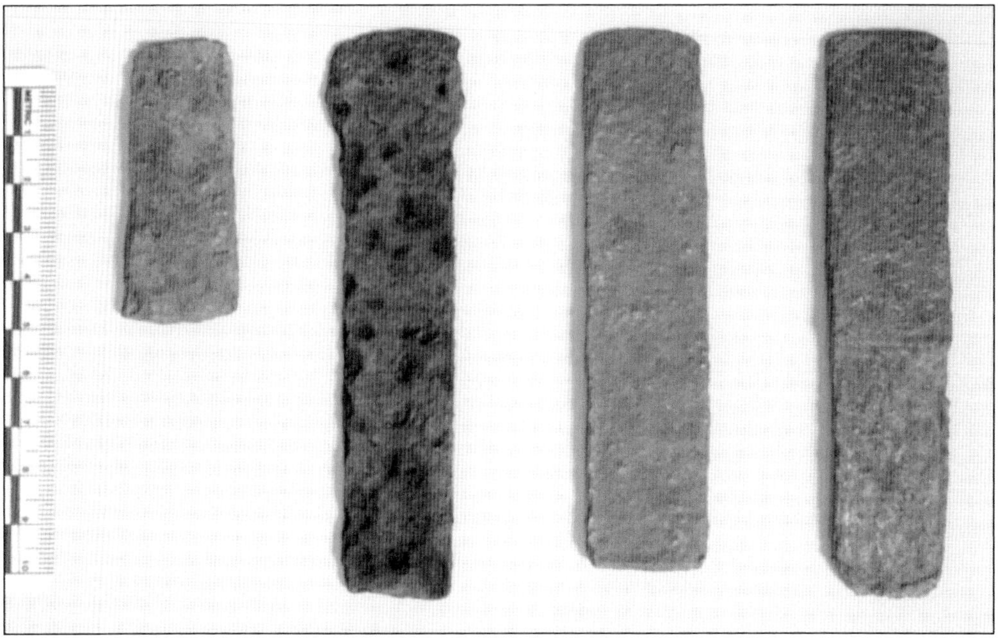

Simple iron chisels are the most frequently discovered Spanish artifacts at the Glass site. These were common trade items, as they were small and easy to carry. (Courtesy of Dr. Dennis Blanton and the Fernbank Museum of Natural History.)

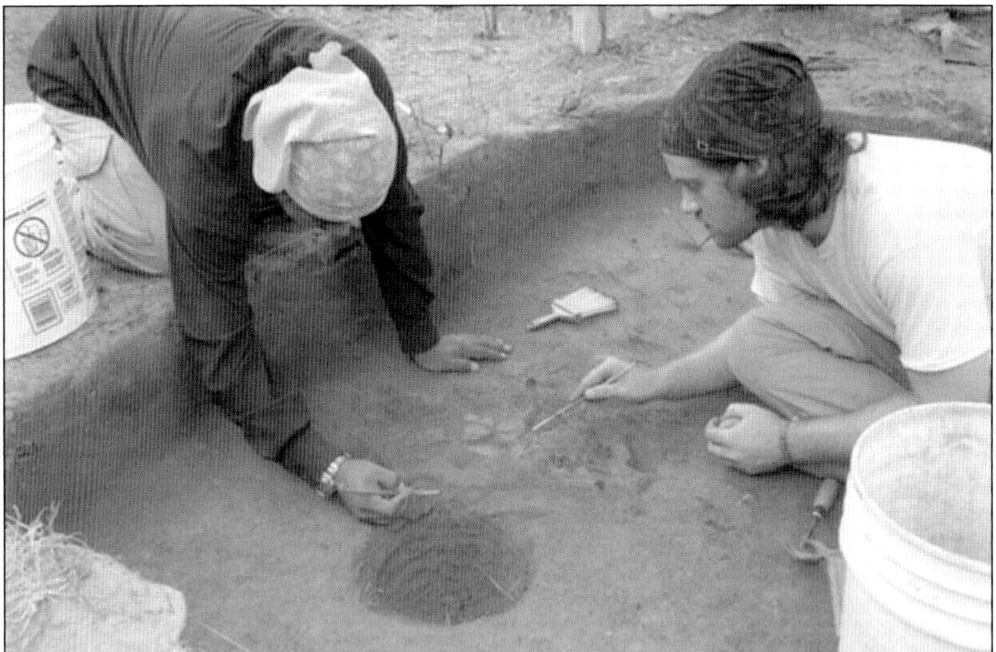

Many Indian houses made up the Glass site village, and here one is being investigated by students. The size and shape of the houses are determined and the type and number of artifacts uncovered. Note the hole that contained a support post 500 years ago. (Courtesy of Dr. Dennis Blanton and the Fernbank Museum of Natural History.)

# *Two*

# The CCC Camp in McRae and the Building of Little Ocmulgee State Park

Before Franklin Delano Roosevelt began his tenure as president of the United States, during the Great Depression, he stated, "I pledge you, I pledge myself, to a new deal for the American people." Many national programs sprang from this simple message, one being the Civilian Conservation Corps (CCC), which was an outgrowth of the Civilian Conservation Corps Reforestation Relief Act passed in March 1933. The unemployed youth of America and veterans took advantage of this opportunity to find work. With an average age of 40, often impaired in body or mind due to the effects of their wartime experiences, these veterans of World War I built Little Ocmulgee State Park near McRae.

McRae's first CCC camp was named Camp Tuggle for one of the original workers who was killed by lightning while sitting under a tree. According to Ruby White, who was a young girl during the 1930s, the camp was located where Southern Charm Personal Care Home is presently located. These men, who were among the hardest hit by the Great Depression, lived in tents. The second camp, which was built within the city limits of McRae, was named Sue-Dan for Sue and Dan McRae; this name was shortened to Sodan. It had all of the city's amenities. Chester Ryals of McRae was the project superintendent of the park's construction.

In 1935, city merchants in McRae gave lands to develop a recreational area for the townspeople. This site was first called Shamrock Springs. The CCC, Department of Forestry Geological Development, and the National Park Service were to help in this endeavor. By 1936, work had already begun on a clubhouse for dancing and parties, which was called the CCC Lakeside Annex. It is now called the Visitors Center. Cottages were constructed around 1938 for overnight guests. The recreational facilities now include a 265-acre lake, boat ramp, fishing dock, an 18-hole golf course, a 60-room lodge, and the 2.6-mile Oak Ridge Trail in the midst of sand hills, scrub oaks, pines, picnic shelters, and a fine restaurant.

Camps of veterans differed from those that housed much younger nonveterans. Those veterans who were married often moved their families into the local area and returned home each evening. Those who were single lived in the barracks. Their legacy is a beautiful park that is a vital part of life in the Telfair area.

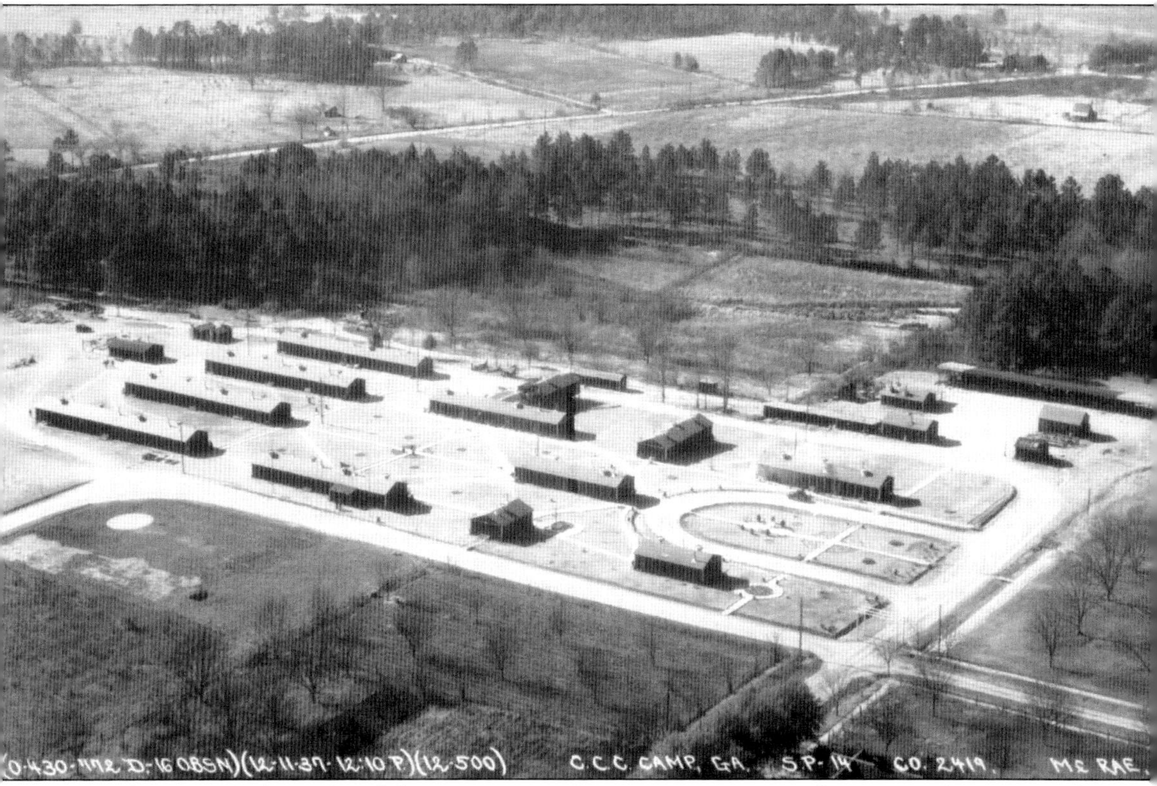


These are the barracks of the CCC camp that was in McRae in the 1930s. The men would travel each day to the site of the park that was being built nearby in Wheeler County. Under the authority of the forest service, these veterans removed dead and diseased timber and planted pine trees. (Courtesy of Connie Huddleston and the National Archives.)

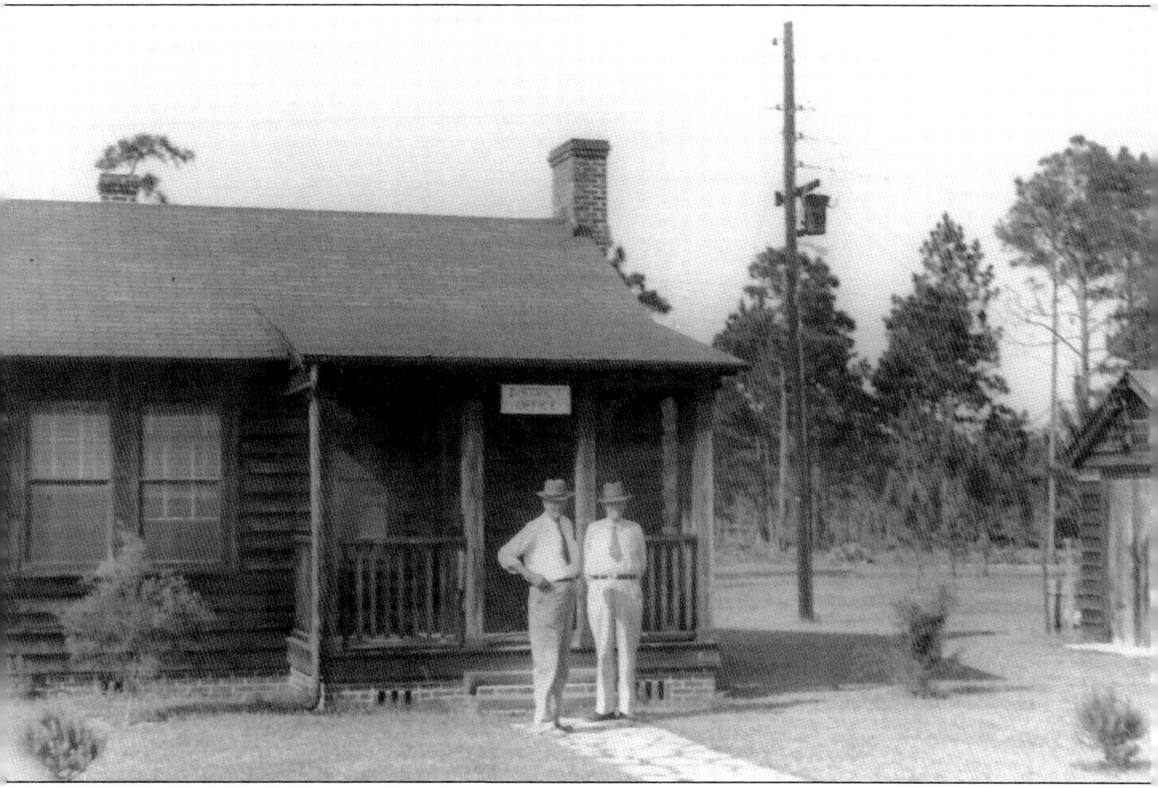

Pictured here is the district office of the CCC camp in McRae, Georgia, during the 1930s. This building could possibly have been in the photograph of the barracks of the CCC camp on the previous page. The CCC camp was located where Southern Charm Personal Care Home is now and probably extended toward Sugar Creek and back past where Eunice Harris now resides. (Courtesy of Margaret Hall.)

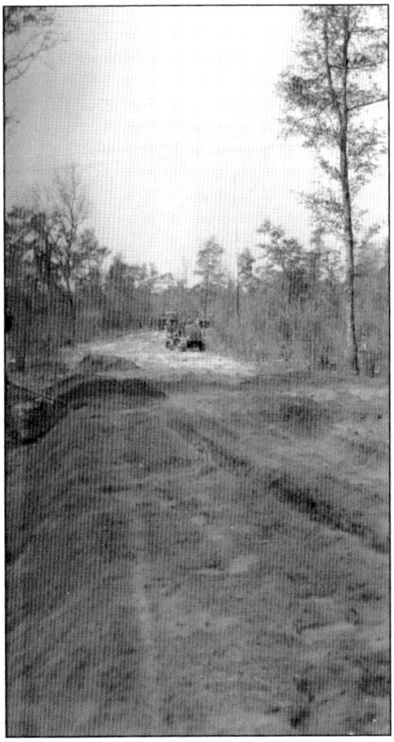

CCC workers carried out the clearing for the park road, and it quickly became apparent that some low areas and dips would need to be filled in to prevent erosion. They brought in dirt and sand from the surrounding areas to complete this task. (Courtesy of Connie Huddleston and the National Archives.)

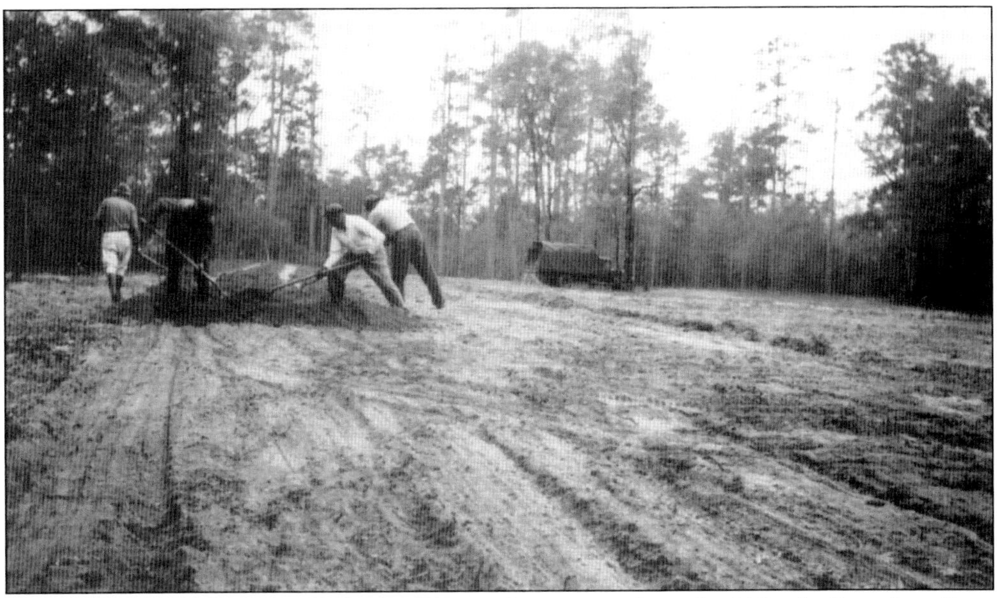

These veterans are clearing the land of diseased trees in order to build Little Ocmulgee State Park. They left old-growth trees in places and removed only the understory. In the final two months of 1935 alone, the men together contributed over 1,000 man-days. In 1936, project superintendent Chester A. Ryals Jr. of McRae noted that more than 30,000 pine seedlings and thousands of hardwood seedlings grown at the state nursery were planted by the veterans. They also transplanted more than 32,000 pines from neighboring lands. (Courtesy of Connie Huddleston and the National Archives.)

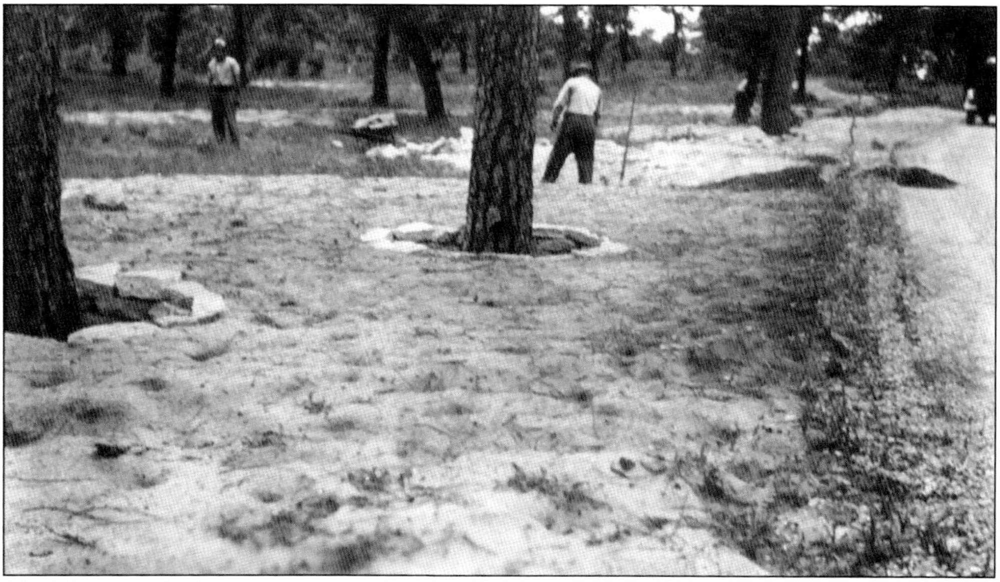

This photograph shows veterans working near the entrance road of the park. They are placing stone borders around some of the trees. This cut stone was brought in from CCC camps in northern Georgia to add landscaping beauty around older trees and new seedlings. (Courtesy of Connie Huddleston and the National Archives.)

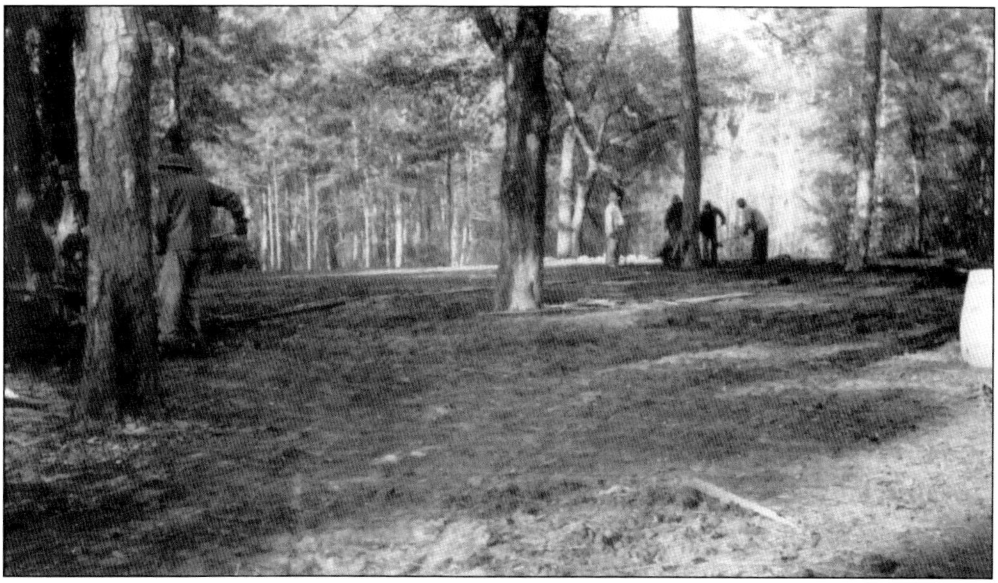

The veterans in this photograph are clearing some old-growth trees of undergrowth. Four men who were immune to poison ivy served on the poisonous plant project. The US Forest Service provided advisors and instructors and landscape architects to each park. The veterans not only learned valuable forestry skills but also landscaping techniques. New landscaping, according to an official plan, had to be watered every day. In areas where water was easily obtained, new growth was watered daily by bucket or hose. (Courtesy of Connie Huddleston and the National Archives.)

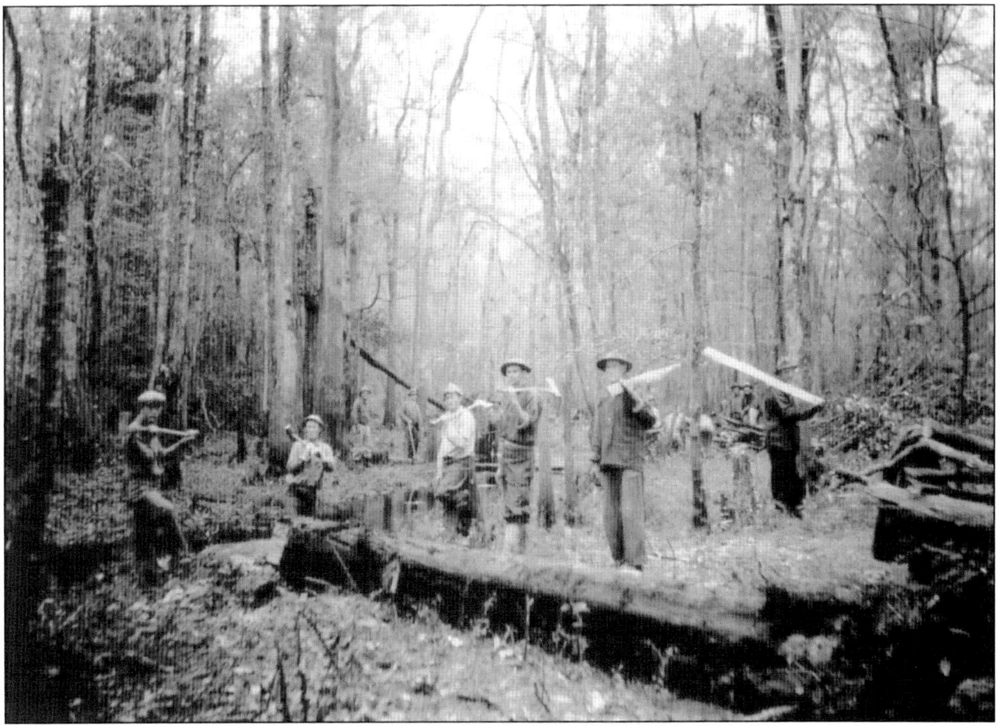

The veterans who built Little Ocmulgee State Park labored under daunting conditions. Taken in 1936, this photograph depicts the rough and untamed wilderness that the veterans encountered in clearing the land for the park. Some of the dense foliage had to be cleared with manual labor alone. (Courtesy of Connie Huddleston and the National Archives.)

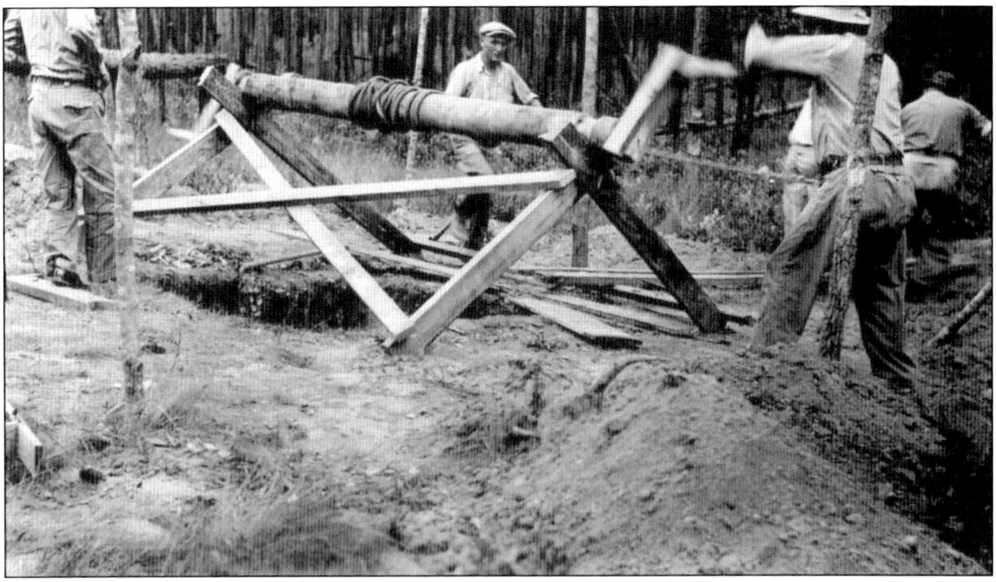

In January 1936, the CCC men began investigations, called soundings, at the site of the proposed dam. Using drills and casings, they dug several tests; samples were taken for analysis. This photograph shows veterans digging a test pit in the area of the proposed dam. (Courtesy of Connie Huddleston and the National Archives.)

Here, workers are observing a core drill, which finally arrived at Little Ocmulgee State Park. It could dig a hole to a depth of over 1,000 feet. It was also capable of bringing up unbroken cylindrical cores. The final tests were conducted at the proposed dam site by driller V.C. Mickle and assistant driller William Sasser, formerly a CCC enrollee at Chehaw, Georgia. Many revisions of the plans, along with the costs involved, delayed dam construction until the late spring of 1938. (Courtesy of Connie Huddleston and the National Archives.)

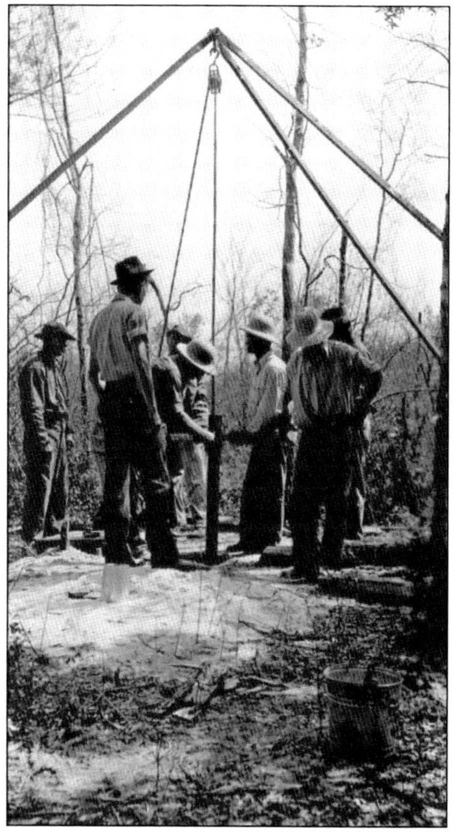

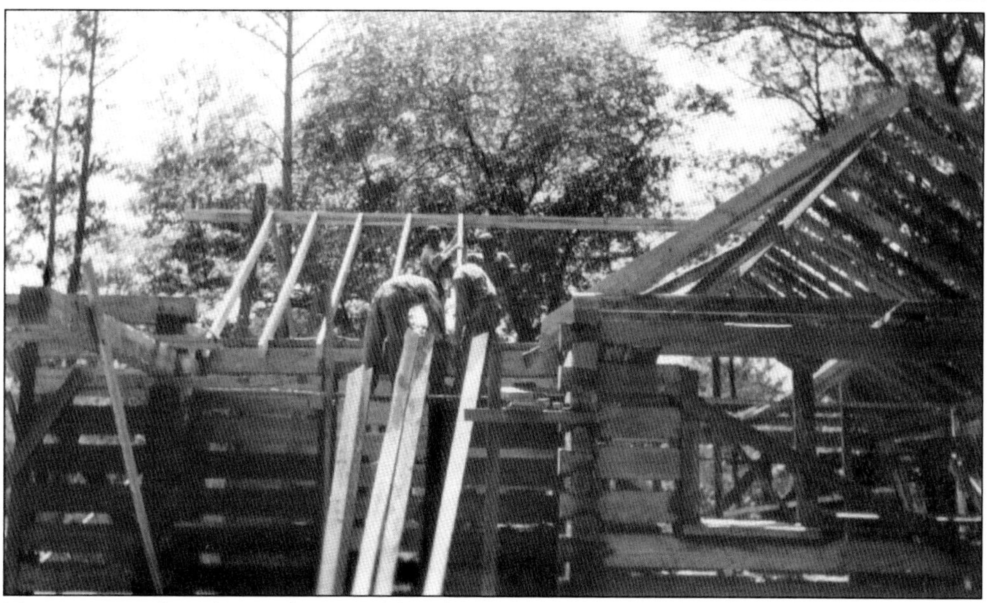

Many men, working hours of intense labor, hewed logs on the site of Little Ocmulgee State Park's main visitors' building, now called the Visitors Center. The men are shown here in June 1936 setting the trusses and rafters for the roof on the Visitors Center. (Courtesy of Connie Huddleston and the National Archives.)

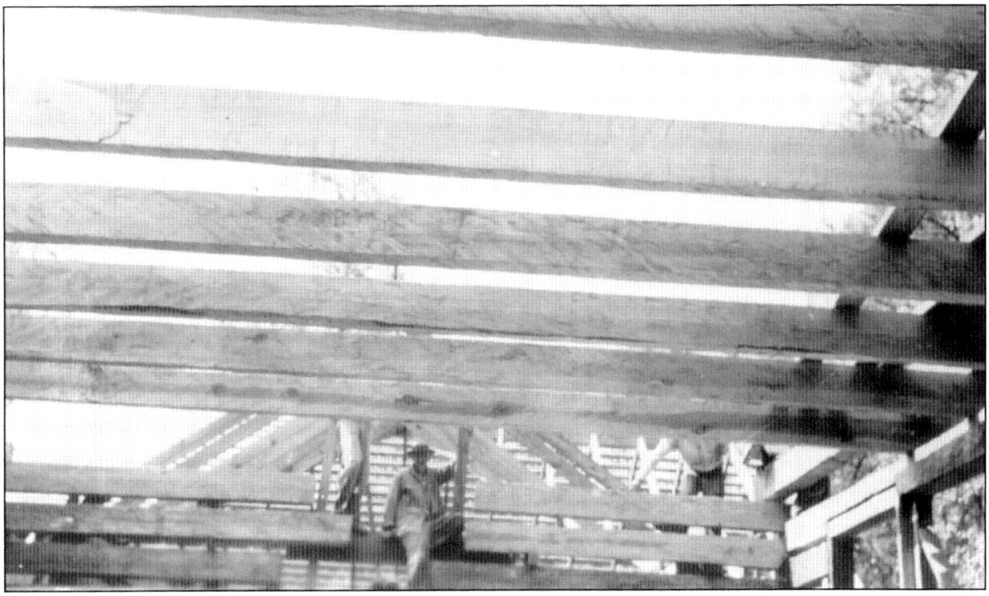

Though most of Little Ocmulgee State Park's veteran labor force had never constructed any buildings, they learned valuable skills while erecting the Visitors Center. The roof was supported by hand-hewn joists that ran across the log structure. (Courtesy of Connie Huddleston and the National Archives.)

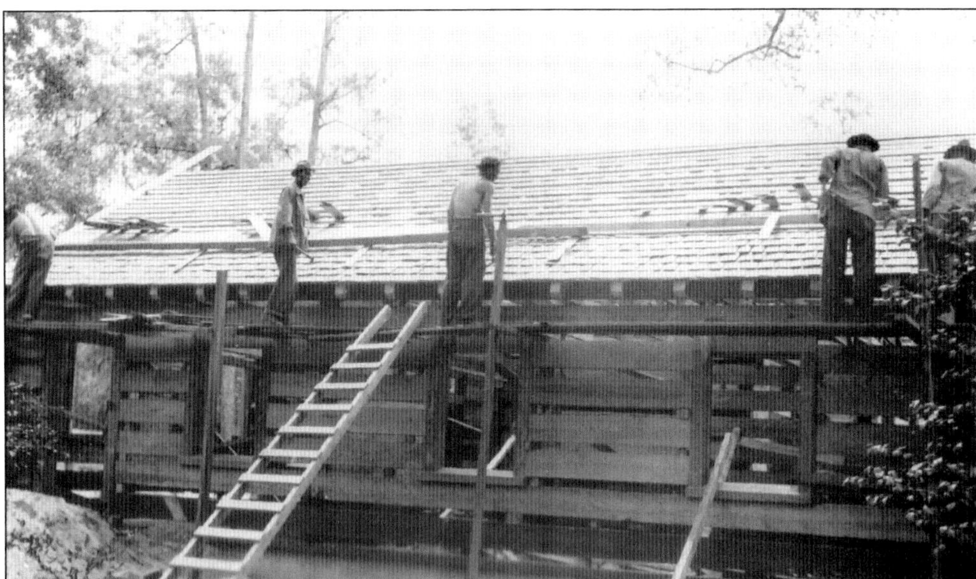

The work of placing decking on the roof was accomplished in mid-July. This was in preparation for the cedar shingles. (Courtesy of Connie Huddleston and the National Archives.)

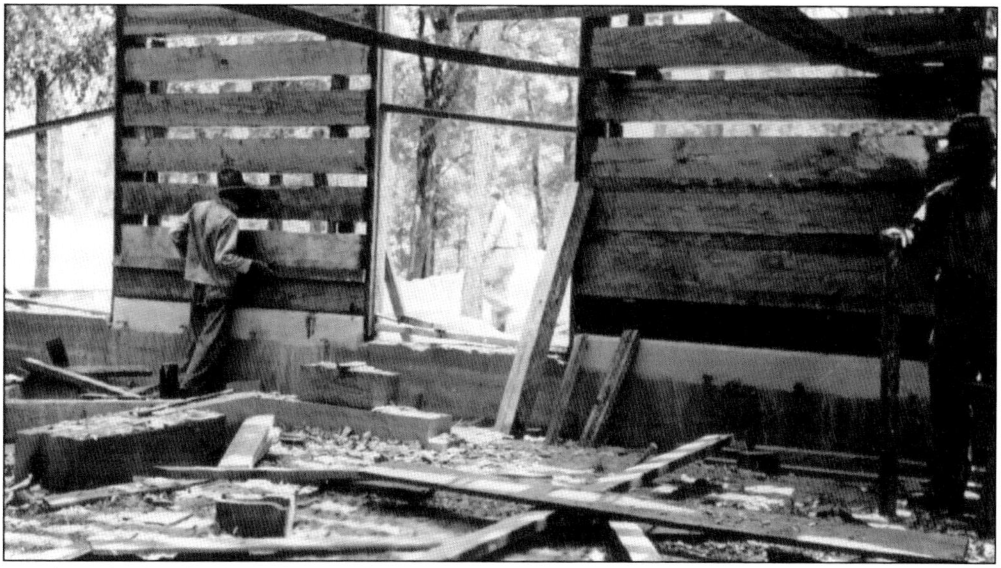

As a base for the chinking that would fill the spaces between the logs, some CCC enrollees placed boards between the hewn logs. (Courtesy of Connie Huddleston and the National Archives.)

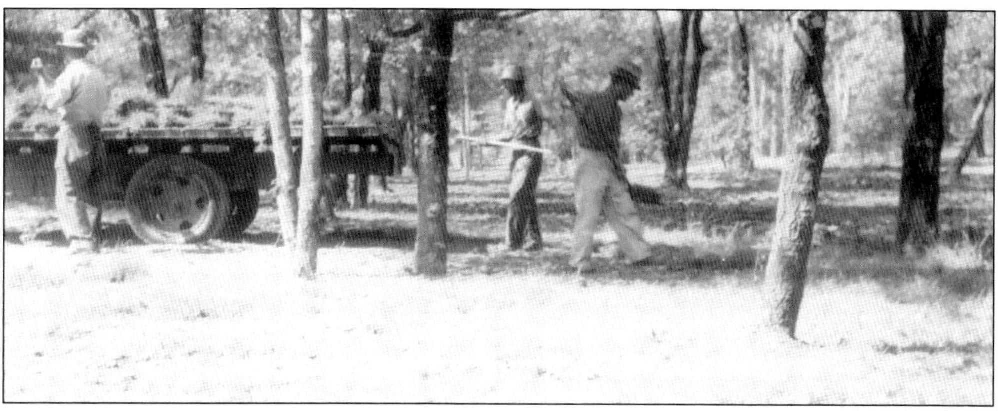

In the autumn of 1936, grounds crews cleared paths and undergrowth in the day-use area of the park. (Courtesy of Connie Huddleston and the National Archives.)

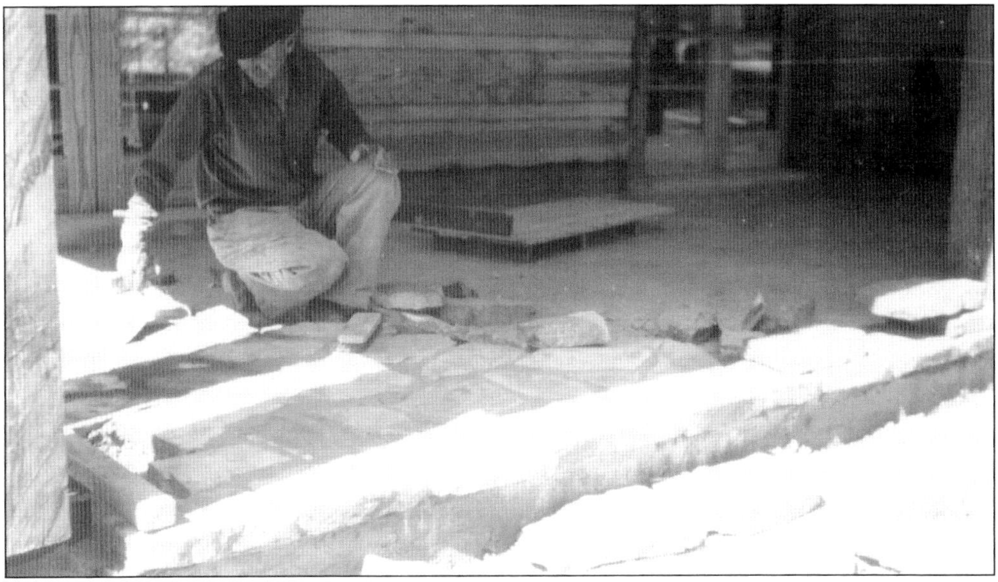

This CCC worker is laying flagstone on the porch of the Little Ocmulgee State Park's combination building. This was a marketable skill that enrollees learned in building the park. (Courtesy of Connie Huddleston and the National Archives.)

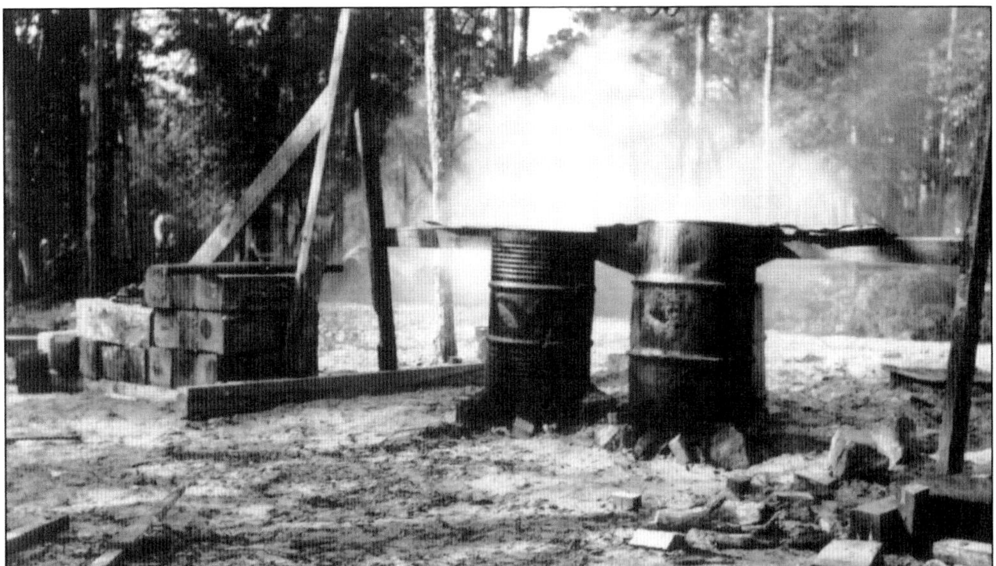

Hot creosote was used as a preservative for the guardrails on the park's roads. This process was repeated into early 1937. (Courtesy of Connie Huddleston and the National Archives.)

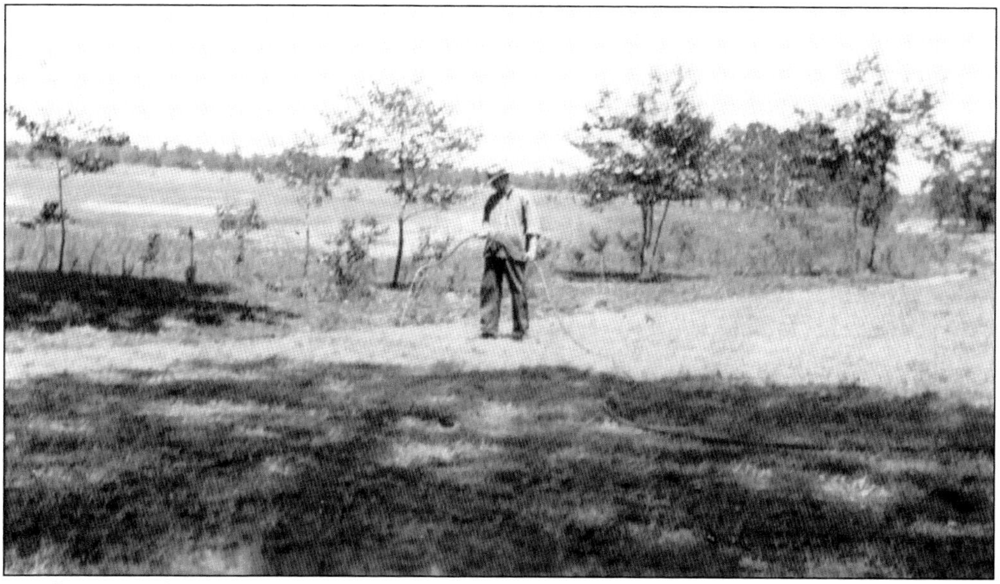

Hand watering the plants was necessary because of the 1936 drought. Surrounding the building under construction and in the day-use area, men planted sod, seedlings, and shrubs. This tedious project took months to complete. (Courtesy of Connie Huddleston and the National Archives.)

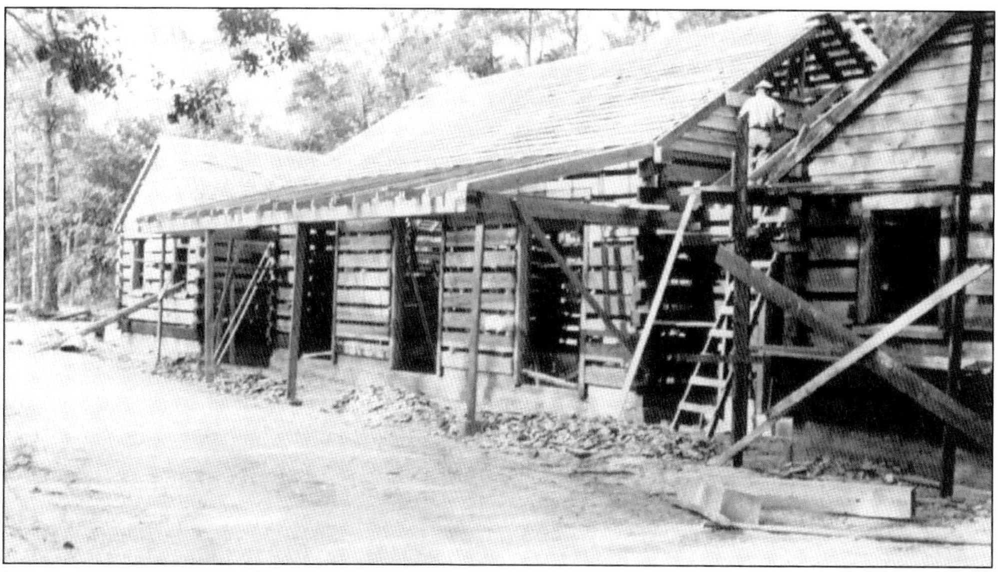

The work of placing decking on the roof in preparation for the application of the cedar shingles was completed. The Visitors Center was definitely taking shape. (Courtesy of Connie Huddleston and the National Archives.)

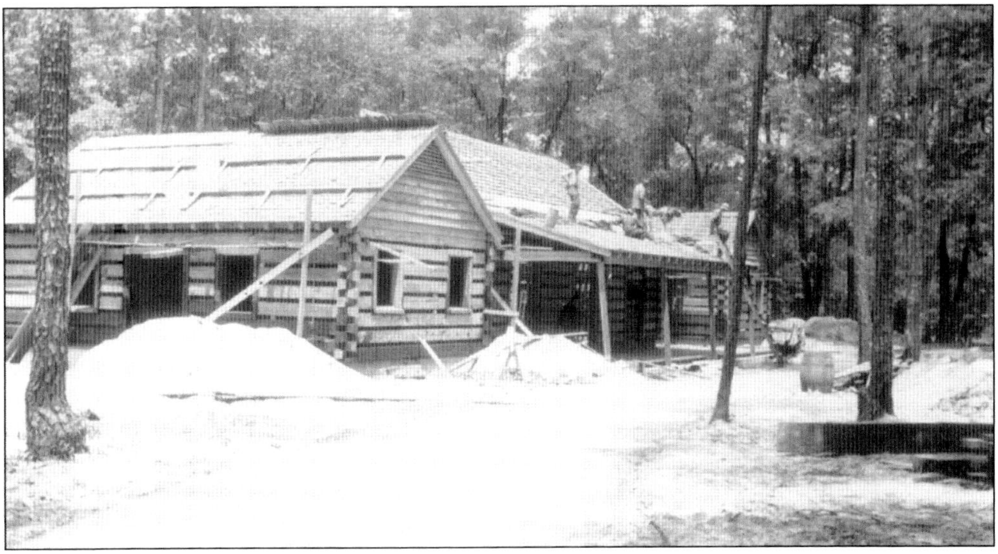

The work of shingling the roof began in late July. The men quickly completed the roof, using cypress shingles made on-site. Extra shingles were shipped to newly constructed CCC buildings at other Georgia state parks for their use. (Courtesy of Connie Huddleston and the National Archives.)

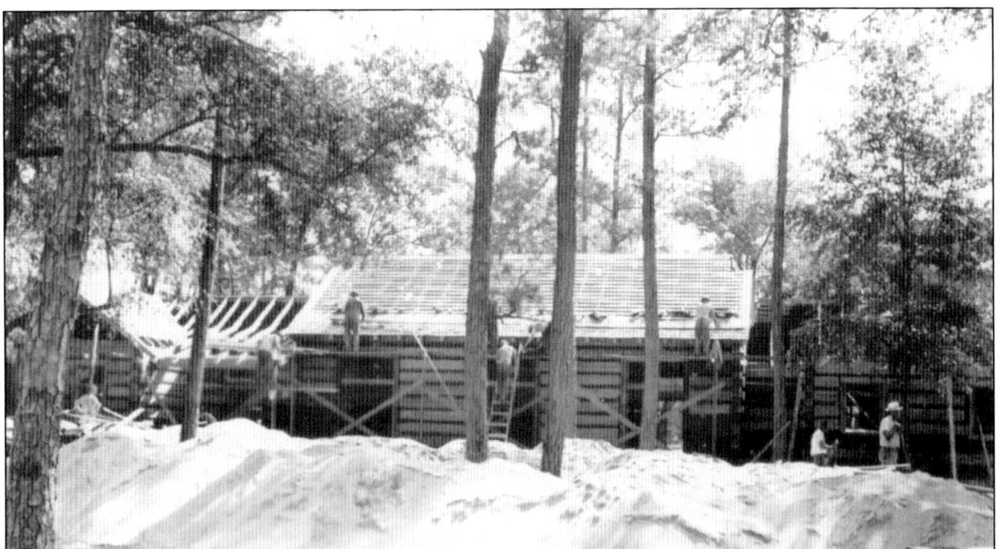

Sand was used for foundation and construction work. Piled high in dunes, the sand looked like snow in the summer of 1936. (Courtesy of Connie Huddleston and the National Archives.)

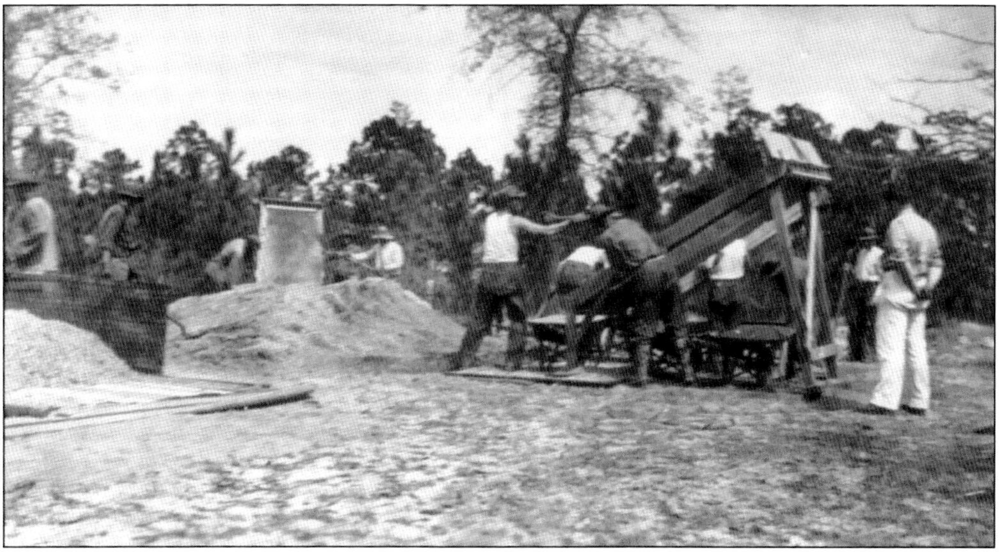

In April 1936, foundation work for the combination building began. The men are seen here mixing and pouring the building's concrete foundations. This is also a view of a wall that has been poured. (Courtesy of Connie Huddleston and the National Archives.)

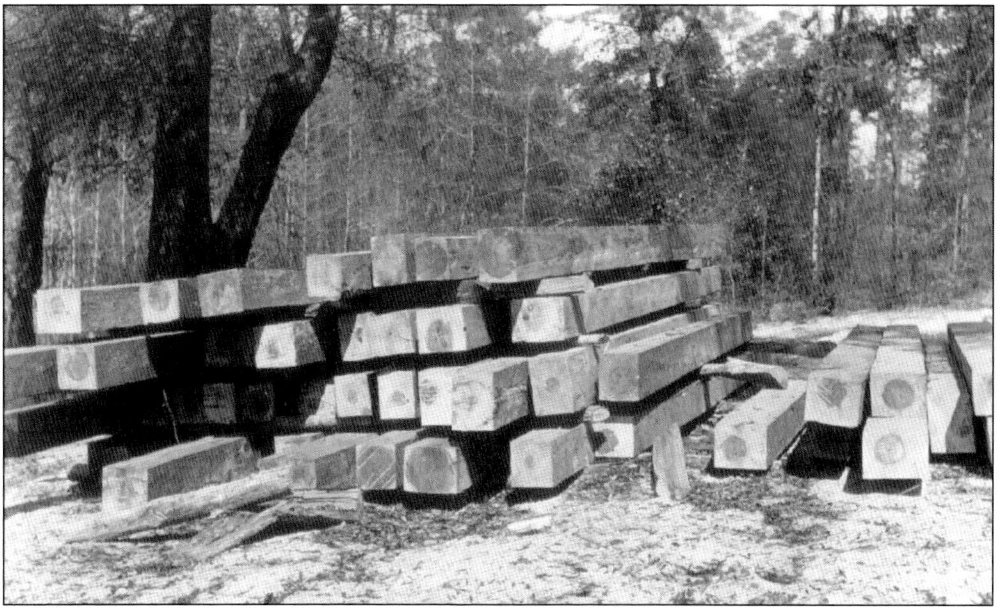

Men were selected by the CCC staff for various tasks. Hewing logs required the strongest of men. Awaiting shipment to the combination building's construction site, these recently hewn logs were cut by hand. (Courtesy of Connie Huddleston and the National Archives.)

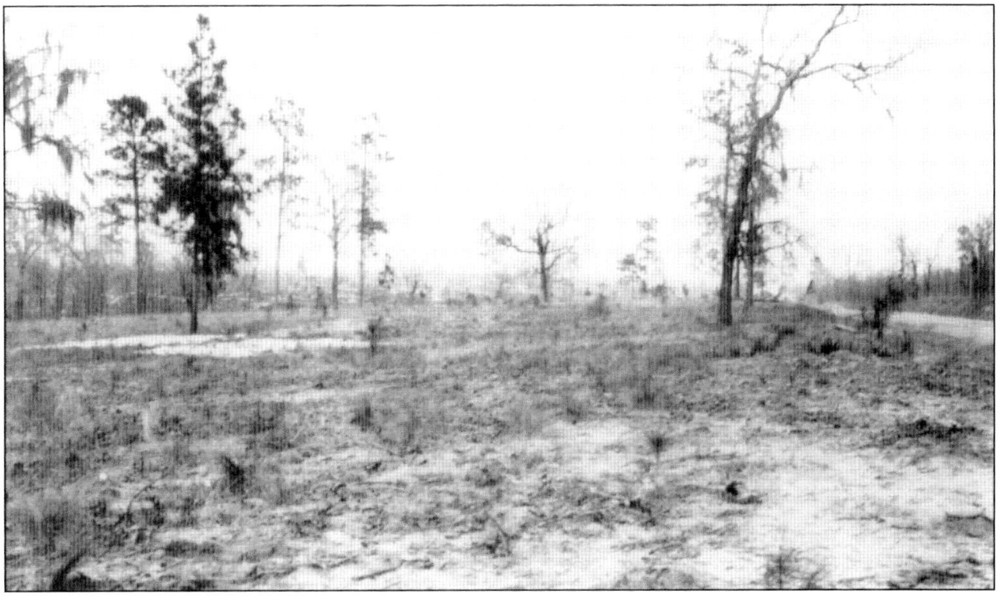

When the Little Ocmulgee State Park project began, acres of land in this area of Georgia were covered with scrub oak. Removing the undergrowth and many of the oaks, the CCC veterans planted the park with a forest of pines, setting out more than 30,000 pine seedlings. (Courtesy of Connie Huddleston and the National Archives.)

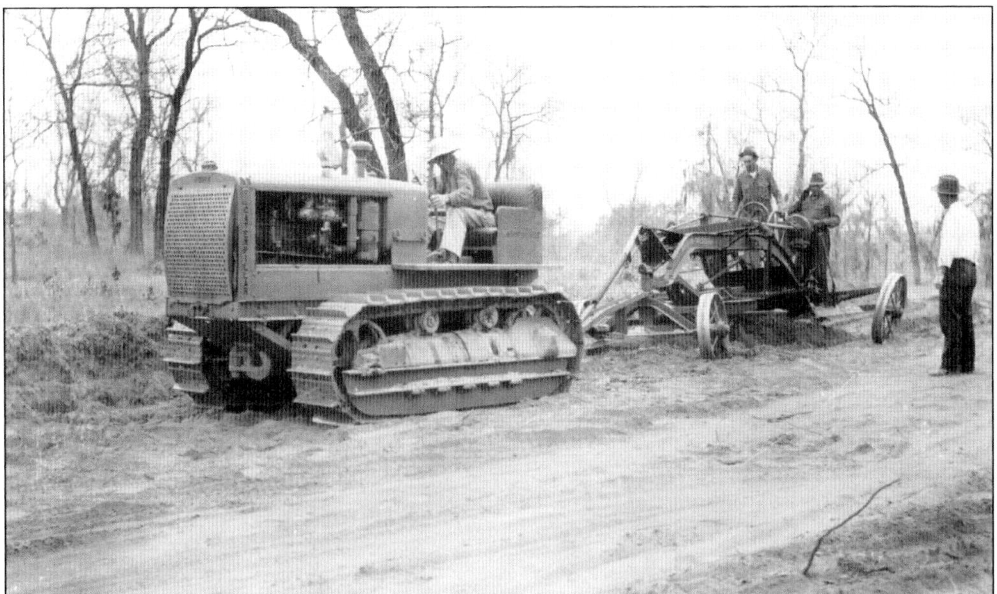

The excavations for the combination building site are shown in this photograph. Though some men used heavy machinery to complete this work, others used shovels and wheelbarrows. (Courtesy of Connie Huddleston and the National Archives.)

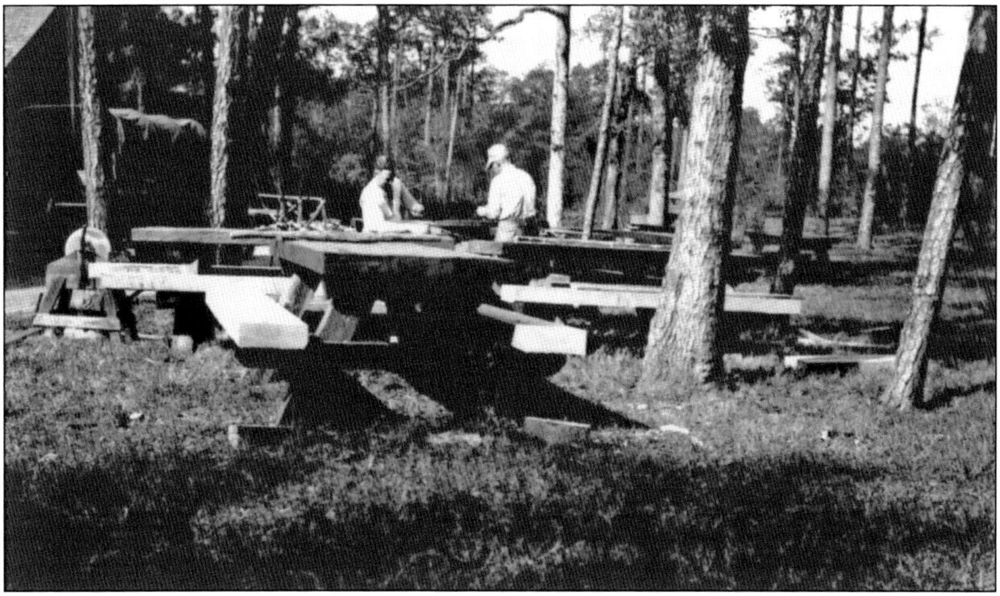

Carpenters built cabins, furniture, a picnic shelter, picnic tables, a bathhouse, and the project supervisor's house. Little Ocmulgee State Park opened to the public in 1940, and many of the original buildings are still in use today. The lake portion of Little Ocmulgee River is a recreation spot, and the park now has a lovely lodge, golf course, and restaurant. (Courtesy of Connie Huddleston and the National Archives.)

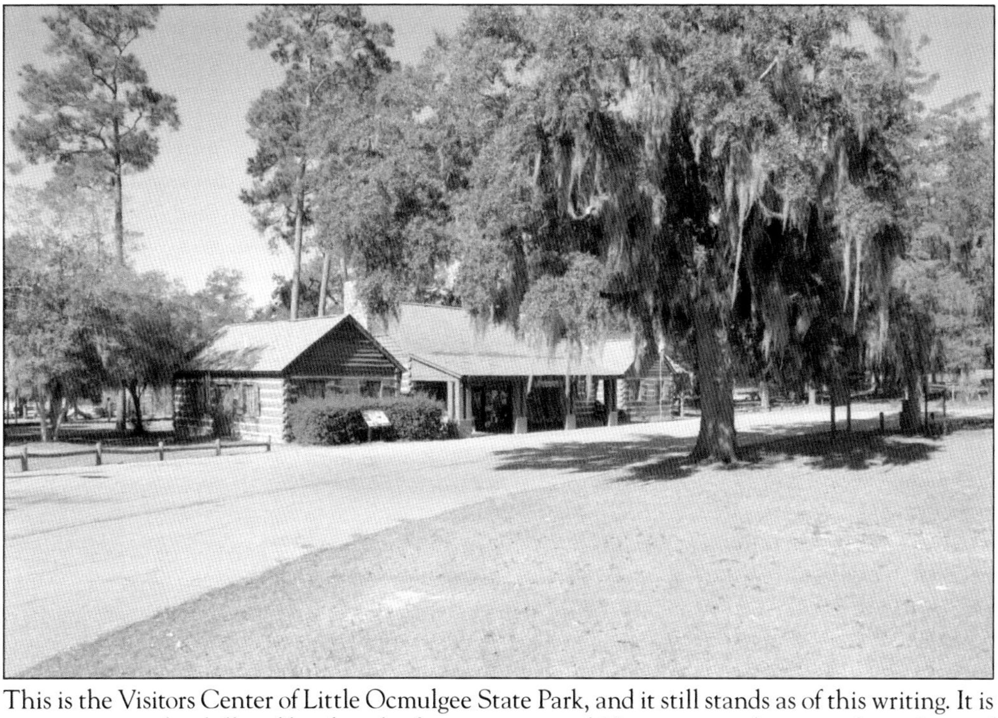

This is the Visitors Center of Little Ocmulgee State Park, and it still stands as of this writing. It is a testament to the skill and hard work of veterans around 80 years ago, who created a park out of wilderness while regaining their own strength and self-esteem. This was all accomplished under the auspices of the CCC camp in McRae. (Courtesy of Billy Ware Walker Jr.)

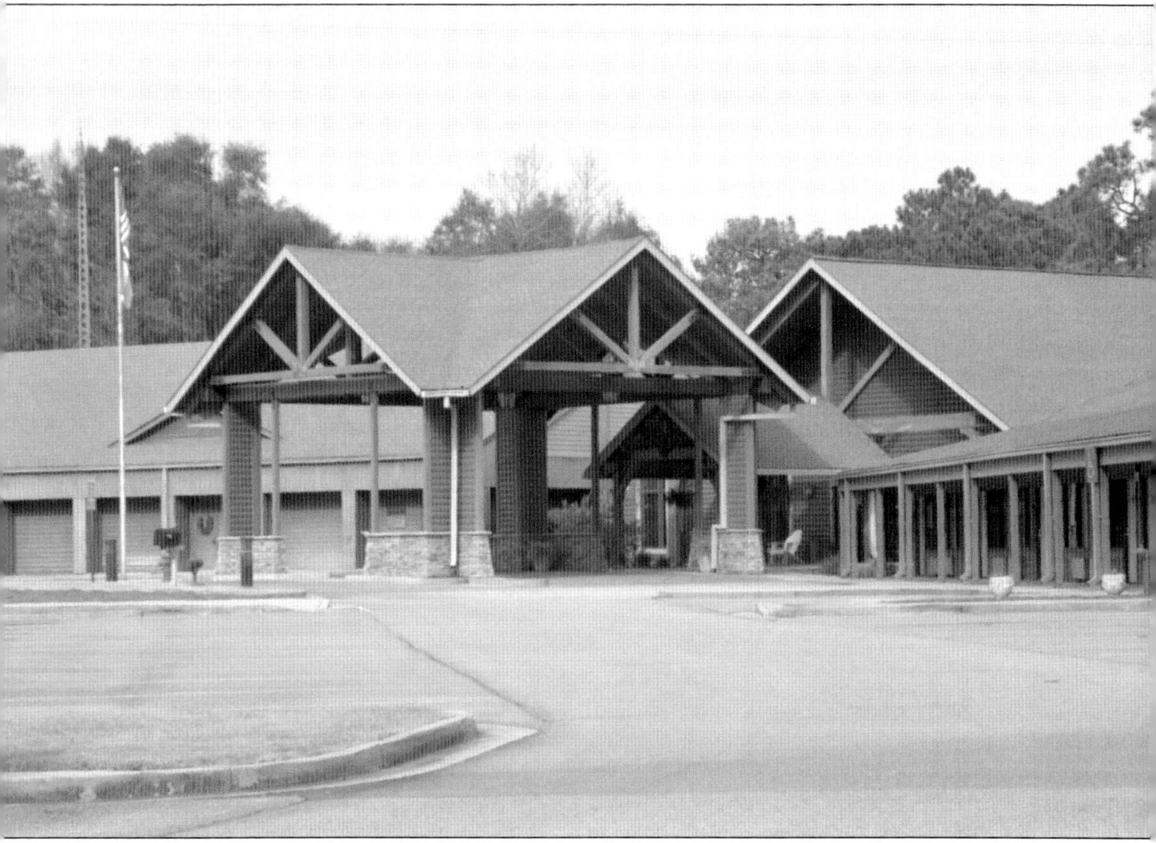

The lodge at the Little Ocmulgee State Park was built in 1988. It has 60 rooms, including five spacious meeting rooms of different sizes that attract many conventions and other groups. Local groups, such as the Pioneer Historical Society, the McRae Rotary, and the McRae Duplicate Bridge Club, meet here on a regular basis. Its fine dining room is also an attraction to locals and visitors alike. (Courtesy of Billy Ware Walker Jr.)

# *Three*

# THE TALMADGE LEGACY

Known for his red suspenders, horn-rimmed glasses, and piercing eyes, Eugene "Gene" Talmadge (1884–1946), with his fiery campaign rhetoric, was elected governor of Georgia four times, but he died before taking office for the fourth term on December 21, 1946. Words attributed to him (though later denied by his son Herman, who claimed they belonged to the person introducing his father) were: "The poor dirt farmer ain't got but three friends on this earth: God Almighty, Sears Roebuck, and Gene Talmadge." Regardless of who actually spoke the words, they conjure a verbal likeness of the man, Eugene Talmadge, and they resonated with the hardscrabble lives of those who consistently voted him into office. The wordage of the quote, however, belied the education and the keen mind of one who held a law degree from the University of Georgia and also the Phi Beta Kappa key.

His son Herman Talmadge (1913–2002) grew up on the family farm near McRae. In his memoir, *Talmadge, a Political Legacy, a Politician's Life*, he paid homage to his father, touting him as "the bravest man I ever knew," and his mother, Mattie "Miss Mitt" Talmadge, as "the most remarkable woman I ever knew." Other memories in Herman Talmadge's book were drawn from his life in McRae as a young boy.

Herman attended the I.J. Davis two-room schoolhouse, heated by a stove, where one had to "go out back to a two-hole privy to go to the bathroom." His lunches brought from home "consisted of a cold biscuit, a little bottle of syrup, some fat meat covered with lard and a sweet potato."

"Young Hummon," as he became known, received his law degree in 1936 from the University of Georgia. He practiced law for several years before joining the Navy, with which he had extensive combat duty in the South Pacific during World War II (1941–1945), eventually earning the rank of lieutenant commander. Elected to the first of four terms in the US Senate in 1956, Herman Talmadge—in spite of his staunch segregationist stance—made his major focus the protection of rural America.

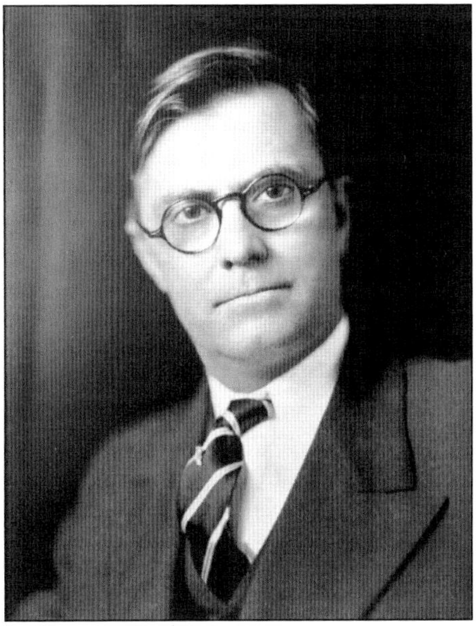

Though no date was given for this photograph of Eugene Talmadge, it was likely made during the 1920s. He served as a three-term commissioner of agriculture, beginning in 1926, and he was elected governor of Georgia for his first term in 1932. Talmadge knew the farmers and their hardships. Known as the "wool-hat boys," the farmers were the constituents who always voted Gene Talmadge into office. (Courtesy of Special Collections and Archives, Georgia State University Library, Atlanta.)

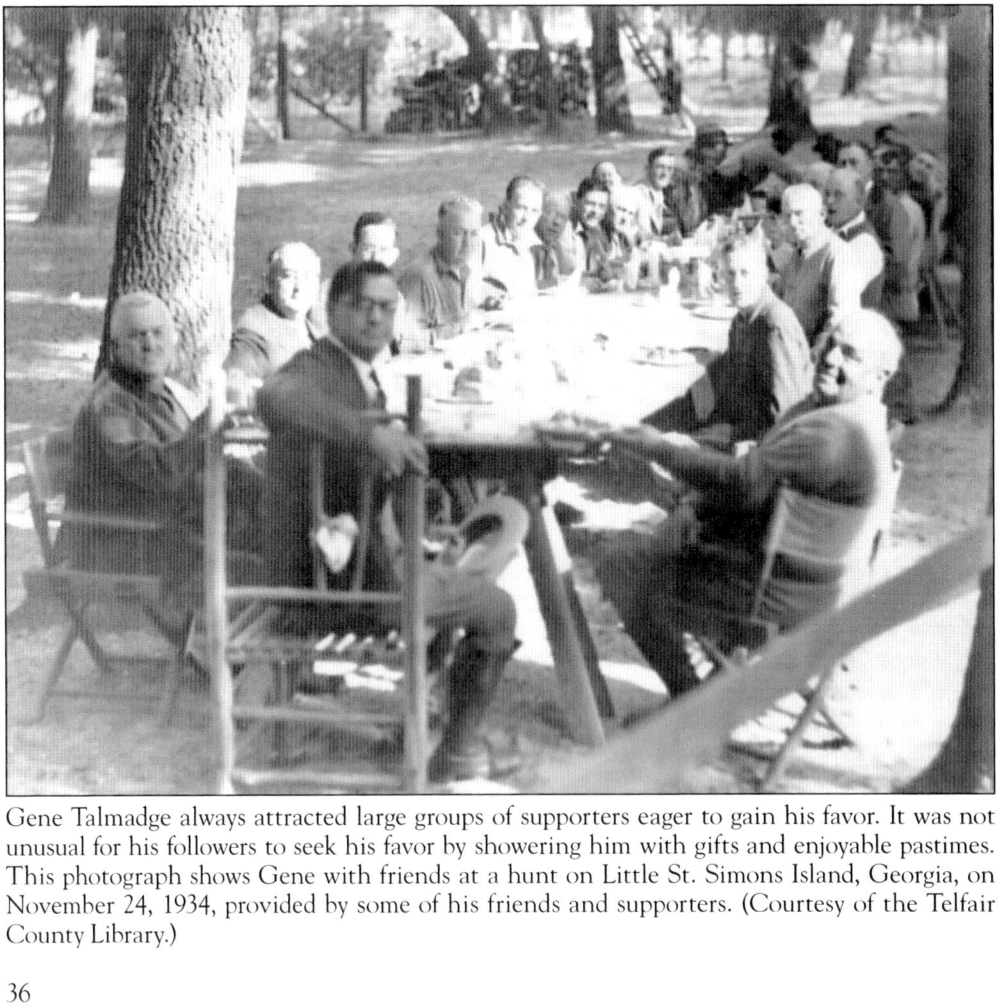

Gene Talmadge always attracted large groups of supporters eager to gain his favor. It was not unusual for his followers to seek his favor by showering him with gifts and enjoyable pastimes. This photograph shows Gene with friends at a hunt on Little St. Simons Island, Georgia, on November 24, 1934, provided by some of his friends and supporters. (Courtesy of the Telfair County Library.)

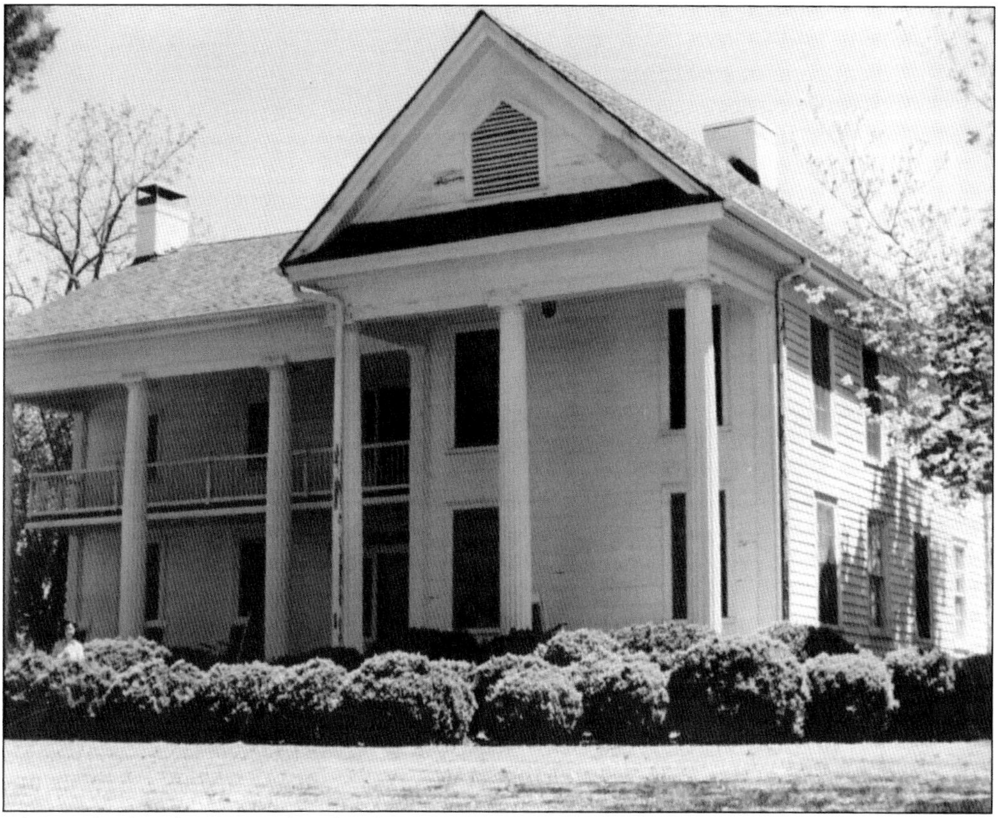

This is the lovely 1836 Talmadge home in Lovejoy, Clayton County, Georgia, which Gene Talmadge bought in 1940. According to field notes, the boxwood came from Betty Talmadge's mother's home. The Lovejoy home was one of the models for Twelve Oaks in *Gone with the Wind.* Cedars line the drive and a scuppernong arbor is at left. (Courtesy of Georgia Archives, Vanishing Georgia Collection, image number clt017-83.)

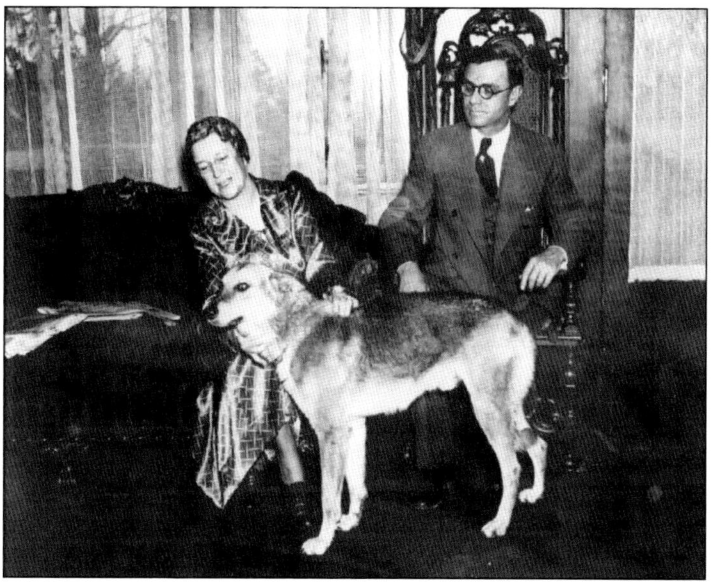

Taken in the 1930s, this is a photograph of Gene Talmadge, his wife, Mitt, and their dog. (Courtesy of Georgia Archives, Vanishing Georgia Collection, image number geo134-83.)

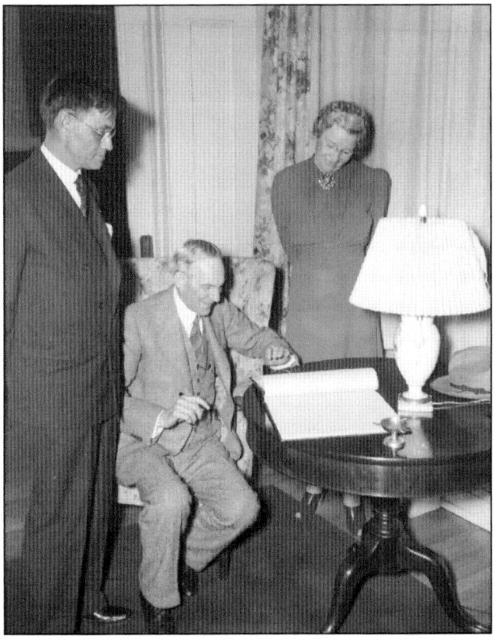

Automobile executive Henry Ford (in chair) with his wife, Clara Bryant, are visiting with Georgia governor Gene Talmadge at the governor's mansion in Atlanta, Georgia. The original photograph was taken around 1935. (Courtesy of the Kenan Research Center at the Atlanta History Center.)

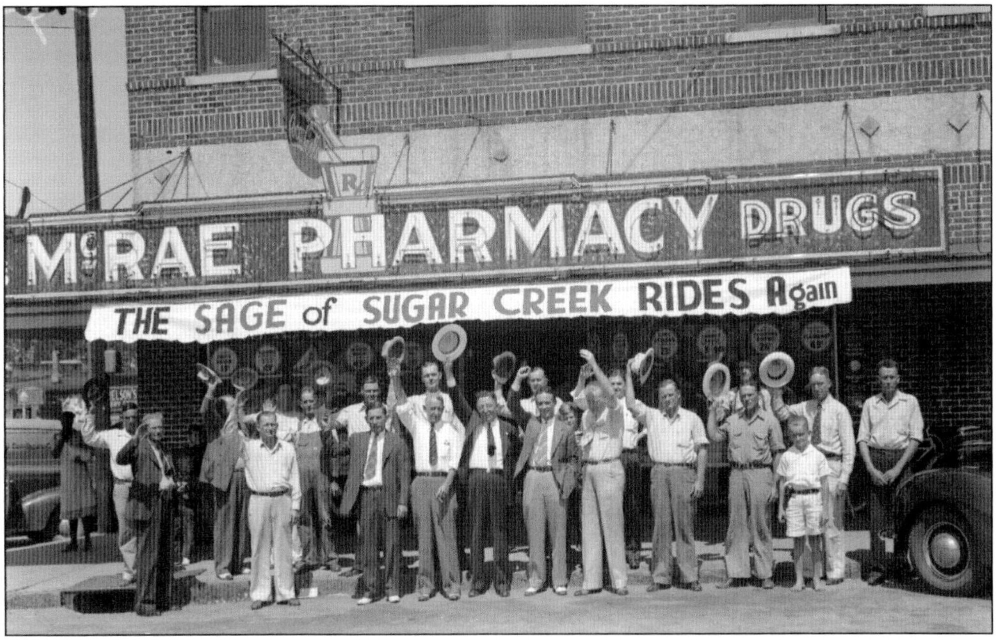


In this 1936 photograph, a crowd of supporters gathers in front of the old McRae's Pharmacy under the banner that refers to Gene Talmadge as the "Sage of Sugar Creek." This was during Talmadge's run for the US Senate. The heated senate race in 1936 pitted then-current senator Richard Russell against Gov. Eugene Talmadge. According to Ralph McGill, noted syndicated columnist, editor, and publisher of the *Atlanta Constitution*, Russell wanted to make a Democrat out of "Republican Gene." He tore up the governor for calling the CCC a bunch of "bums and loafers" and denied Talmadge's claim that Russell had befriended Northern African Americans. Russell defeated Talmadge 263,154 to 134,695. The county unit vote was 378 to 143. (Courtesy of the Kenan Research Center at the Atlanta History Center.)

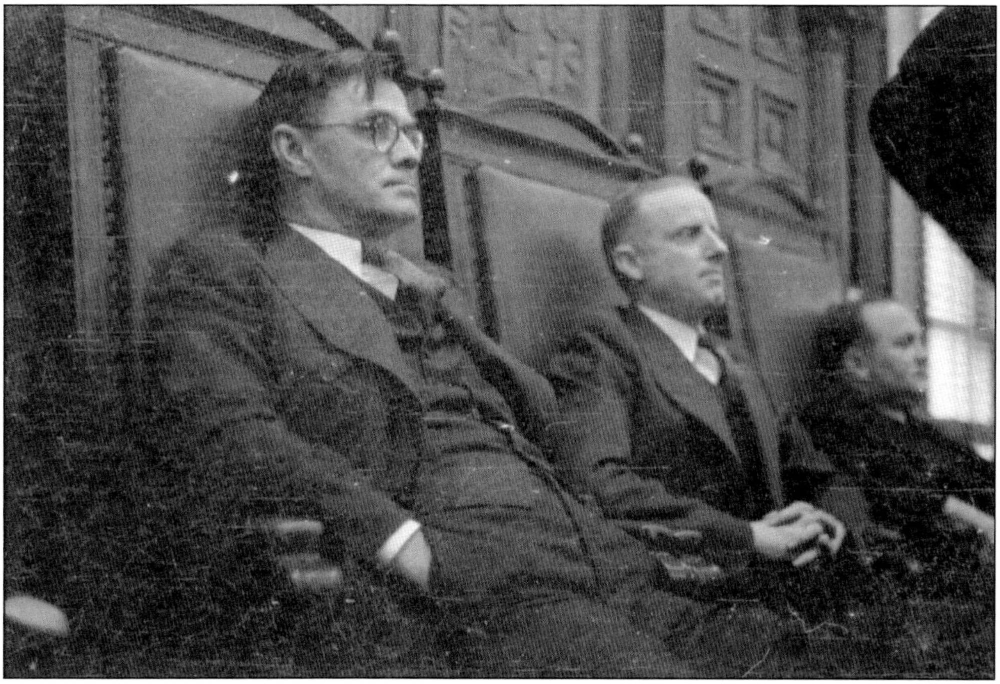

Former governor Gene Talmadge sits in the Georgia State Senate in this photograph, taken in 1939. During his three-term tenure as governor of Georgia, Talmadge reduced the cost of license tags, as well as utility charges and property taxes. (Courtesy of Special Collections and Archives, Georgia State University Library, Atlanta.)

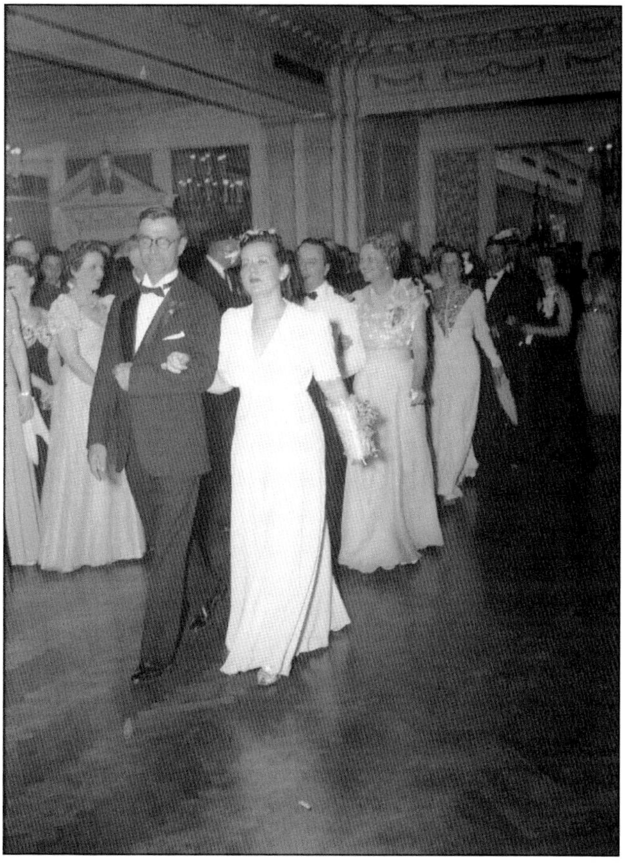

Gov. Gene Talmadge is shown at his inauguration in 1941. His wife, Mitt Talmadge, is in the procession behind her husband and the unidentified woman in the white gown. (Courtesy of Special Collections and Archives, Georgia State University Library, Atlanta.)

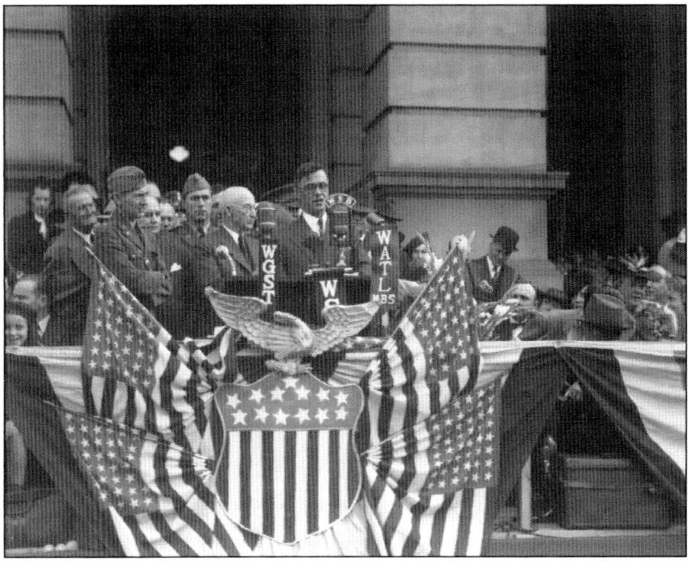


In 1941, Gov. Gene Talmadge is making his inaugural address in Atlanta before serving his third term as governor. He was convinced that farmers should not enlist in the Army and that married farmers should be released because the war was destroying rural Georgia. (Courtesy of Special Collections and Archives, Georgia State University Library, Atlanta.)

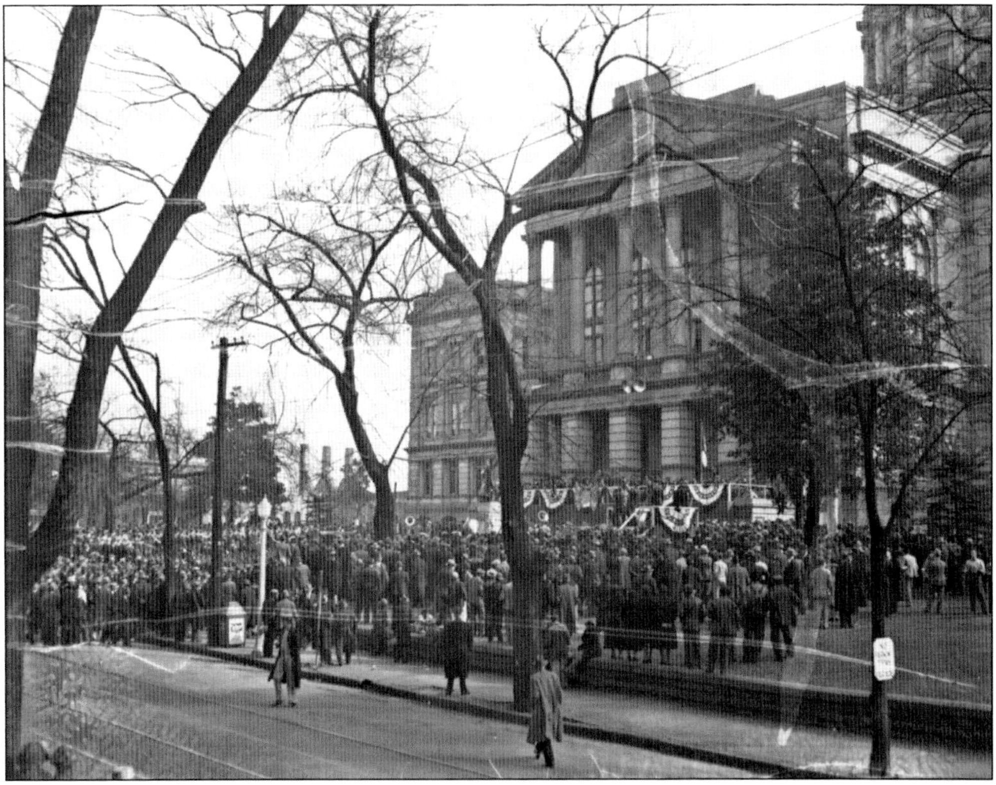

Decked out in patriotic bunting for Gene Talmadge's inauguration in 1941, Fulton County was the wintry scene of Talmadge's commencement of his third term as governor of Georgia. The photograph is dated January 14, 1941. (Courtesy of Special Collections and Archives, Georgia State University Library, Atlanta.)

Former governor Gene Talmadge campaigns in Lyons, Toombs County, Georgia, in this photograph, dated May 18, 1946. He died several months later in December after winning his fourth election and before beginning his fourth term in January. (Courtesy of Special Collections and Archives, Georgia State University Library, Atlanta)

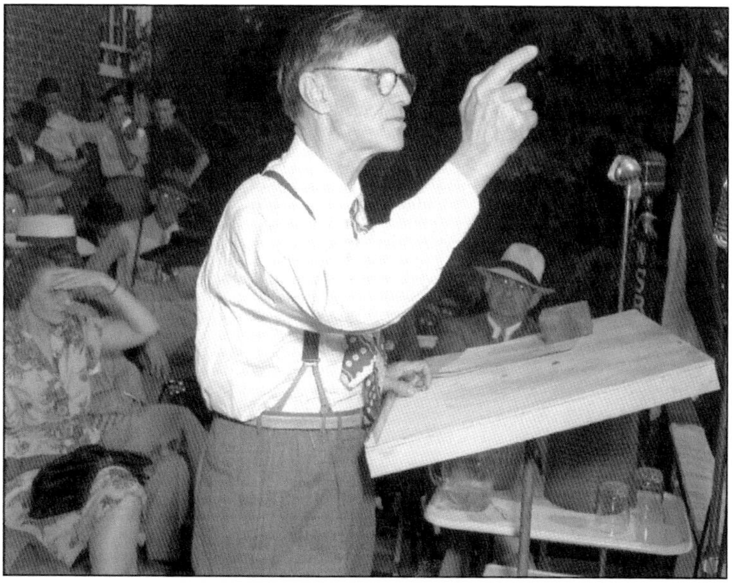

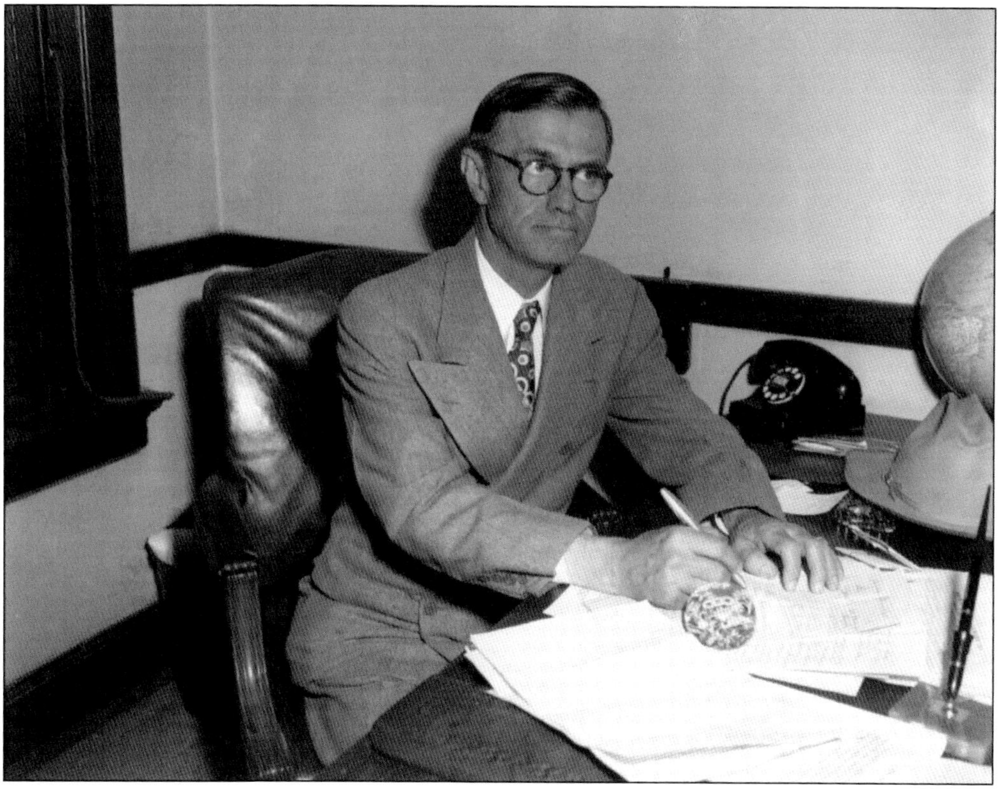

Dressed nattily in a double-breasted suit and tie, with his hat within easy reach, Gov. Gene Talmadge is shown prior to the July 1946 Democratic Party gubernatorial primary. The illness to which he would succumb in December is showing in his face. Though he would be elected governor, defeating Ellis Arnall, he would die within six months before beginning his fourth term. The photograph is dated June 3, 1946. (Courtesy of Special Collections and Archives, Georgia State University Library, Atlanta.)

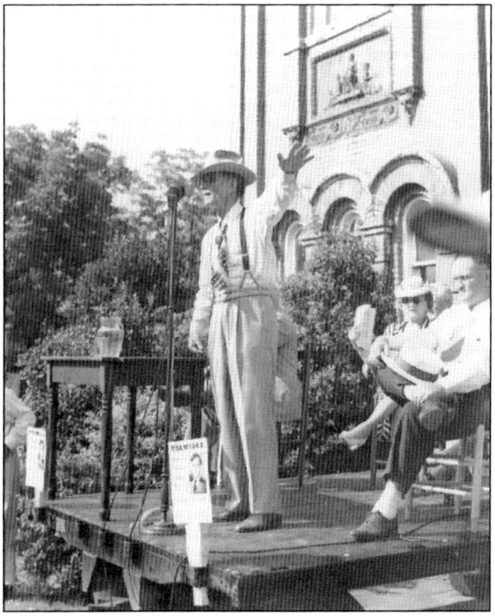

Eugene Talmadge represented himself as a champion of the common man. To emphasize this, he often doffed his suit coat and spoke to his supporters in his shirt sleeves, showing off his trademark red suspenders as seen in this 1946 campaign stump speech in Dublin, Georgia. (Courtesy of the Telfair Museum of History.)

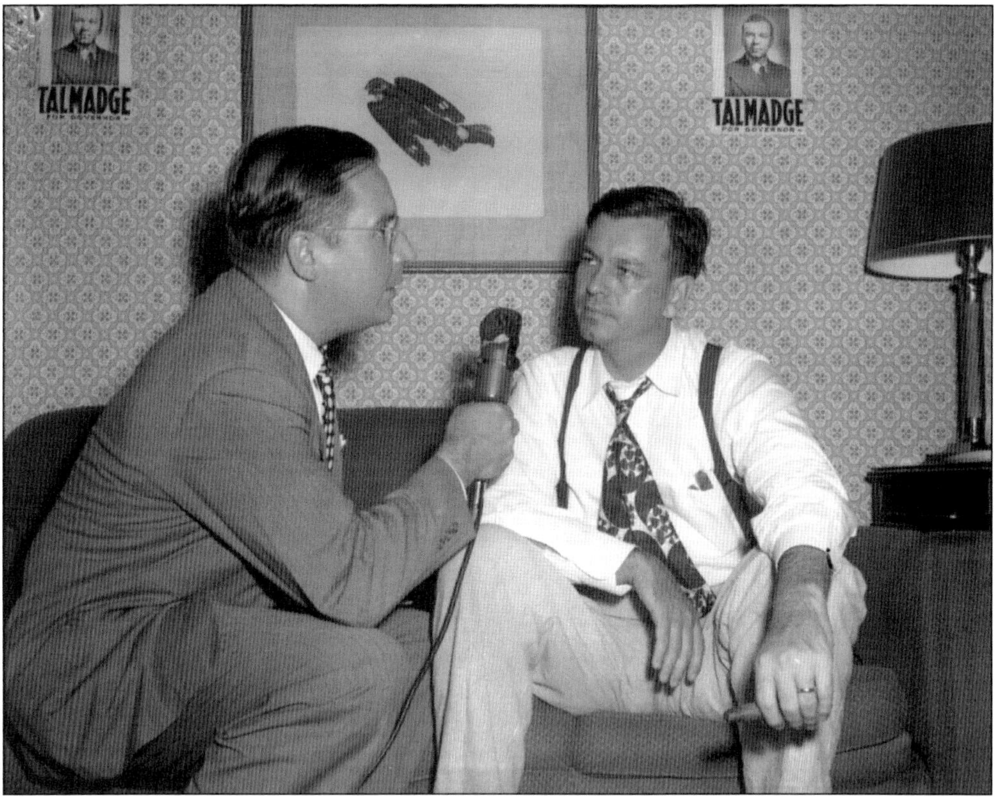


Herman Talmadge is being interviewed by John Fulton of WGST Radio in Atlanta in this photograph, taken September 8, 1948. He could have been talking about the fact that in 1948 "forest industries were bringing $300 million a year into Georgia's economy." This is an excerpt from Herman Talmadge's book *Talmadge, a Political Legacy, a Politician's Life*. (Courtesy of Special Collections and Archives, Georgia State University Library, Atlanta.)

Young Margaret Talmadge is either telling her father a secret or maybe she is kissing him on his cheek. Margaret married Scott Shepherd, and they lived in the Talmadge home in McRae for many years. After Shepherd's death in 1982, Margaret continued to reside in her family's ancestral home until her death on December 5, 2001. (Courtesy of the Telfair County Library.)

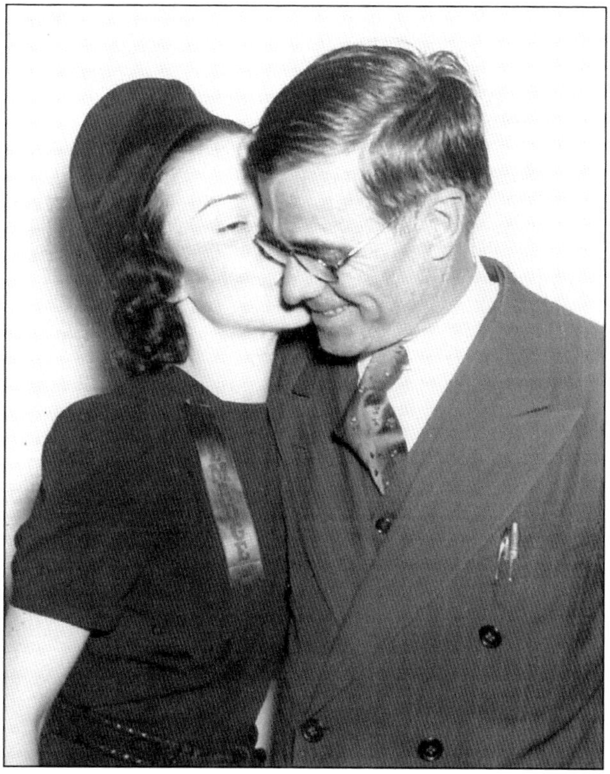

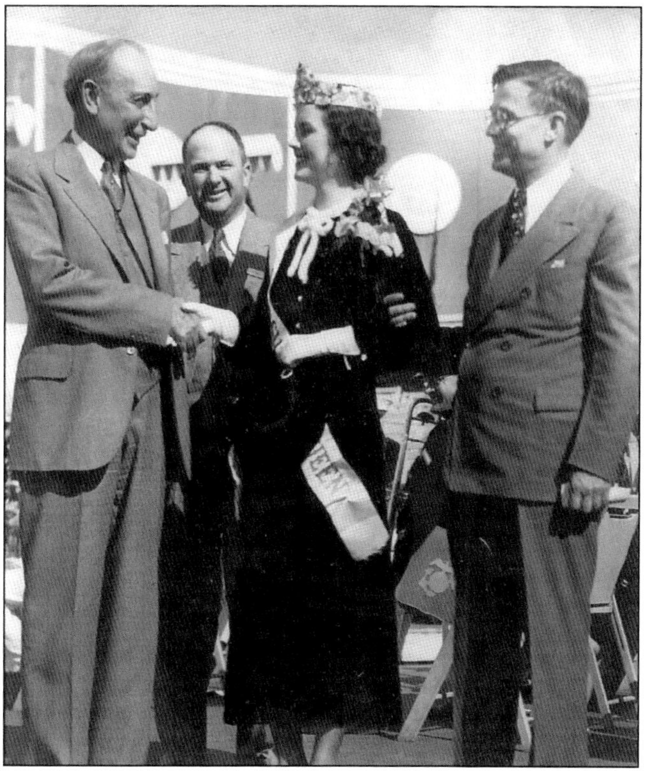

Both of Gene and Mitt Talmadge's daughters were beautiful. Here we see Vera Talmadge with a crown on her head and a sash that proclaims her queen in an unknown competition. Her father, Gene (right), looks on with obvious pride. (Courtesy of the Telfair County Library.)

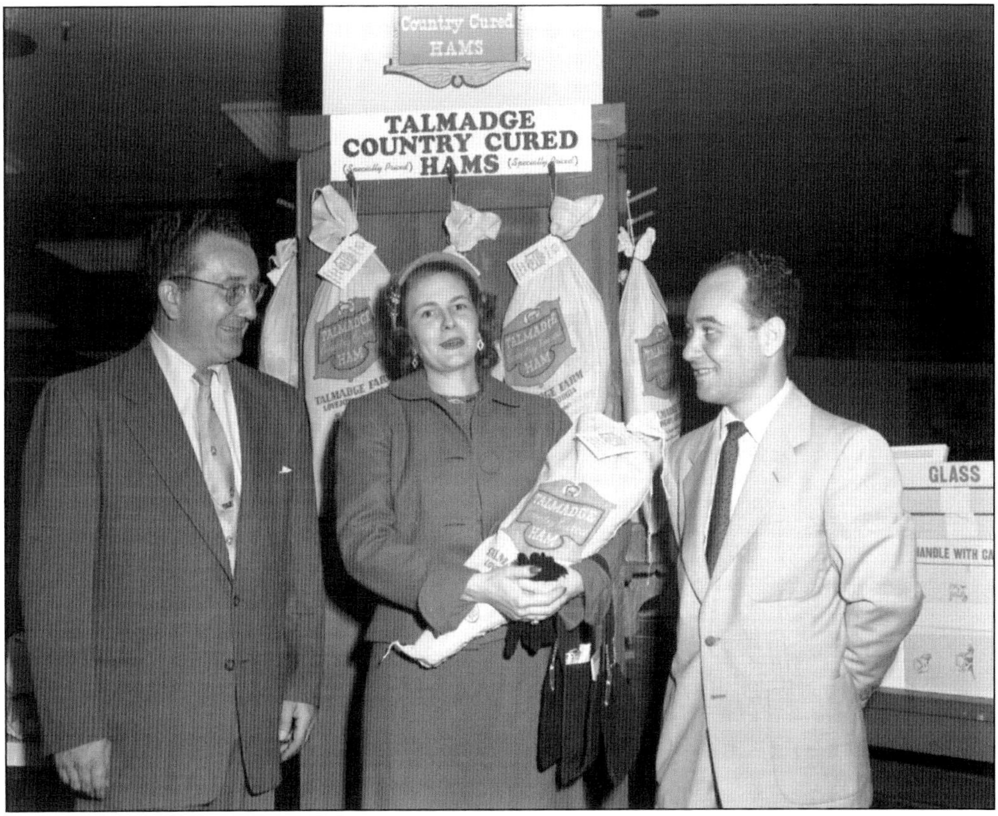


In this 1953 photograph, Betty Talmadge is holding a Talmadge Farm ham. She built the company into a business worth $6 million before selling it in 1969. She was a prominent socialite and hostess in Washington, DC, and a frequent bridge partner of Lady Bird Johnson. When her autobiographical cookbook was published in 1977, a *New York Times* reporter asked her how she found the nerve to slaughter her first pig. "Real easy, honey," she replied, "I first thought, 'you little male chauvinist, you,' and I went to it." (Courtesy of Special Collections and Archives, Georgia State University Library, Atlanta.)

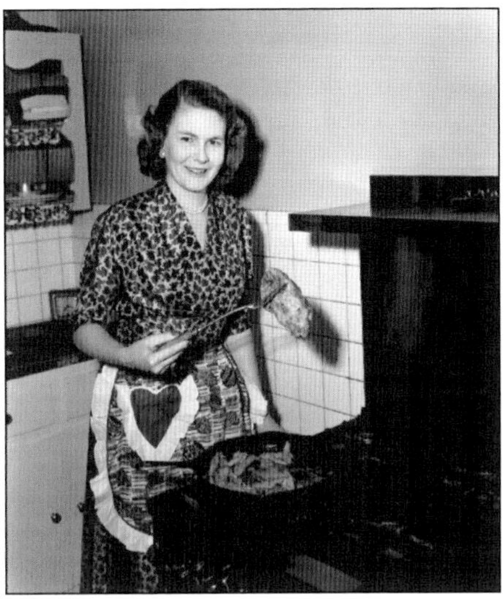

Betty Talmadge is shown frying chicken in a photograph taken in Atlanta on April 21, 1954. Her husband, Herman Talmadge, was governor of Georgia. Betty hosted elaborate parties for media and political guests at Lovejoy Plantation with her pet goat walking about as guests sipped cocktails. She claimed that Lovejoy was the inspiration for the home Twelve Oaks in the book *Gone with the Wind*. In 1977, Betty Talmadge's cookbook *How to Cook a Pig and Other Back-to-the-Farm Recipes* was published. She also wrote *Betty Talmadge's Lovejoy Plantation Cookbook*. (Courtesy of Special Collections and Archives, Georgia State University Library, Atlanta.)

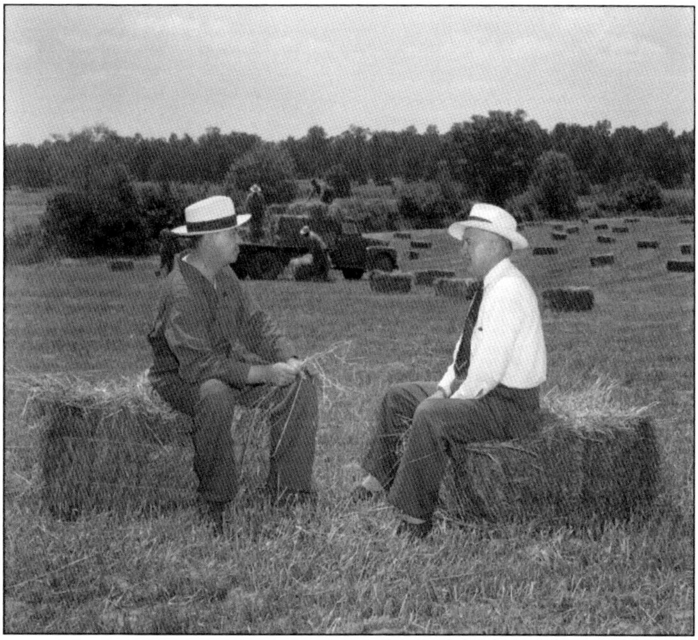

In the late 1940s or early 1950s, Gov. Herman Talmadge (left) and an unidentified man are having a chat at Talmadge Farms in Lovejoy. Lovejoy was a 1,200-acre tract 20 miles south of Atlanta in Jonesboro, which Gene Talmadge purchased in 1940. After Herman Talmadge's divorce from his second wife, Betty Talmadge, she retained control of the 1836 Lovejoy Plantation. (Courtesy of Special Collections and Archives, Georgia State University Library, Atlanta.)

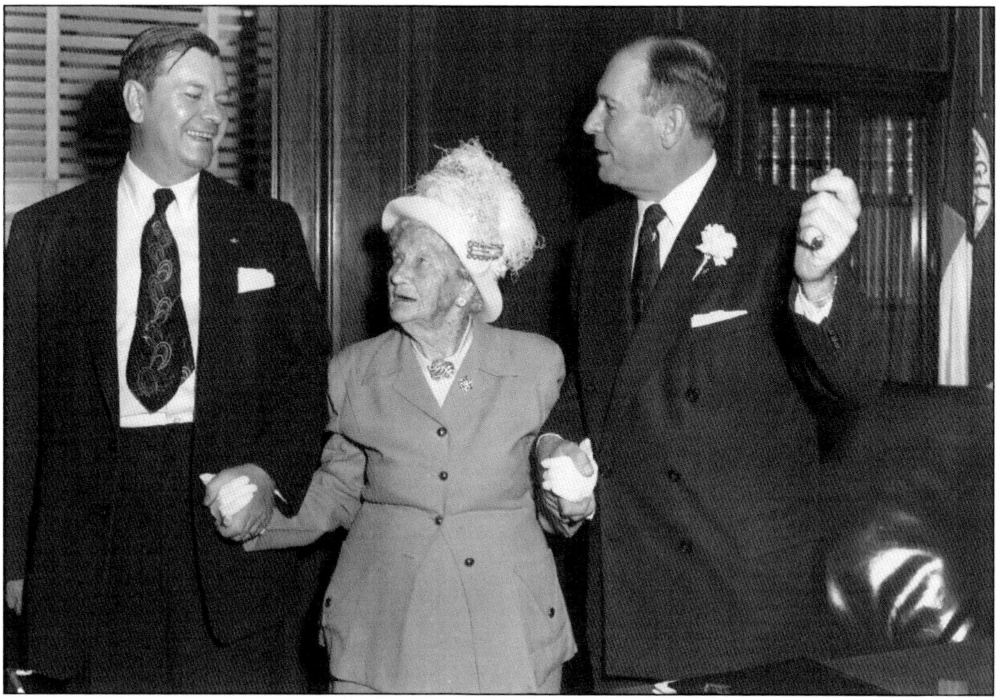

Governors Herman Talmadge (left) and Marvin Griffin met together with an unidentified supporter for the Georgia Governors Parade on January 11, 1955. Though *Harper's* magazine stated that Herman Talmadge was the "Best Southern Governor," when the publisher of *Time* asked what he thought of his magazine, Talmadge gave him an irate but candid answer: "The most significant news story in America today is the industrialization of the South, and I haven't read one word about it in your magazine." About six weeks later, the cover story in *Time* was "The Industrialization of the South." (Courtesy of Special Collections and Archives, Georgia State University Library, Atlanta.)

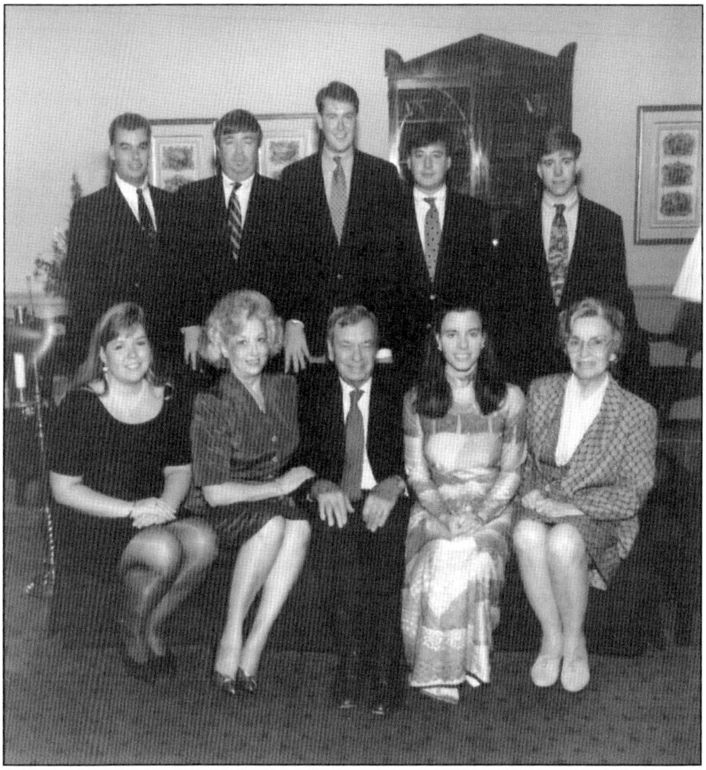

This Talmadge family photograph was taken when Herman Talmadge celebrated his 80th birthday on August 9, 1993. Pictured here from left to right are (first row) Mitt Talmadge, Lynda Talmadge, Herman E. Talmadge, Elizabeth Talmadge, and Margaret Talmadge Shepherd; (second row) David Pierce (Lynda's son), Gene Talmadge, Herman Talmadge III, Tyler Talmadge, and Robert Talmadge. Not pictured are Ramsey Talmadge, Murphy Talmadge, and Katherine Talmadge. (Courtesy of Lynda C. Talmadge.)

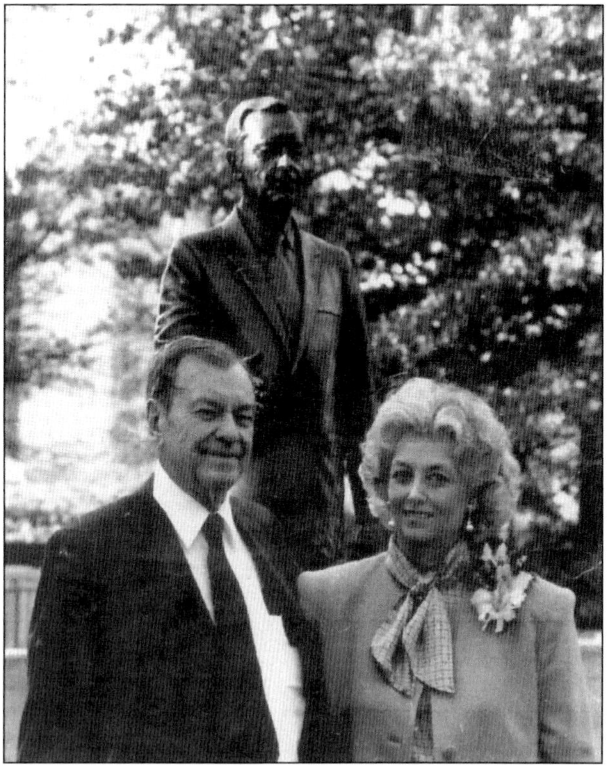

Herman E. Talmadge and Lynda C. Talmadge stand before the statue of Herman at the statue dedication at the Georgia Capitol on November 15, 1990. (Courtesy of Lynda C. Talmadge.)

Though it rained on the day of their wedding on September 30, 1984, Herman and Lynda Talmadge radiate their happiness as they stand together under an umbrella. They were married for 18 years. (Courtesy of Lynda C. Talmadge.)

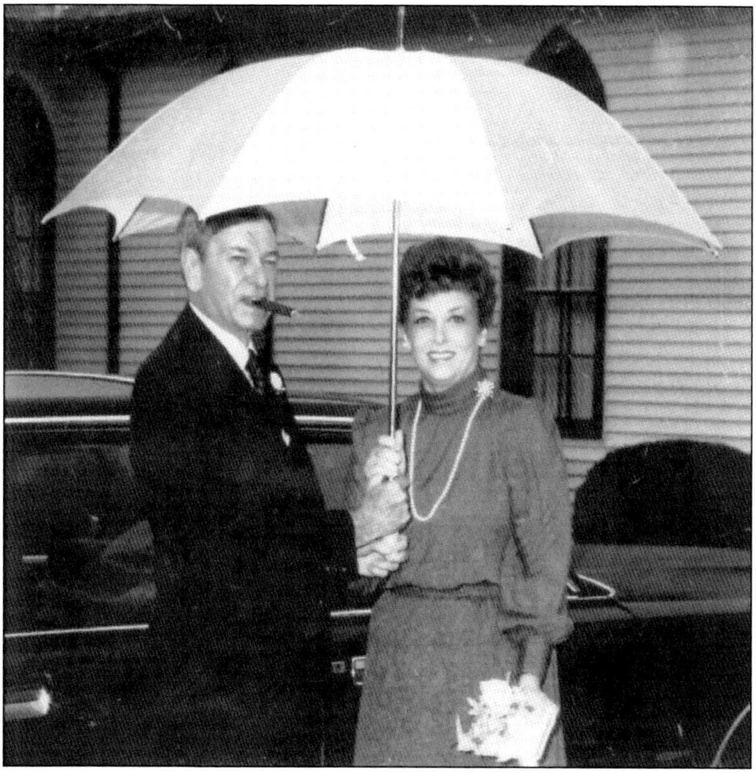

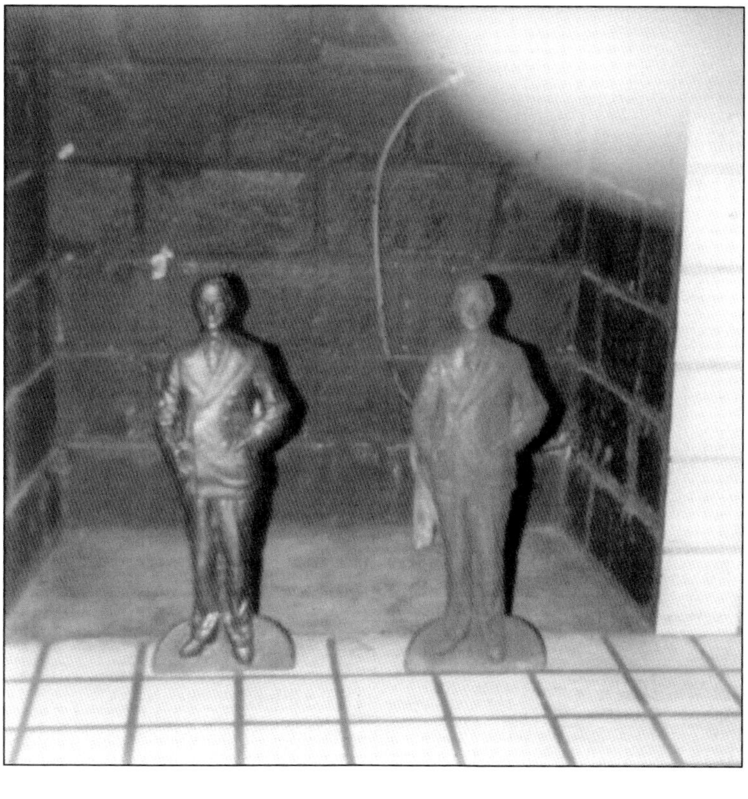

These are very intriguing andirons found in one of the upstairs bedrooms of the Talmadge home in McRae. They were made in the likeness of Gene Talmadge, who received many unusual gifts throughout his political career. (Courtesy of Norwood Davidson.)

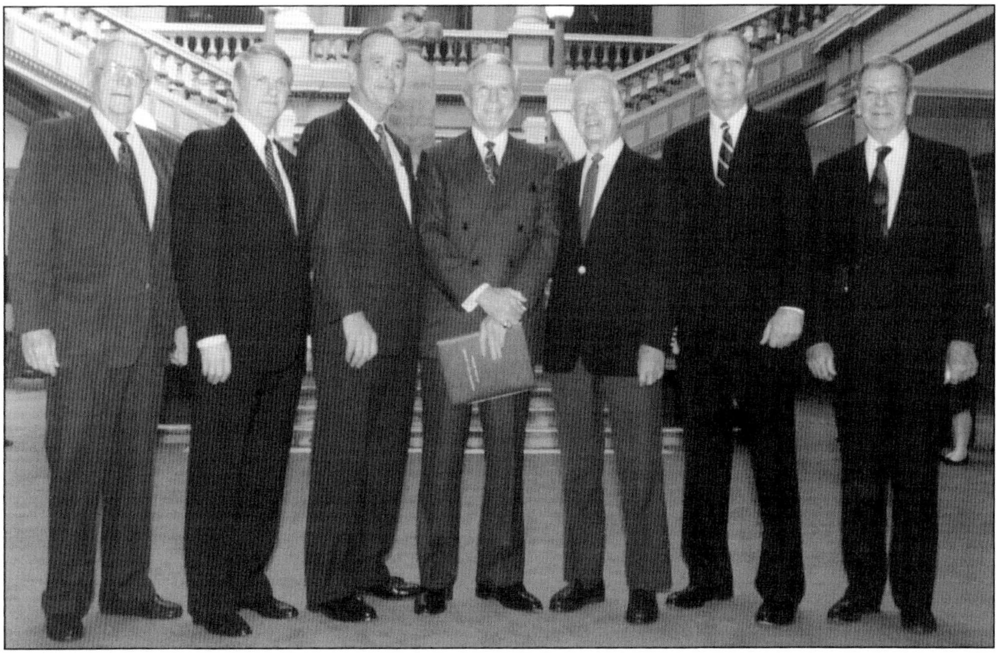

Seven Georgia governors posed for this photograph at the Georgia Capitol on January 25, 1991. Pictured here from left to right are Ernest Vandiver, Zell Miller, George Busbee, Carl Sanders, Jimmy Carter, Joe Frank Harris, and Herman Talmadge. Of the seven, only three are still living: Miller, Carter, and Harris. (Photograph by Joe Sports, courtesy of the Georgia Historical Society.)

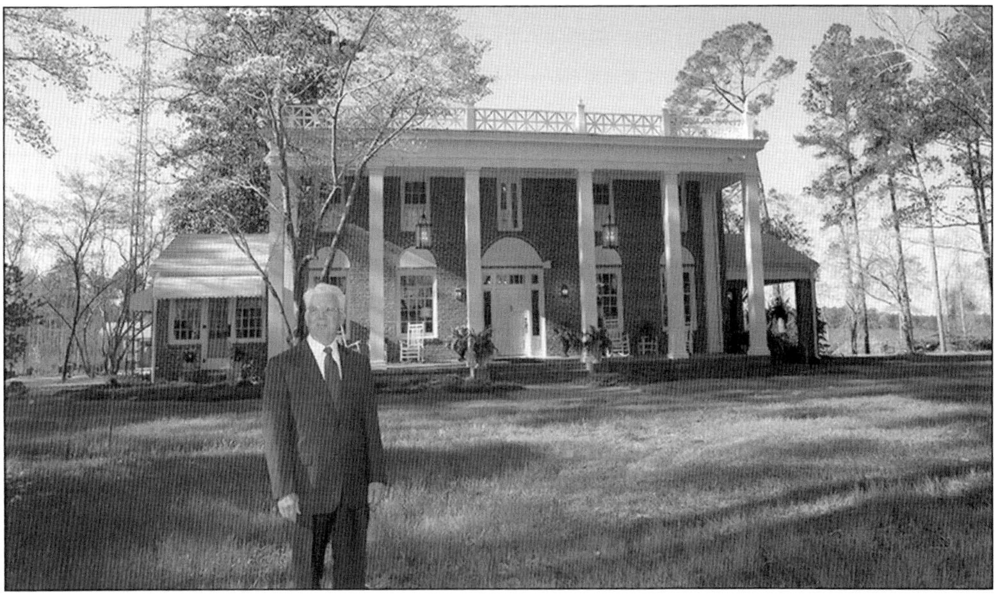

Jim Wooten stands before the lovely and historic Talmadge home, now called Sugar Creek Plantation, which he and his wife, Ann, bought in 2011 and restored. Home to two Georgia governors, Gene and Herman Talmadge, the house was built in 1937. Retiring in 2009 after nearly 40 years in journalism, Jim Wooten was former southeastern bureau chief for *U.S. News & World Report*, editorial page editor of the *Atlanta Journal*, and later associate editor of the combined *Journal-Constitution*. (Courtesy of Donnie Swanson.)

# *Four*

# People, Places, and Events

Telfair County, one of the oldest counties in Georgia, was established in 1807. The county is named for Edward Telfair, a two-term governor of Georgia. Telfair was a member of the Continental Congress and a signatory of the Articles of Confederation.

The county is located on the big bend of the Ocmulgee River near the confluence of the Ocmulgee, Oconee, and Altamaha Rivers in central Georgia. First inhabited by Native Americans, the area was viewed in high regard for its location on the river and its fertile soil. It provided easy access to the ocean and the interior of Georgia.

Shaped like an exotic dancer's fan, Telfair County's towns and communities are situated along the county's borders. McRae, the county seat, is located in the triangle at the top of the fan, while Milan, Jacksonville, Lumber City, and Scotland border the county lines east, south, and west of McRae. These communities have long and storied histories that long to be explored.

Jacksonville, located about 20 miles south of McRae, was the county seat until it was moved to McRae in 1871. Although largely untouched by both the Revolutionary War and the Civil War, many stories abound, including a possible path of de Soto as he traversed the Southeast in search of gold and the escape route of Jefferson Davis as he fled Union soldiers at the end of the Civil War.

Many prominent people called Telfair County home, including two former governors, Gene Talmadge and his son Herman. Herman also was a US senator. Marion Folsom, former assistant secretary of the treasury and secretary of health, education, and welfare under President Eisenhower, also called Telfair County home. Brainard Cheney, author of *Lightwood*, *River Rogue*, *This Is Adam*, and *Devil's Elbow*, was raised in Lumber City. In 1932, the world's largest bass on record was caught in Telfair County by George W. Perry.

Common man and celebrity alike have worked together to make Telfair County a great place to live.

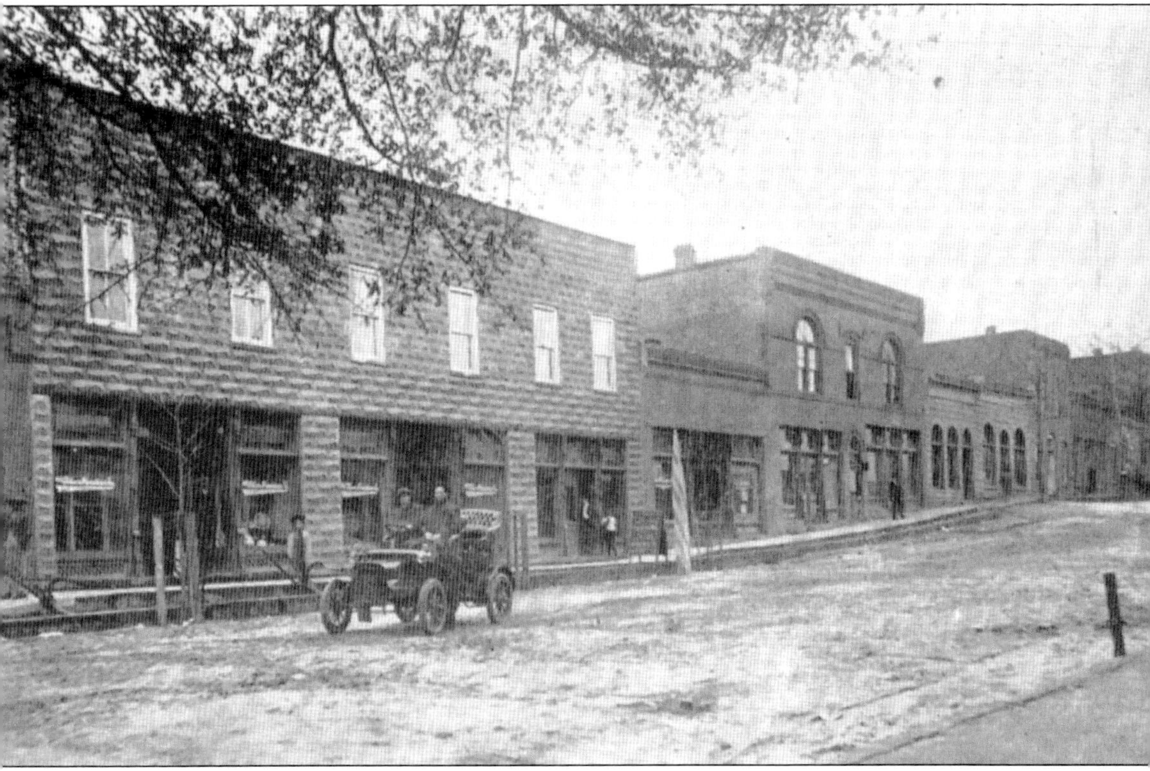

This early-1900s photograph of McRae, Georgia, features a horseless carriage, one of the first in town. The streets are unpaved, and the photograph appears to be looking east on the main street. In the right foreground, note the hitching post as horse and carriage were still the typical modes of transportation. In the center, there appears to be a barber's pole. (Courtesy of the Telfair Museum of History.)

McRae was a bustling small town in the 1920s. This photograph shows the town as it looked west from Oak Street to Second Avenue. Notice the tree-lined street and the newly paved sidewalk. (Courtesy of Bill Hunt Jr.)

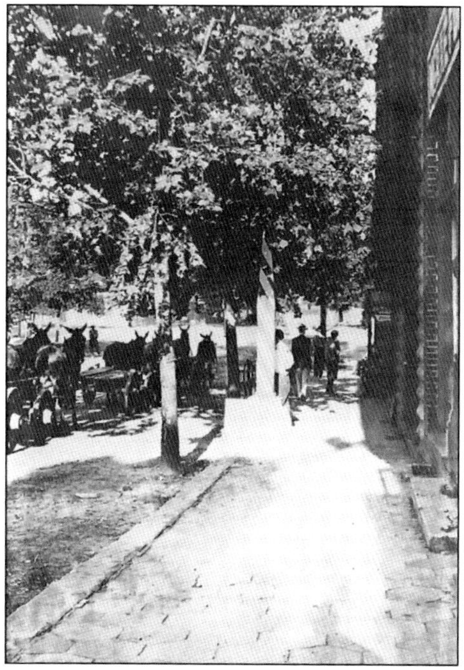

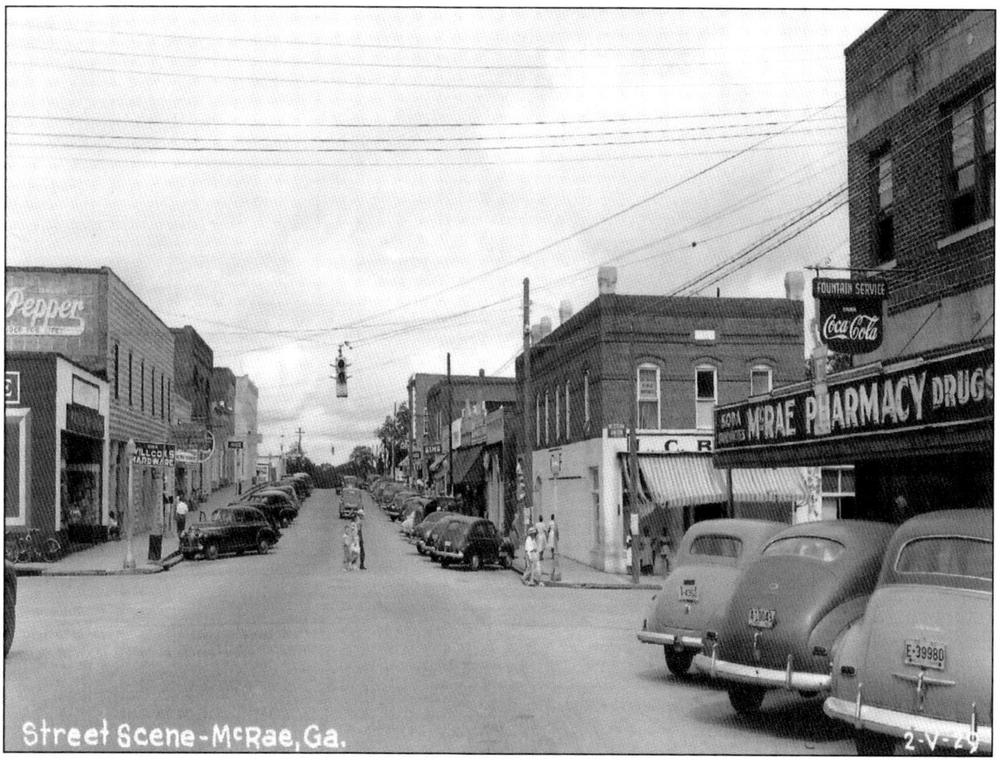


McRae, Georgia, was named for Daniel McRae, an early resident of the community. In the late 1940s, McRae was home to many area businesses, including McRae's Pharmacy, Willcox Hardware, and the *Telfair Enterprise*. This scene looks north on Oak Street, the main highway through town at the time. (Courtesy of Chris McRae.)

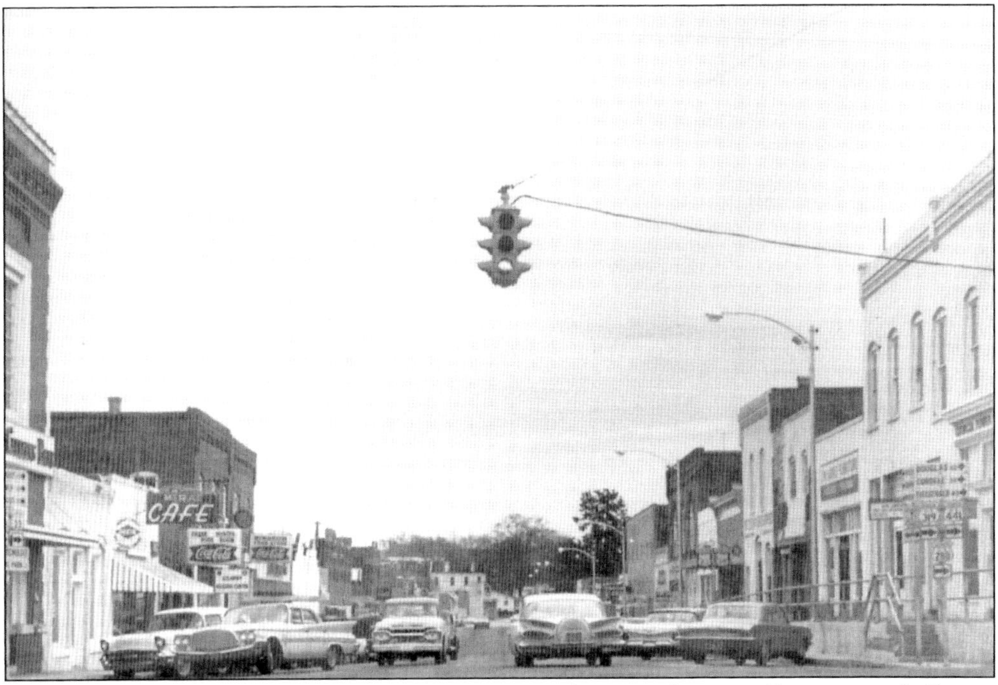


In the late 1940s and 1950s, McRae, Georgia, emerged as a modern city. Businesses of all sorts lined both sides of the main street. (Courtesy of the *Telfair Enterprise*.)

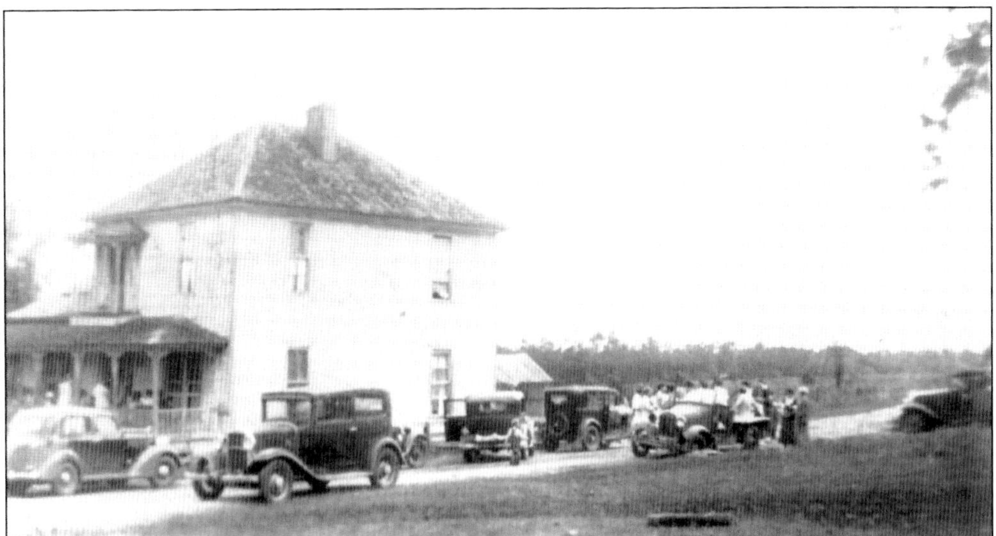

The Boney family migrated to Telfair County sometime before 1840. Cullen and Pheby Boney settled in the China Hill area. Their son Stephen and grandson Lucius remained on the homestead. Lucius built a two-story house on this site. This became the center of the Boney family until it was destroyed by a tornado in 1944. (Courtesy of LaJoy Boney.)

C.B. Parker was in the naval stores business. He built this Victorian house on Second Avenue in 1890, but it is no longer standing. He challenged any community to match his $10,000 for the building of a college. Mount Vernon did so, and Brewton Parker College was constructed there. Parker was also instrumental in the building of the First Baptist Church in McRae. (Courtesy of Harriette McClung and Eddie Taylor.)

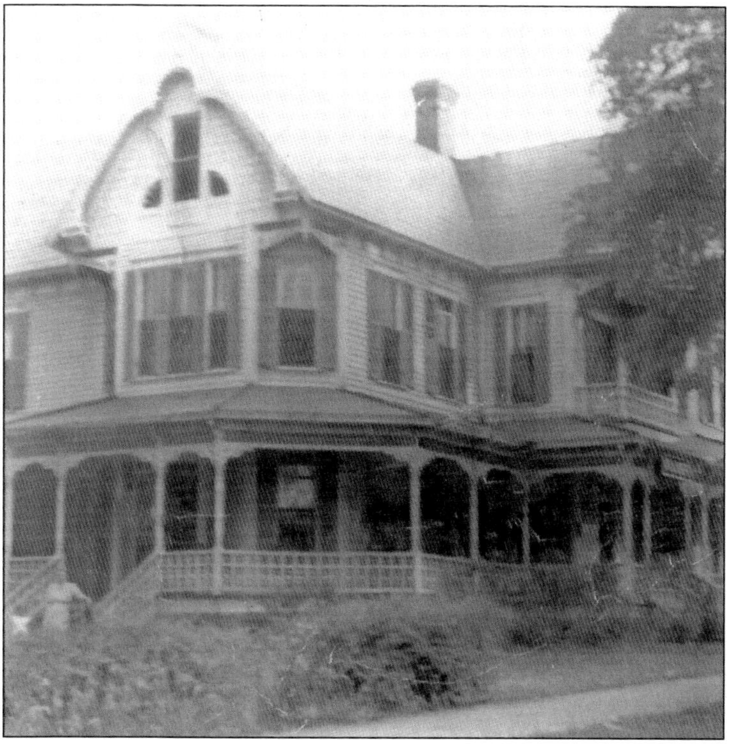

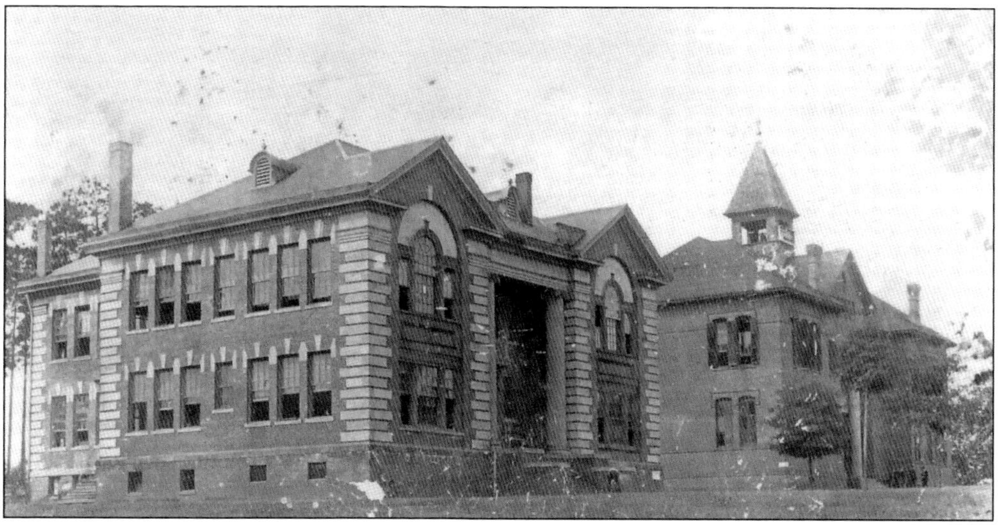

South Georgia College was chartered in 1892 and opened in 1893. The college was founded as a result of the initiative of Rev. W.A. Huckabee, pastor of the McRae Methodist Church, who persuaded the South Georgia Conference of the Methodist Church of the need for such an institution. It remained under the auspices of the Methodist Church until financial difficulties forced its closure in 1928. (Courtesy of the Telfair Museum of History.)

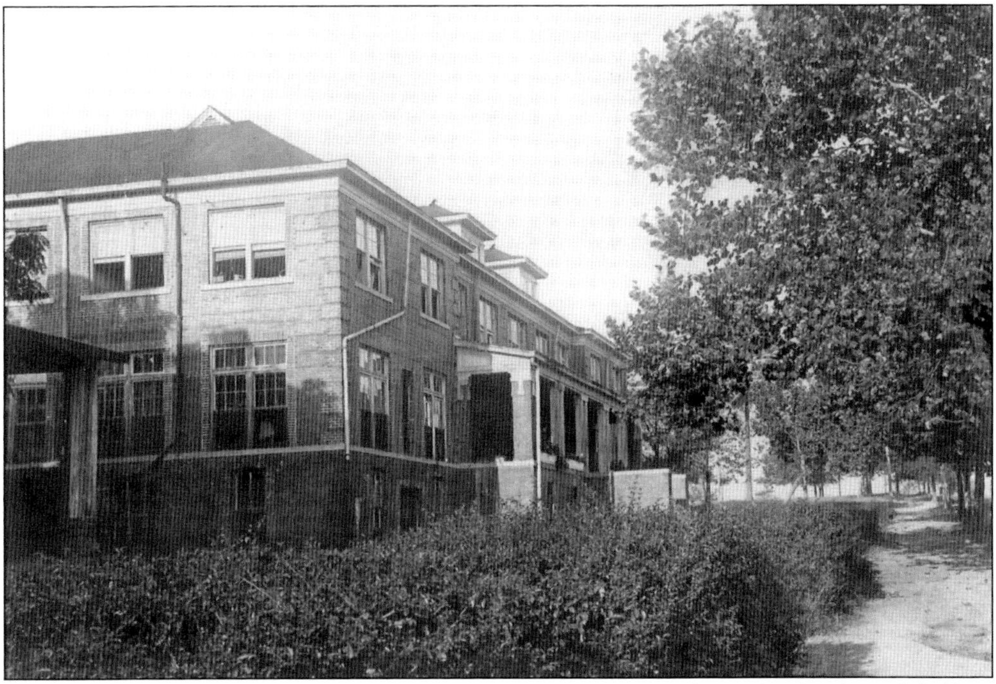

Despite its name, South Georgia College was opened in 1893 to serve the grade school–aged children of the area as well as those attending their first two years of college. The girls were lodged in the girls' dormitory pictured here. The boys' dormitory was separated by a fence, and the two sexes were not to meet except in class and at the coed cafeteria. (Courtesy of the *Telfair Enterprise.*)

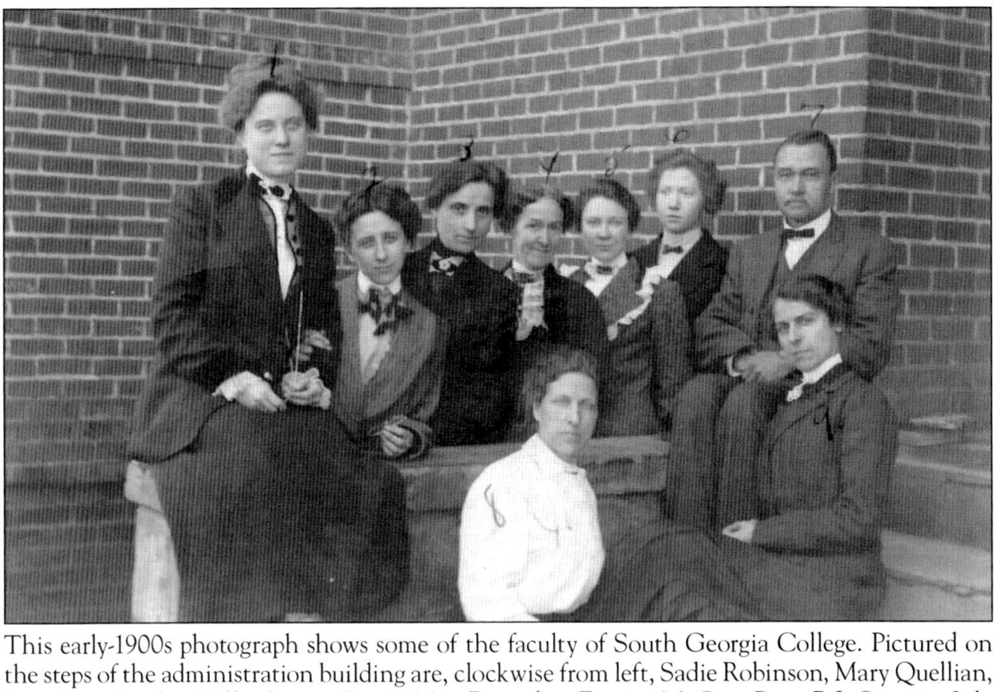

This early-1900s photograph shows some of the faculty of South Georgia College. Pictured on the steps of the administration building are, clockwise from left, Sadie Robinson, Mary Quellian, Josephine Banks, Willie Jones, Carrie Mae Brounlee, Eunice McGee, Pres. R.J. Strozier, Lila Windsor, and Newton Swinney. (Courtesy of the Telfair Museum of History.)

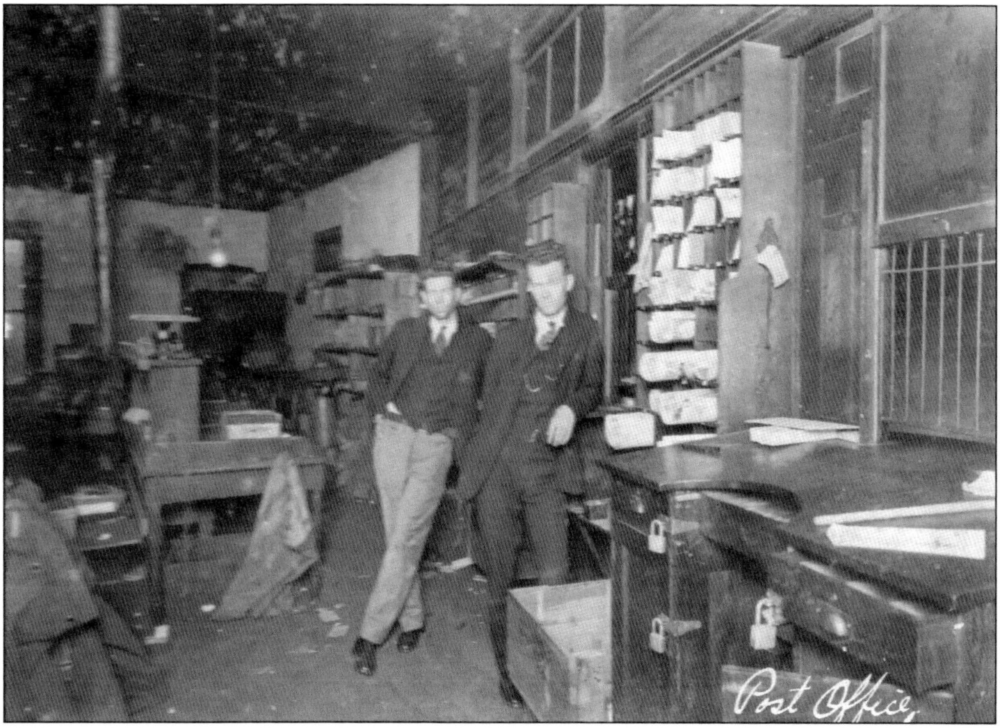


McRae's post office was originally located on Railroad Street. June Harbin (right) was one of the rural mail carriers for this post office. The original post office was established on February 3, 1891. The first postmaster, even predating the post office shown here, was John W. Griffin. In 1937, a new post office was built on the corner of Second Avenue and Pine Street. (Courtesy of Danny Harbin.)

Milan Methodist Church, as it stood in 1936, was originally built in 1894 on the west side of Milan. The land and materials to build the church were donated by interested citizens of the community. The lumber for the building was obtained from trees on the property. In 1949, a new brick church was built on the east side of Milan. (Courtesy of Patricia Cravey.)

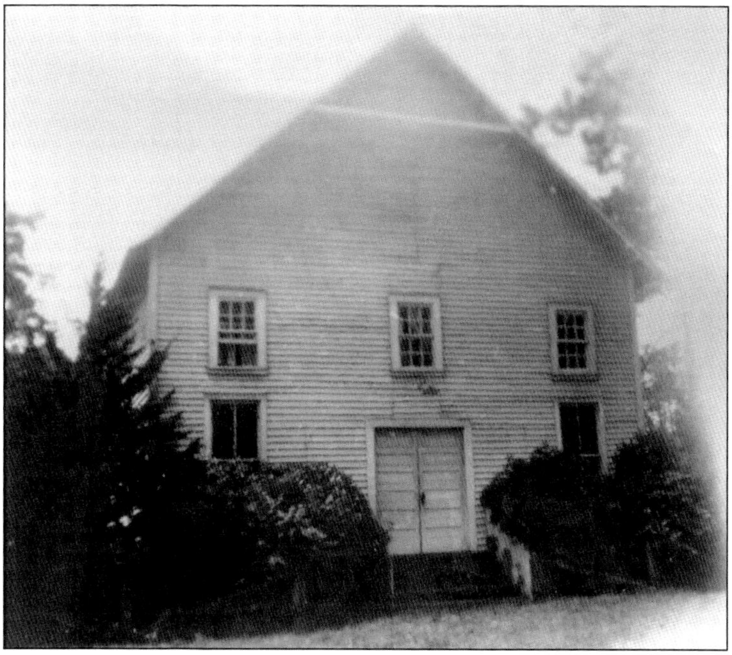

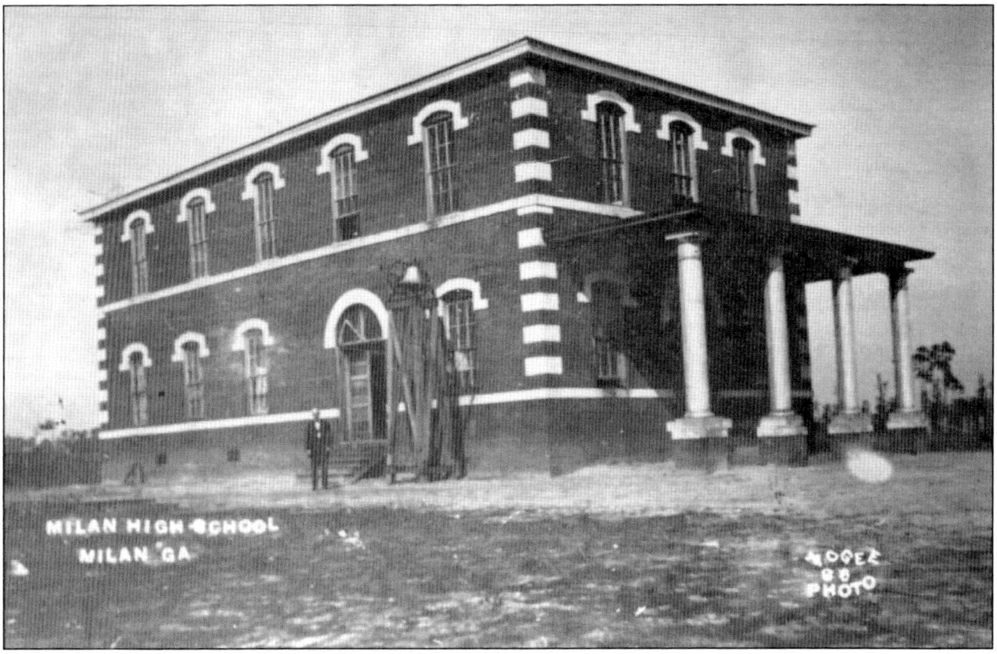


Milan High School was a modern-looking brick structure around the turn of the 20th century. Note the faux arched windows, the school bell in the yard, and the Greek columns on the front of the building—modern looking for the times. This building burned sometime after 1906. (Courtesy of Donnie Swanson.)

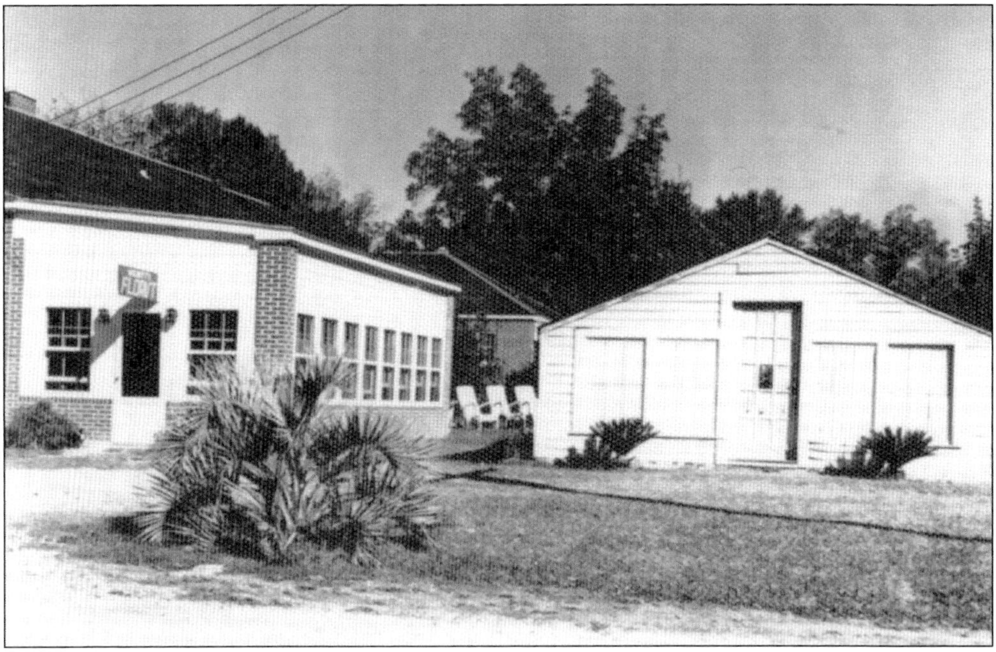

Essie McGinty opened her florist business in Helena in the 1940s. At one time, she was the only florist in the area. In 1939, the McGintys built a new home on Third Avenue in McRae with a florist shop included in the layout. Essie McGinty was self-taught in the trade. Her florist shop was unique in that it had a greenhouse. (Courtesy of Melissa McGinty Carroll.)

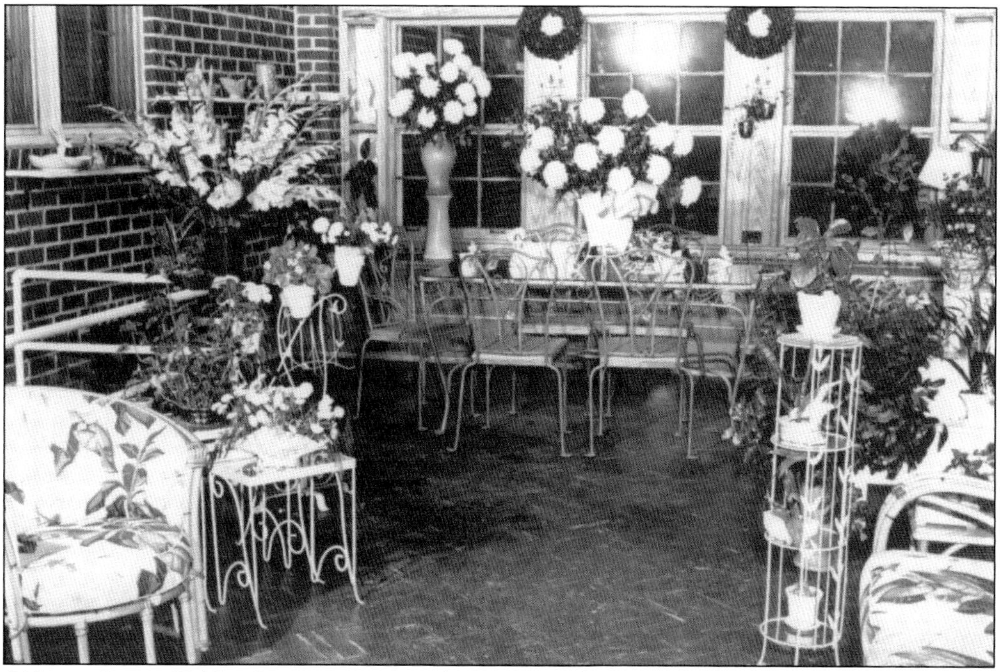

Older residents of Telfair County may remember going inside McGinty's Florist shop. This photograph captures an antiquated and interesting business. (Courtesy of Melissa McGinty Carroll.)

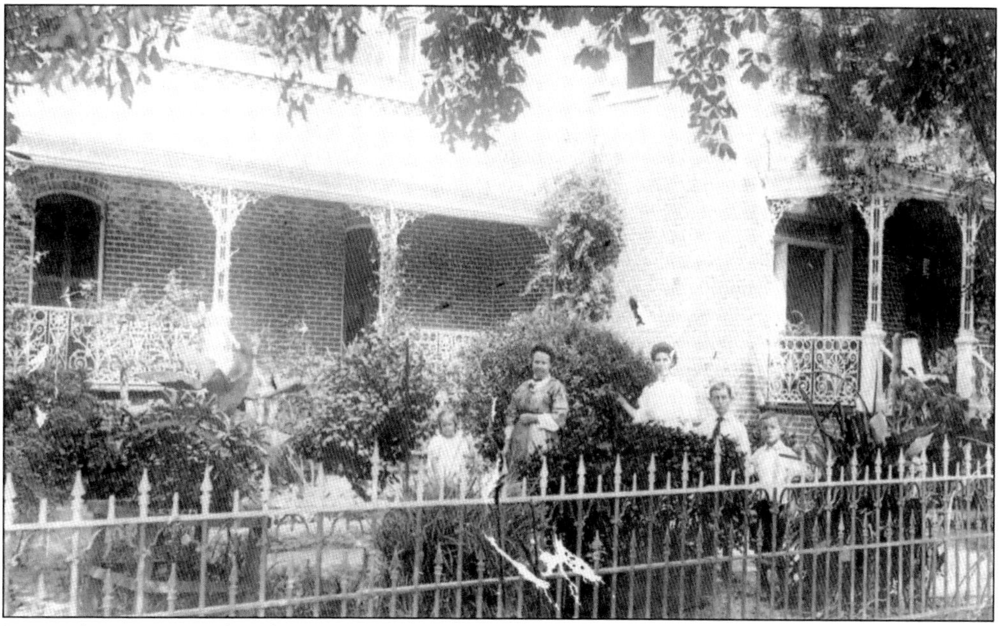

Located on West Railroad Street in Lumber City, this two-story brick building, constructed in 1885, was originally owned by Capt. John L. Day. He owned three steamboats on the Ocmulgee River and was a riverboat captain. This early photograph of the Day house shows, from left to right, Elizabeth Funderburke, Christian Day, Betty Massey McRae Funderburke, Alan Funderburke, and Paul Funderburke. (Courtesy of Thomas Wayne Anderson and Paula R. Anderson.)

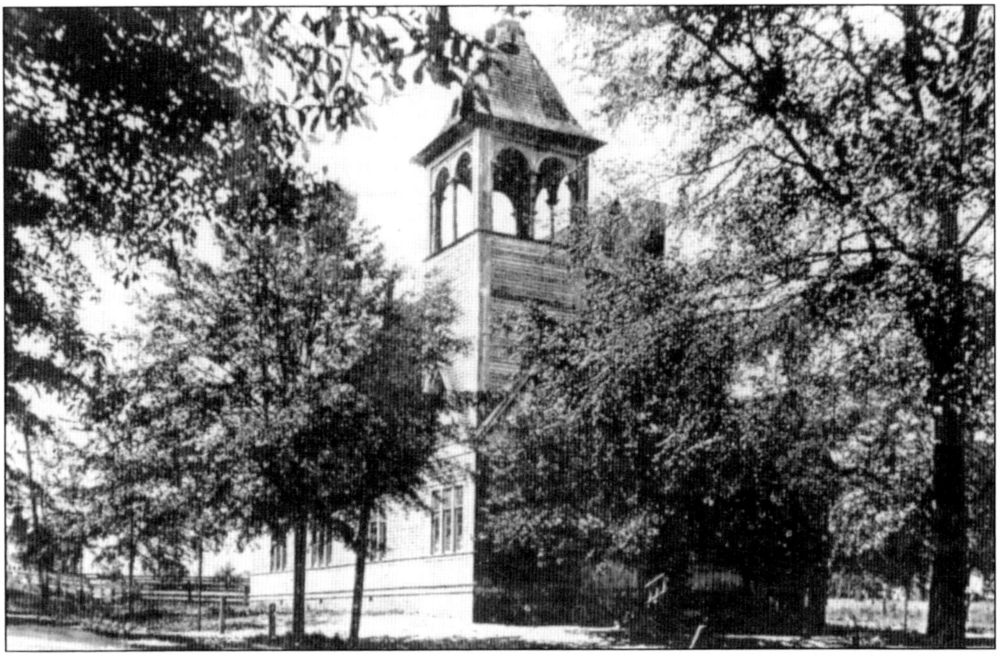

The second church building of the McRae Methodist Church was constructed on the corner of College Street and Second Avenue in 1899. The first church building, constructed in 1882, was on the corner of Parsonage Street and Telfair Avenue. The bell in the belfry was removed when the present building was erected in 1928. (Courtesy of the McRae United Methodist Church History Committee.)

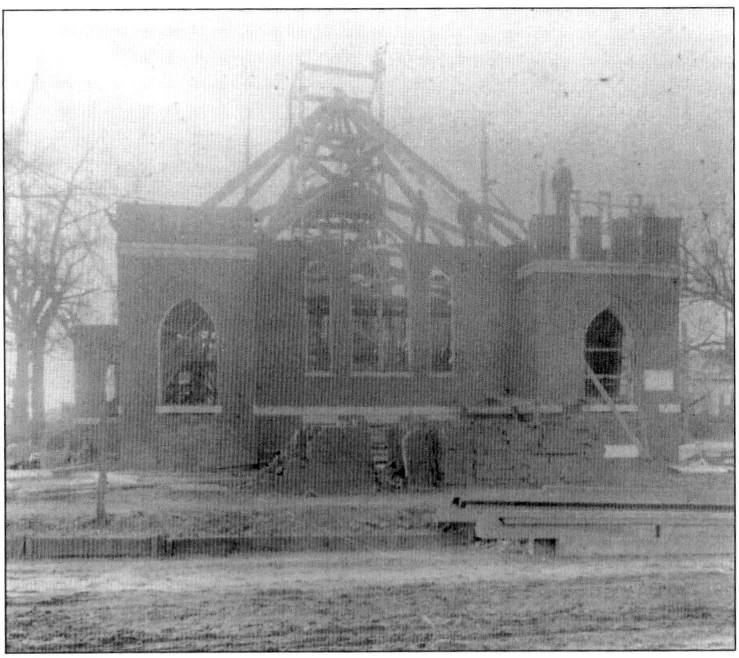

The First Baptist Church of McRae was established in 1890. A small church was built to accommodate a growing congregation. Soon it became apparent the small structure would not hold the number attending. In the early years of the 1900s, a decision was made to build a new, larger sanctuary. This photograph shows the present sanctuary being built during 1904–1908. (Courtesy of the McRae First Baptist Church.)

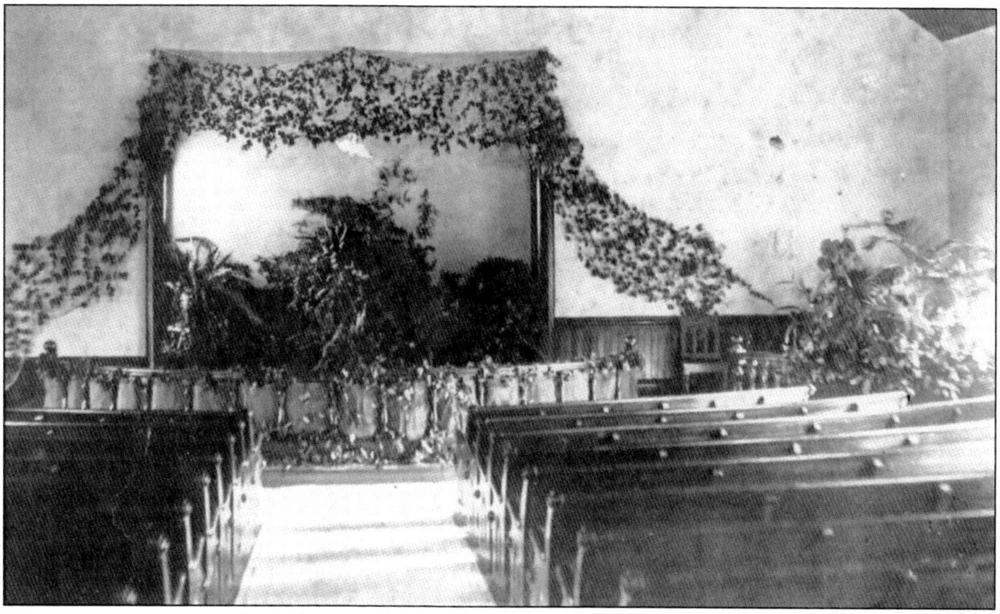

The sanctuary of the 1899 McRae Methodist Church was decorated for the wedding of E.F. McRae and Fannie Griffith in 1906. (Courtesy of the McRae United Methodist Church History Committee.)

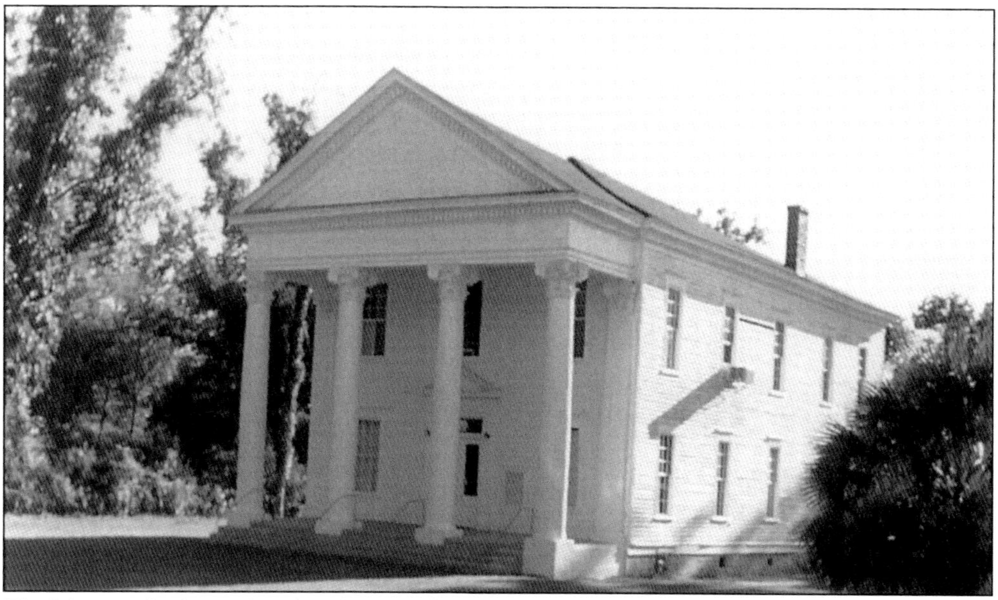

The Masonic Lodge in Lumber City was built in 1908. It was covered in weatherboard, and the interior consisted of a central hallway with rooms on either side. There was a main meeting room for group meetings. The front had four large columns, two pilasters, and dentils. This landmark burned in the 1930s. (Courtesy of Norwood Davidson.)

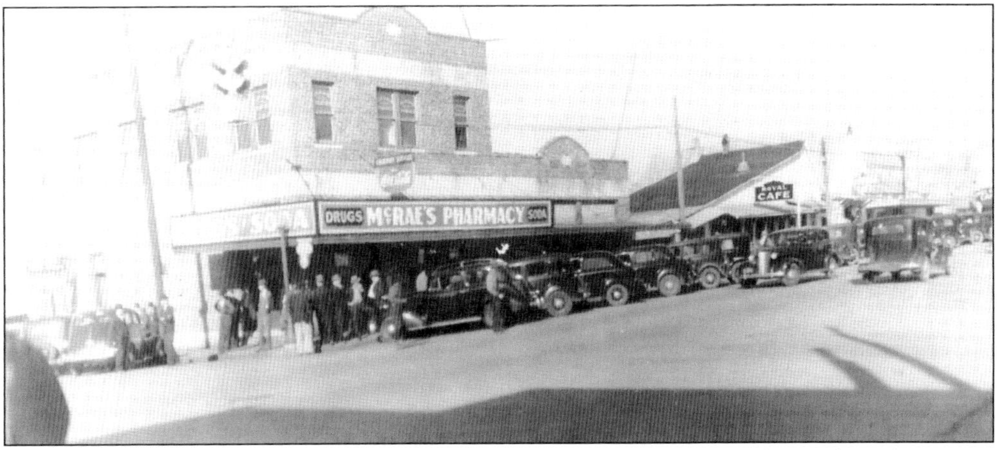


Opened in 1924 by Dr. W.A. "Billy" McRae Sr., McRae's Pharmacy was located on the corner of Oak Street and Second Avenue. At the time of Dr. McRae's retirement, it was recognized as the oldest privately owned pharmacy in the state. The establishment had a soda fountain where hamburgers and sandwiches were served. The pharmacy was relocated to a building on Oak Street in 1964. (Courtesy of Chris McRae.)

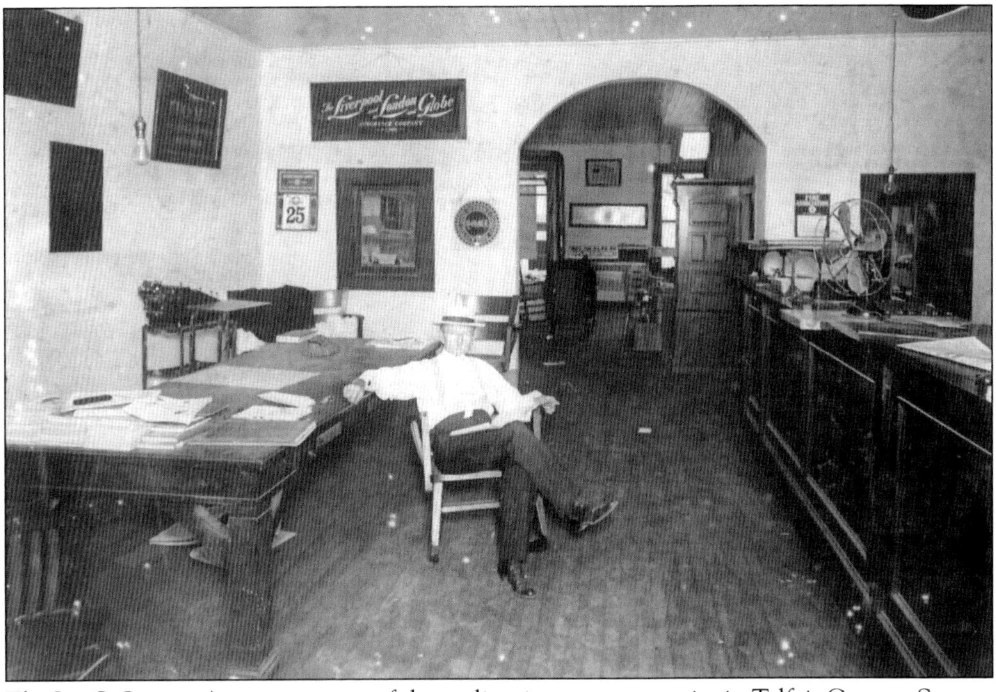

The Jon S. Stamps Agency was one of the earliest insurance agencies in Telfair County. Stamps purchased it from Judge Max L. McRae in 1914. He was the proprietor until his death in 1961. It was taken over by his son Jon S. Stamps Jr., who sold it to Henry Walker in 1977. This 1928 photograph shows Rudolph Oberley in the office. Oberley served as agent for the Georgia Land and Lumber Company after the murder of John C. Forsyth in 1890. Until that time, McRae had never had a city clerk, but the city hired Oberley as the very first. Since the city did not have an office, Oberley operated out of the insurance agency office. He moved his desk, likely the one used by John C. Forsyth, to the insurance office. William Dopson now owns this desk after purchasing it from Jon Stamps Jr. (Courtesy of Stamps-Walker Insurance Agency and William Dopson.)

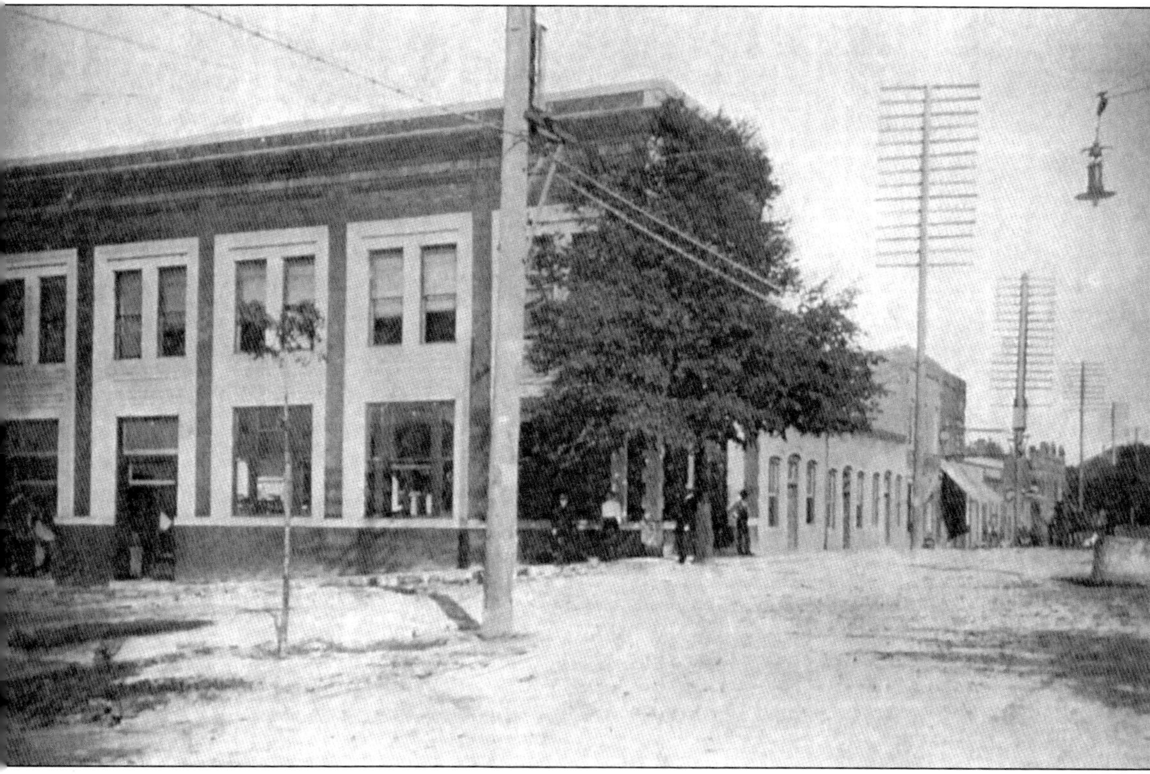

Merchants Bank of McRae, shown here, merged with Citizens Bank of Helena during the Great Depression. The two banks joined so that the newly created Merchants and Citizens Bank could survive the hard economic times. Merchants Bank was located on the corner of Oak Street and Third Avenue in McRae. (Courtesy of Dr. Mickey Nelson.)

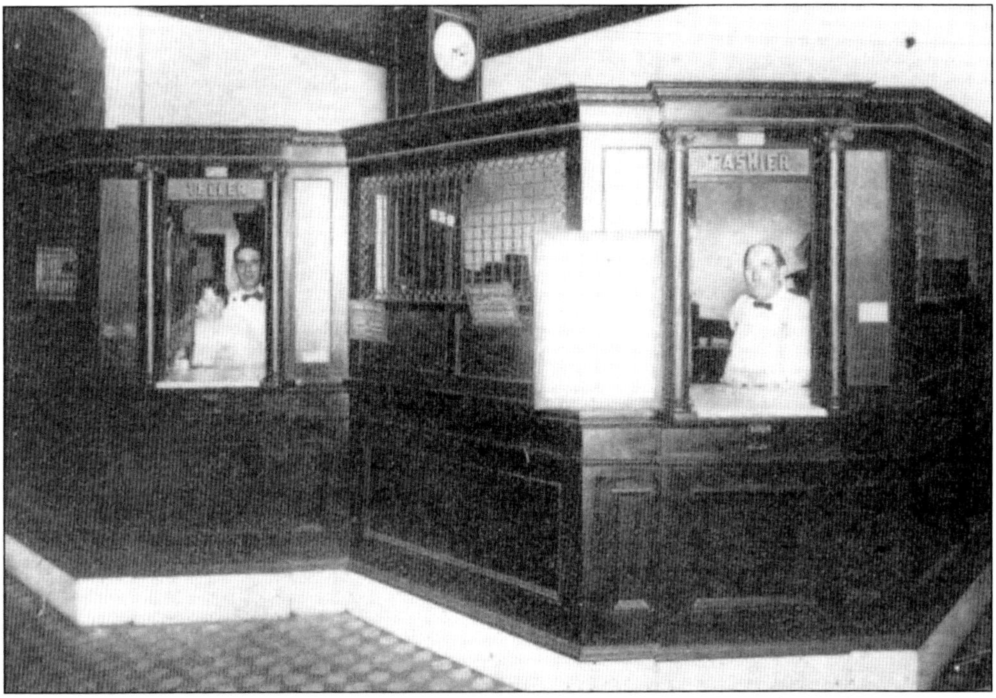


Merchants and Citizens Bank was established in 1929 with the merger of Merchants Bank of McRae and Citizens Bank of Helena. Its charter was granted on March 28, 1929. O.F. McRae was the first president and cashier of the bank. Shown here is the interior of Old Merchants Bank around 1908. Pictured in the interior are, from left to right, Annie Whidden, E.F. McRae, and O.F. McRae. (Courtesy of Merchants and Citizens Bank.)

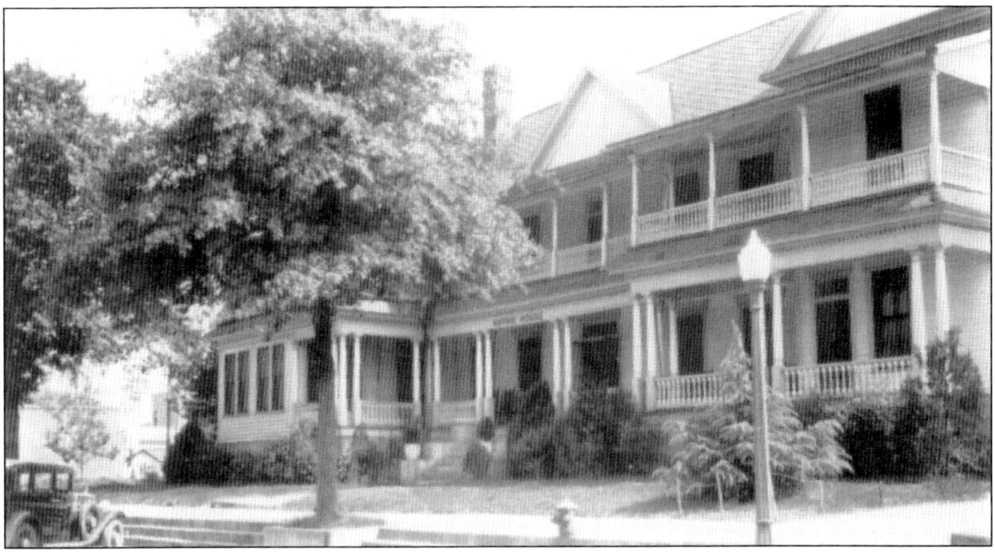

A well-known hotel in McRae was the Harris House. It was established by a Mrs. Guerry and managed by her and later her sister T.A. "Grand Ma" Harris. The establishment was later managed by a Mrs. Marquis, and Mrs. H. Fenchel succeeded her. The hotel was outfitted in the most modern way, and its services were equal to any city hotel. (Courtesy of Harriette McClung and Eddie Taylor.)

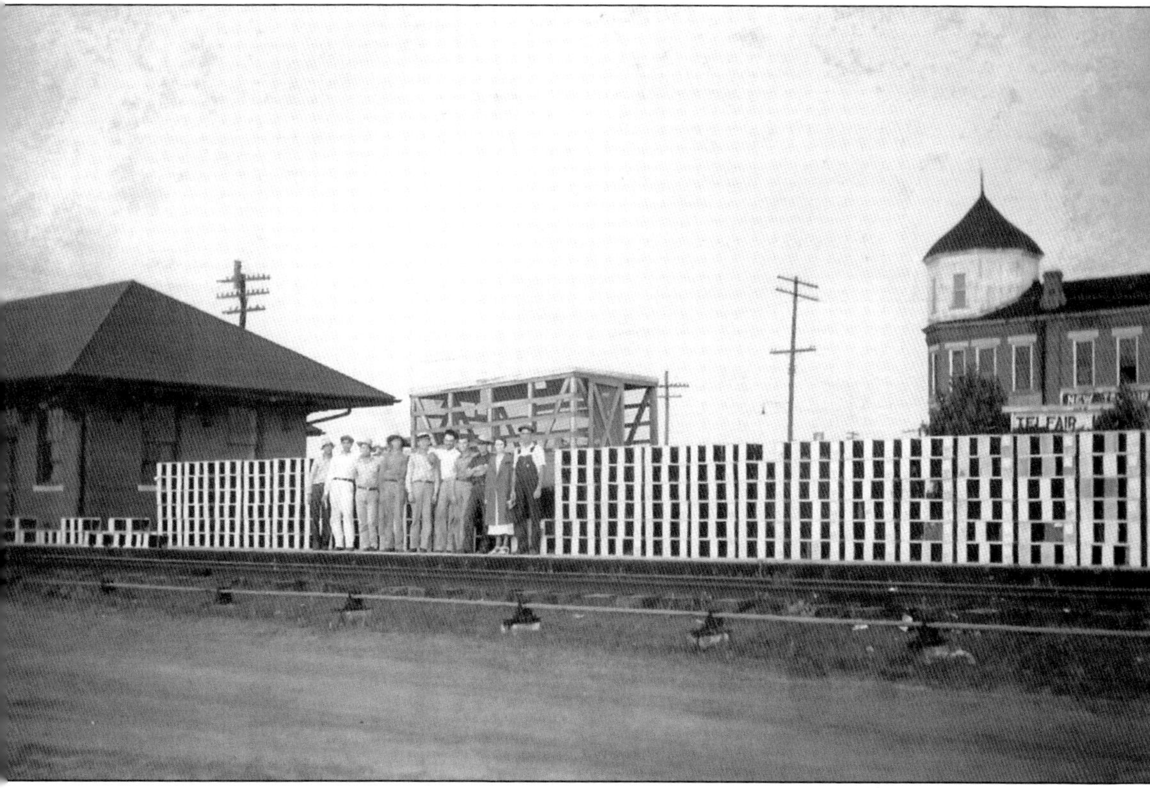


Old Union Railroad depot in Helena, located at the intersection of the Seaboard and Southern Railroads, provided transportation to the many passengers who boarded at the old Willard Hotel, shown in the background. Freight was important to the railroad. On the loading platform are stacks of bee boxes containing bees and beehives, probably from Stover Apiaries in McRae, to be shipped to locations in the Southeast. The old depot is no longer standing. (Courtesy of the Telfair Museum of History.)

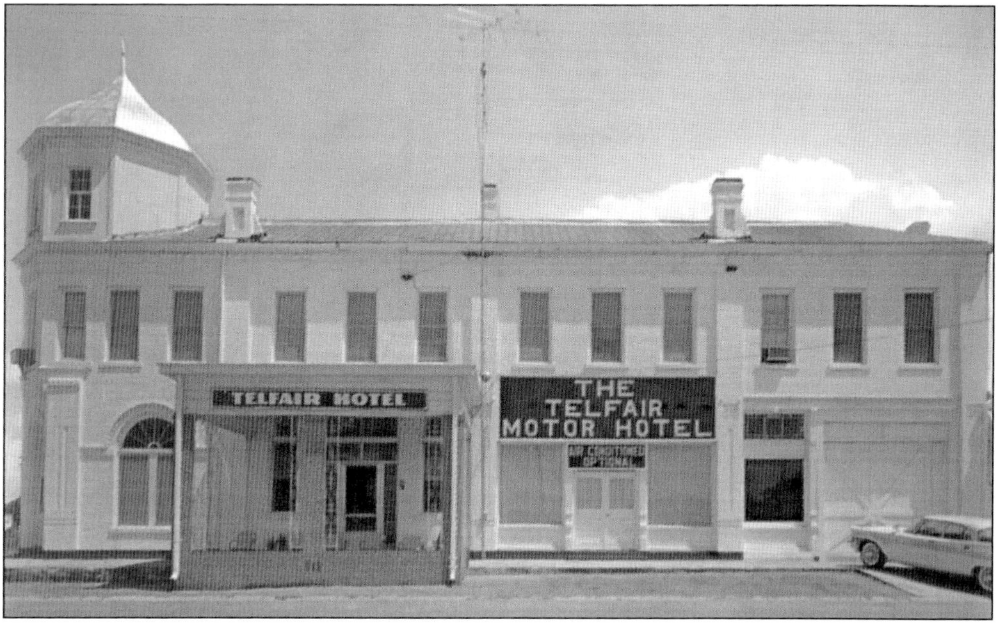


The old hotel building in Helena has been known by many names over the years: the Brick Hotel, Helena Inn, Hotel Willard, and the Telfair Hotel. It was built by the president of the Seaboard Railroad to house train passengers. The hotel emphasized the importance of the railroad to the area. It was located near the old Union Station at the junction of the Seaboard and Southern Railroads. (Courtesy of Julian Williams.)

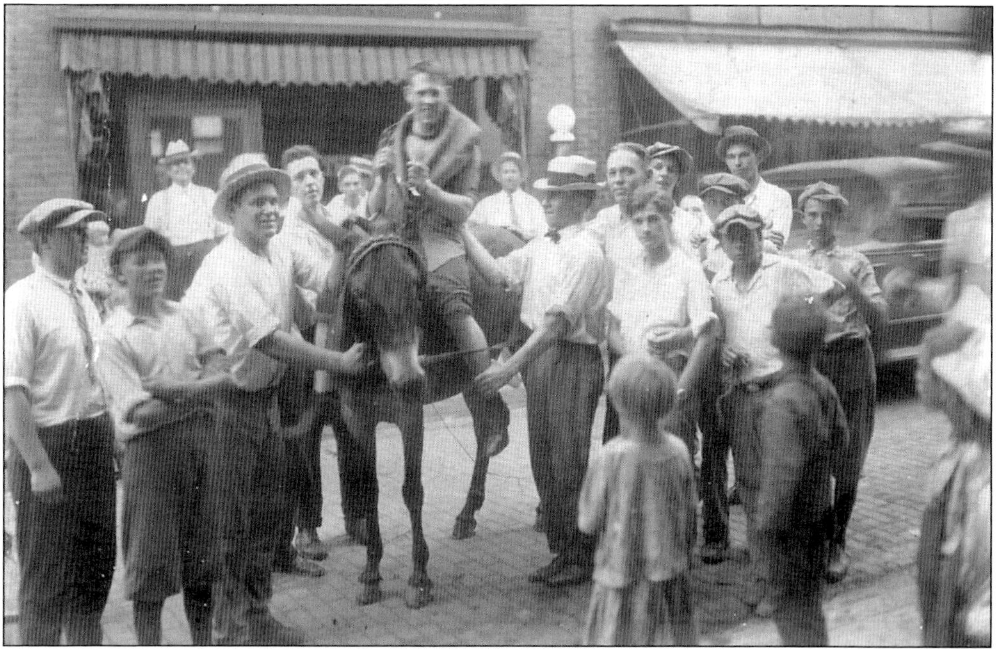

Early in the history of McRae, citizens came to town on the weekends. They used any means of transportation that was available to them: horses, mules, and later automobiles. A young man rides a mule into downtown McRae in this undated photograph, garnering a great deal of attention from those in town. Note the brick-paved street. (Courtesy of Bill Hunt Jr.)

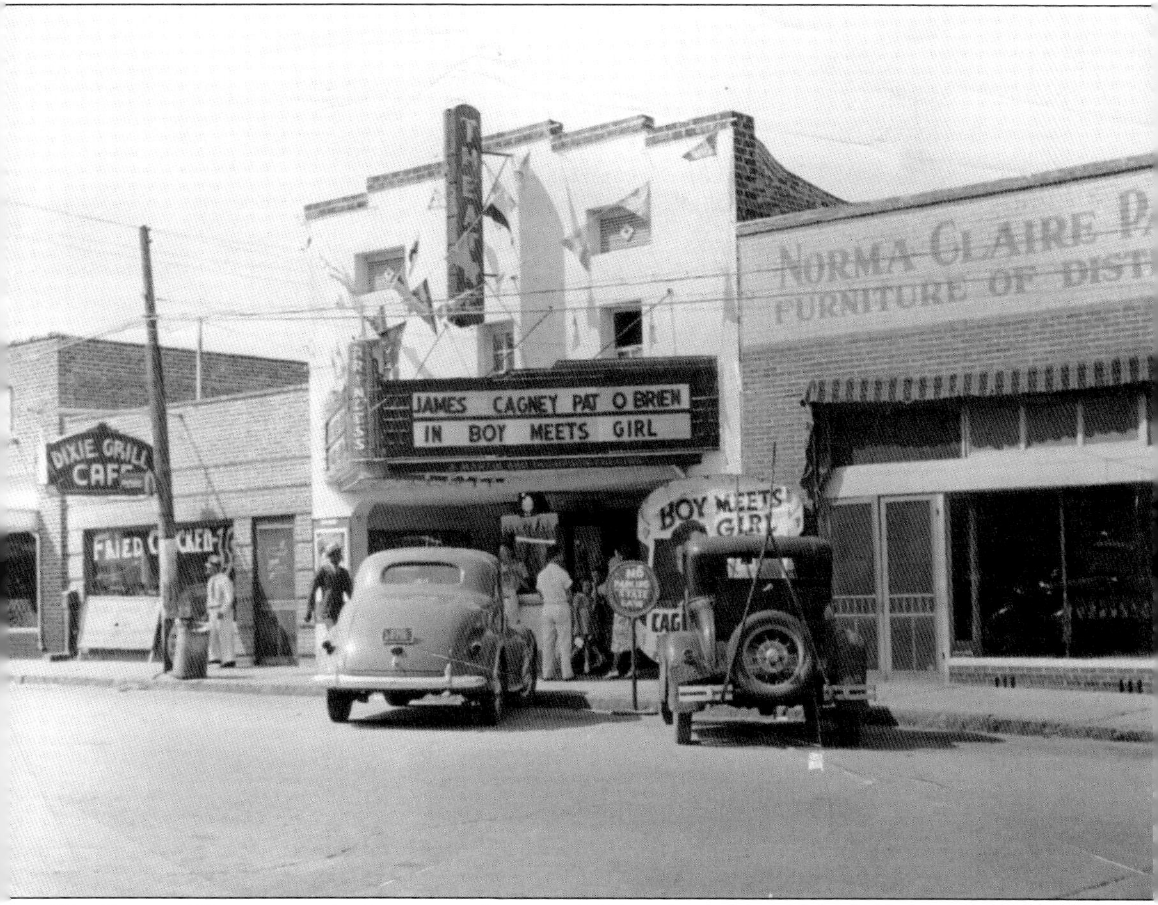


The Princess Theater was the first movie theater in McRae. It was located on the main street next to the present-day Chas-Mar Hardware store. The location of the theater is now vacant, serving as the parking lot of Chas-Mar. Next door and to the left of the Princess Theater was the Dixie Grill, owned and operated by Bethel Harbin. (Courtesy of Chris McRae.)

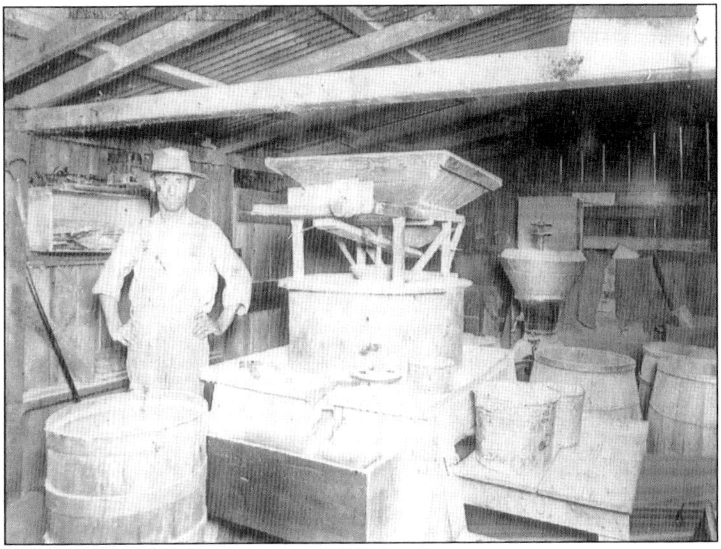

In the early 1900s, people used mills to grind their corn. This was true in the early years of Lumber City. William Conly Varnadoe is shown at his mill in Lumber City, where he ground corn in an early gristmill in the mid-1920s. Varnadoe is the great-grandfather of Mike Varnadoe, a Lumber City businessman. (Courtesy of Mike Varnadoe.)

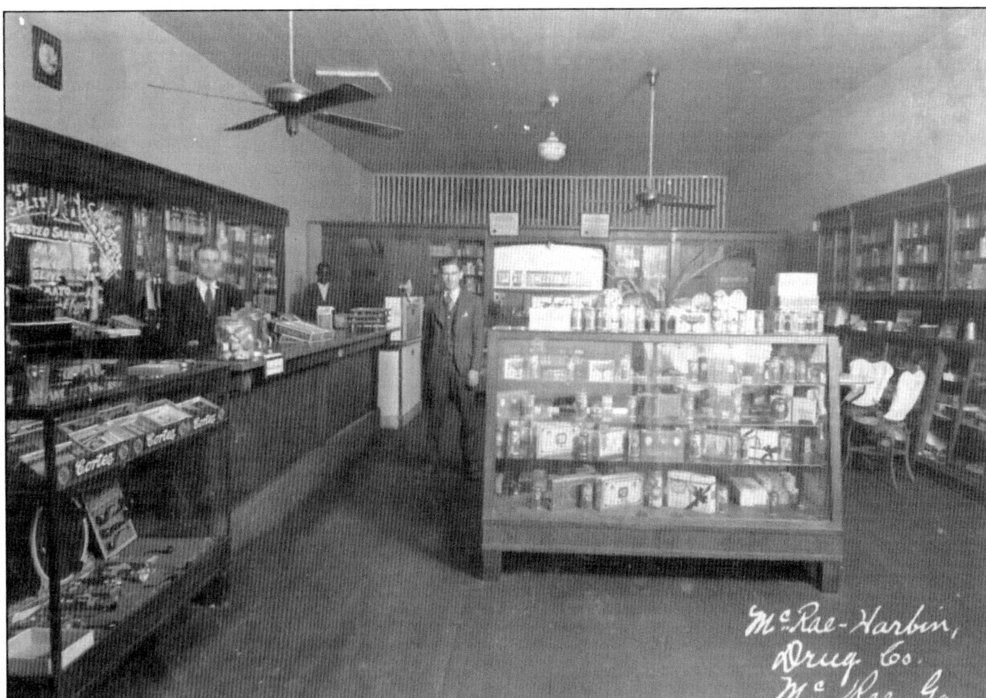


The McRae-Harbin Drug Company was one of the first drugstores in McRae. It was owned by Dr. Bill McRae, later pharmacist and owner of McRae's Pharmacy, and Bethel Harbin. The store was located on the main street next door to Crossroads Music Production. The building has been gutted, and a temporary wall has been erected. (Courtesy of Chris McRae.)

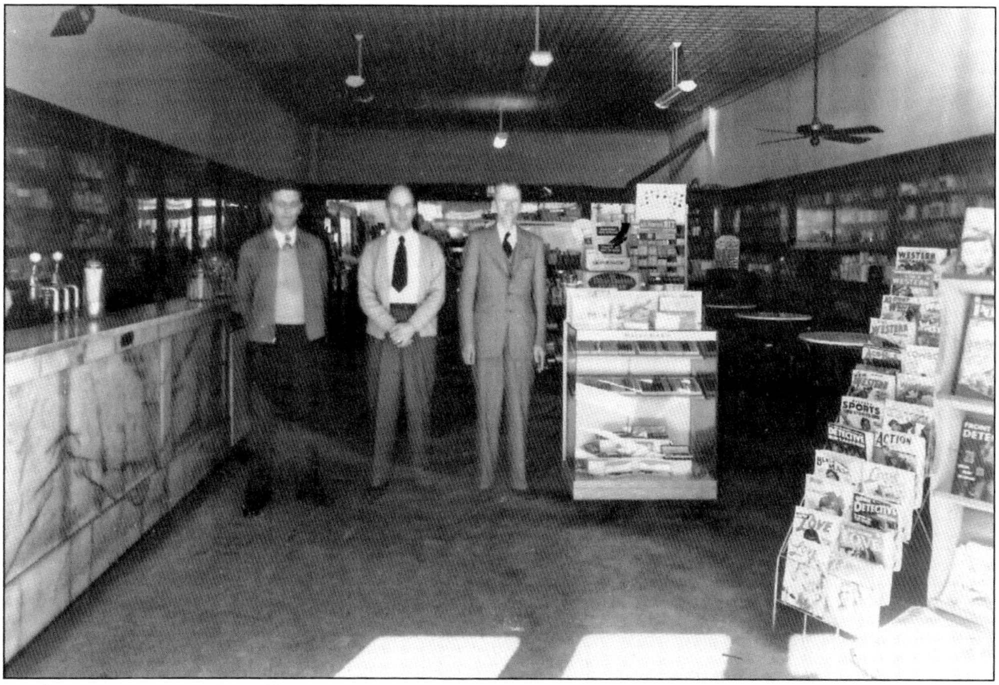

Ryals Drug Store is the oldest continuously operating business in McRae. Purchased by Chester A. Ryals Sr. in 1889, it was originally located at the corner of Third Avenue and Oak Street. In 1923, it was relocated to its present site on Second Avenue. A special bench was located to the right of the entrance, where folks came to sit and talk politics. It was almost always full. (Courtesy of Norwood Davidson.)

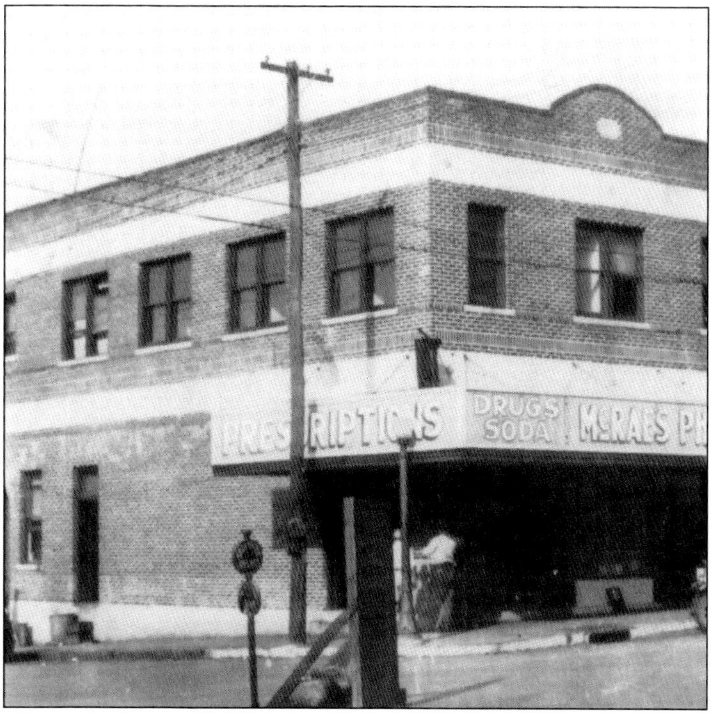


McRae's Pharmacy was one of three pharmacies in McRae in the 1960s, the others being Ocmulgee Drugs and Ryals Drug Store. Dr. Billy McRae Jr. owned and operated McRae's Pharmacy after his father's death. (Courtesy of Elizabeth Garrett.)

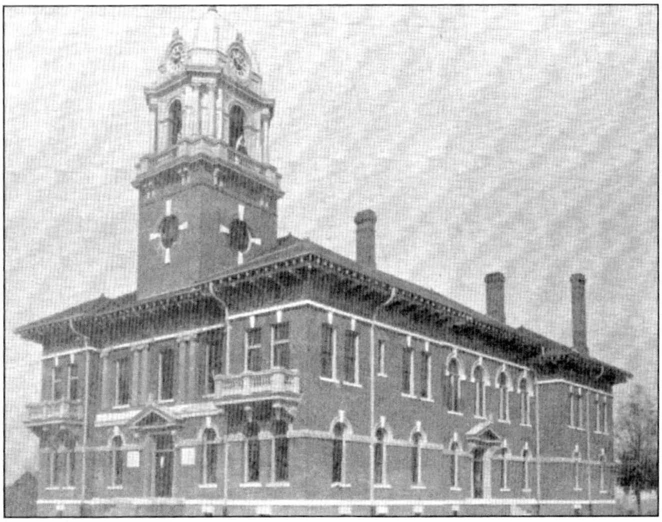

The Telfair County Courthouse is located in McRae, the county seat. The county seat was moved from Jacksonville to McRae in 1871. The first courthouse was a frame structure and used until 1888, when a brick structure was built on the same site; however, that structure, shown here, burned in 1934. The present structure was built at that time, and it has been remodeled several times since. (Courtesy of the Telfair Museum of History.)

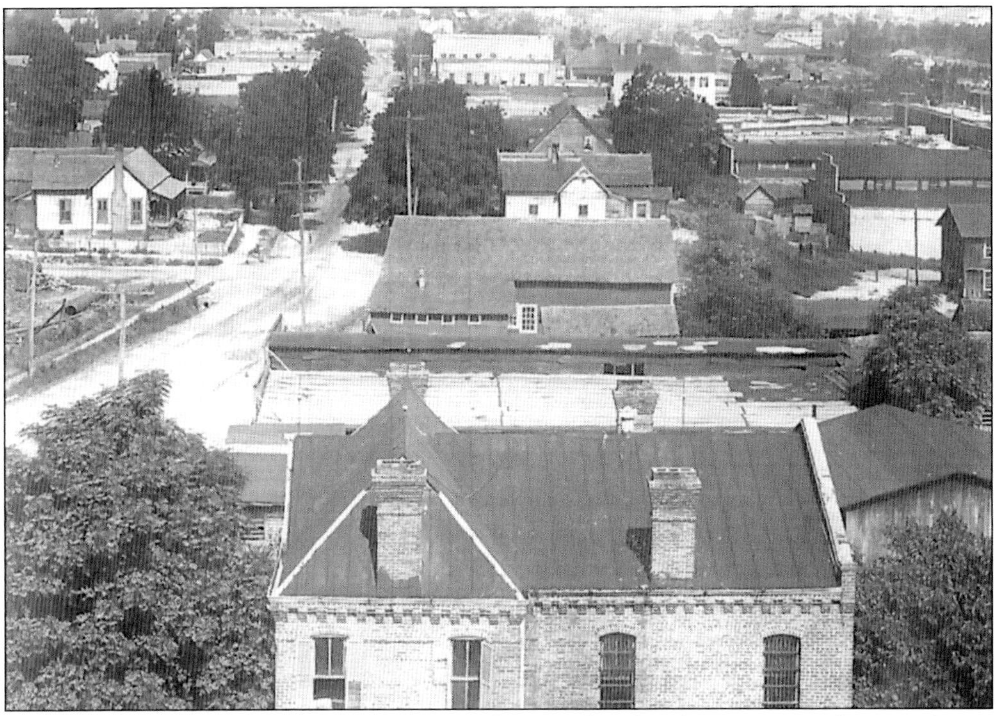

The Telfair County Jail is shown in this 1920s photograph, taken from an upper-floor window at the Telfair County Courthouse. The jail, built in the late 19th century, is listed in the National Register of Historic Places. The photograph captures McRae looking west from the courthouse. (Courtesy of Bill Hunt Jr.)

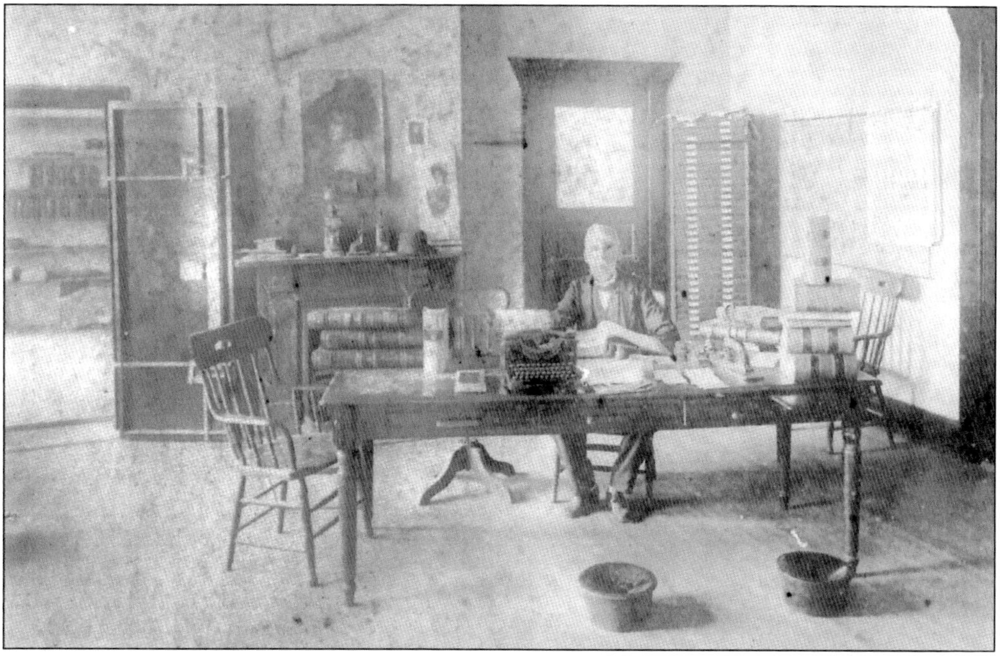

In the Telfair County Courthouse that burned in the mid-1930s, county official Henry Cook sits at his desk. Notice the fireplace in the background. Each office had a fireplace for winter heat. When the present courthouse was built in 1935, this room retained the fireplace, and it is still there today. Today, the clerk of court's office is located in this room. (Courtesy of Norwood Davidson.)

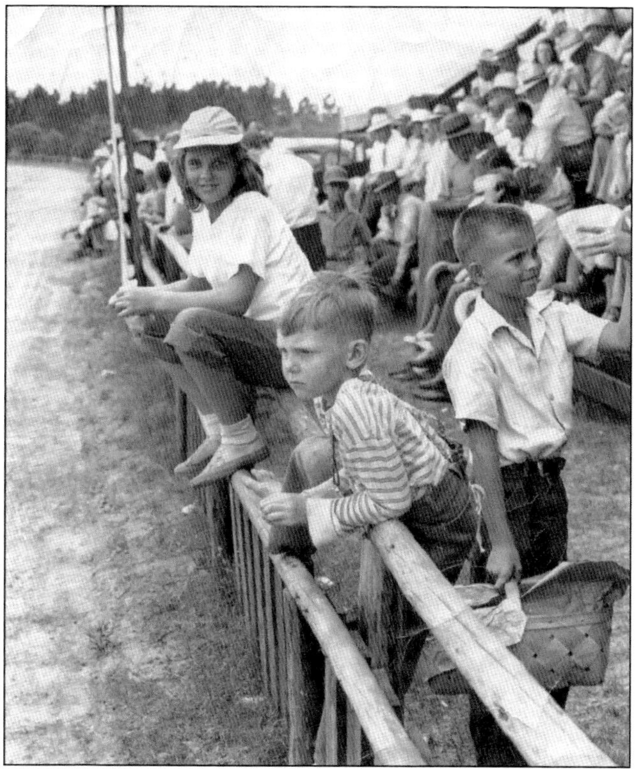

In addition to an automobile racetrack south of McRae, citizens enjoyed horse racing as well. Dr. George Callihan, a local dentist, owned the old racetrack. Located in the area of present-day Southside Baptist Church, football and baseball games were held there as well as the county fair. Danny Harbin (foreground, leaning on rail) and Ann Whiddon (on rail) enjoy a day at the races in this 1940s photograph. (Courtesy of Danny Harbin.)

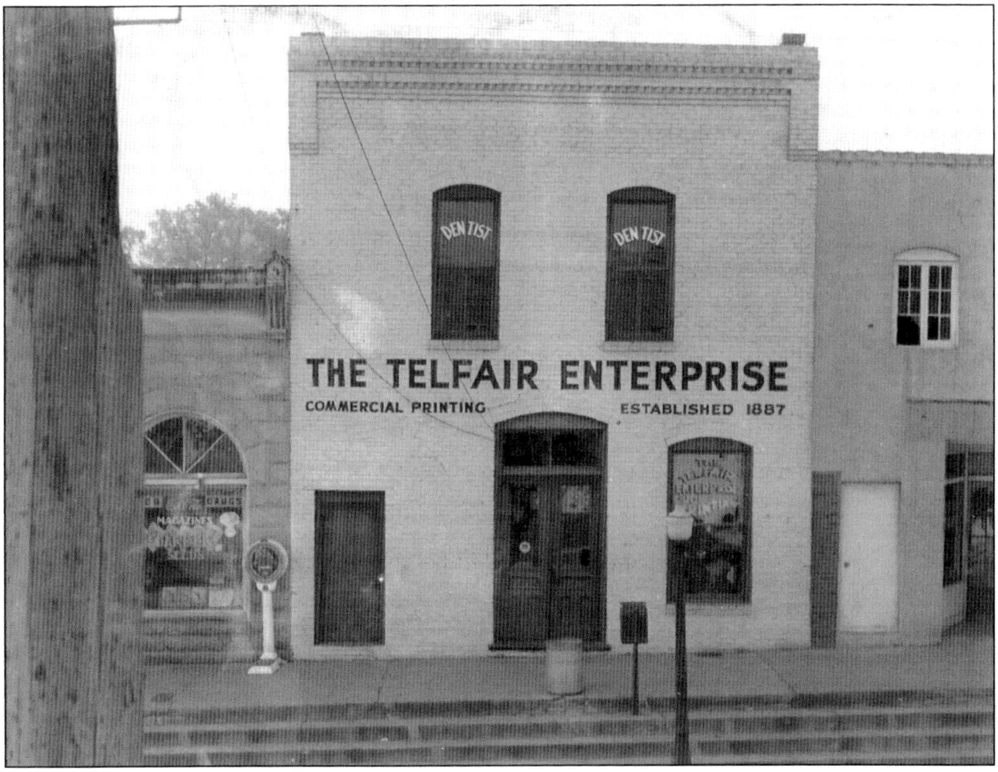


The *Telfair Enterprise* is the oldest continuously published newspaper in Telfair County. The first edition of the paper was published by A.L. Ryals from his home in 1887, and O.F. McRae bought the paper in 1902. Other owners included Claude Methvin, J. Kelly Simmons, W.D. Horton, and W.L. Bowen. Later purchased by Edwin and Sarah Bowen, it is now published by a regional newspaper group. (Courtesy of the *Telfair Enterprise*.)

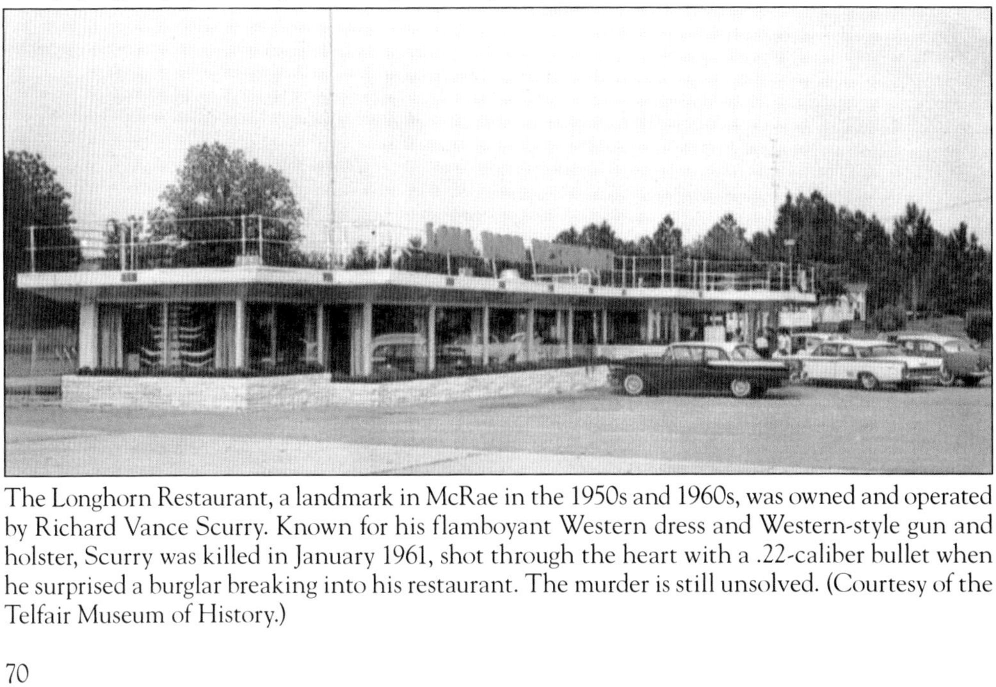

The Longhorn Restaurant, a landmark in McRae in the 1950s and 1960s, was owned and operated by Richard Vance Scurry. Known for his flamboyant Western dress and Western-style gun and holster, Scurry was killed in January 1961, shot through the heart with a .22-caliber bullet when he surprised a burglar breaking into his restaurant. The murder is still unsolved. (Courtesy of the Telfair Museum of History.)

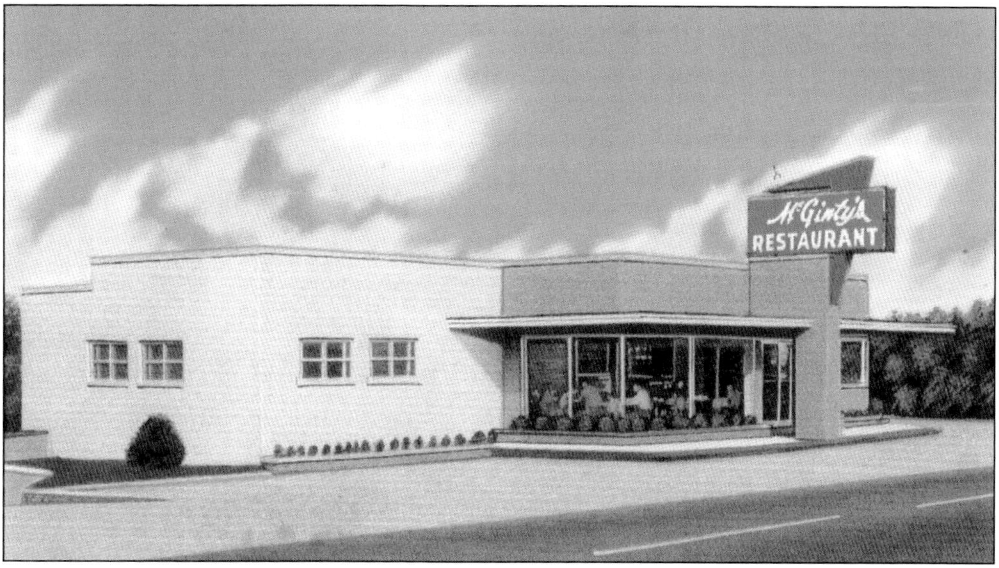


In 1928, Truman and Essie McGinty opened McGinty's Restaurant. It was located near the Seaboard and Southern Railroad tracks in Helena. McGinty's Restaurant was reported to be the place where the best barbeque (pronounced "Bobby-Q" by Truman) sandwiches could be found. It was also a meeting place for social gatherings, business meetings, and civic clubs. The restaurant burned on March 19, 1987. (Courtesy of the Telfair Museum of History.)

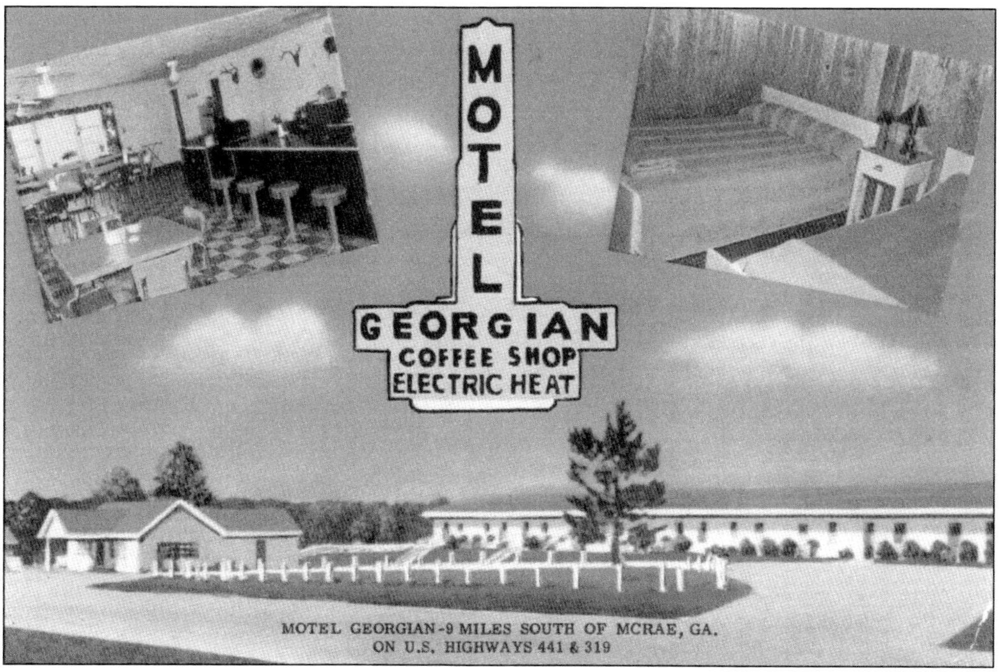


Billed as one of the best motels on US Highway 441 and Highway 319 in Telfair County, the Motel Georgian was located nine miles south of McRae. It featured electric radiant heat and was modern throughout, with pine-paneled floors and walls. It had a coffee shop for the travelers' convenience. The motel is still in operation in the Workmore community. The restaurant caters to hunters and fishermen. (Courtesy of Rita Williams.)

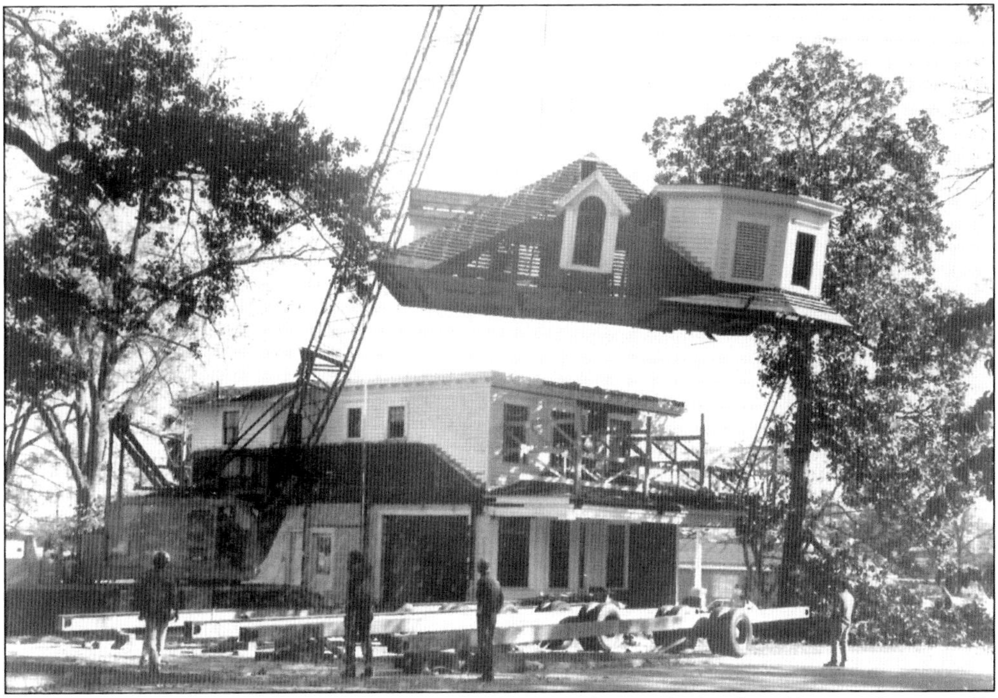

The two-story house being dismantled in this photograph was the boyhood home of Marion B. Folsom. Known for his active work as a primary architect of the 1935 Social Security Act, Folsom also was secretary of health, education, and welfare in the Eisenhower administration. His house was dismantled and moved to Wheeler County. Merchants and Citizens Bank now sits on the site. (Courtesy of Elizabeth Garrett.)

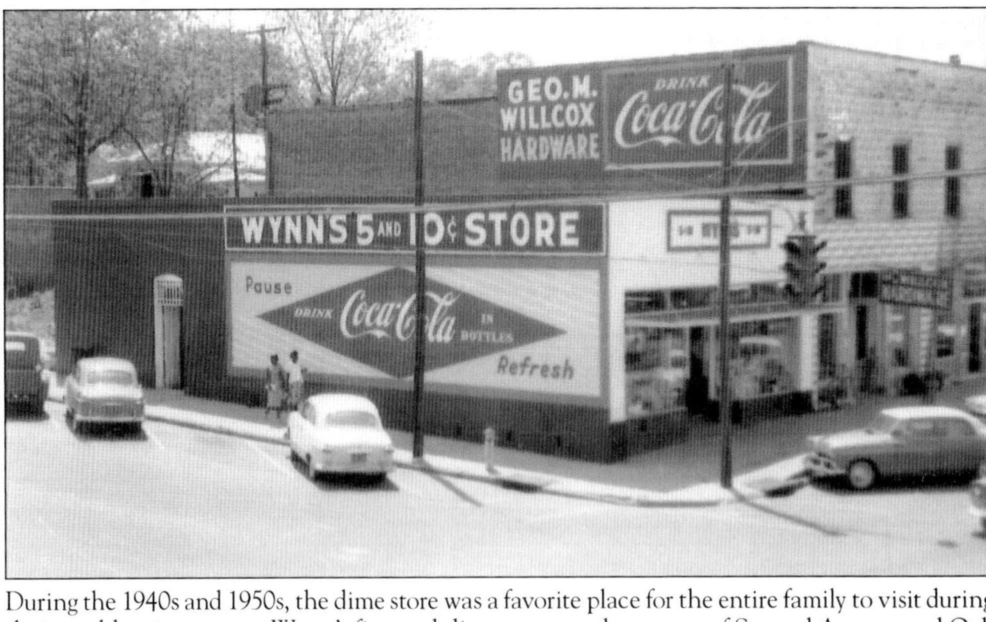


During the 1940s and 1950s, the dime store was a favorite place for the entire family to visit during their weekly trip to town. Wynn's five-and-dime store on the corner of Second Avenue and Oak Street in McRae was no exception. The business is long gone now, at one time replaced by a hardware store. The building is now vacant. (Courtesy of the Telfair Museum of History.)

Bradfield's Department Store was a must-visit business when the family came to McRae. It provided all the family's clothing needs, both work clothes and "Sunday-go-to-meeting" attire. The business is no longer in operation, having succumbed to the larger retail outlets that provided better selections at less cost. (Courtesy of the Telfair Museum of History.)

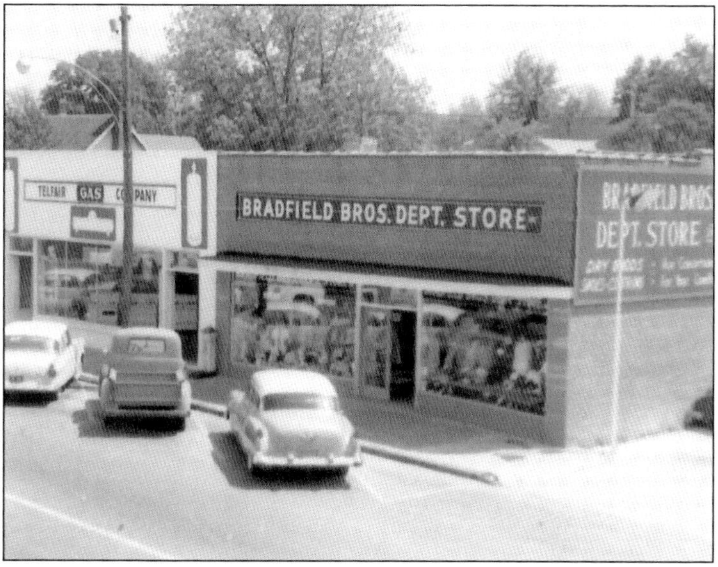


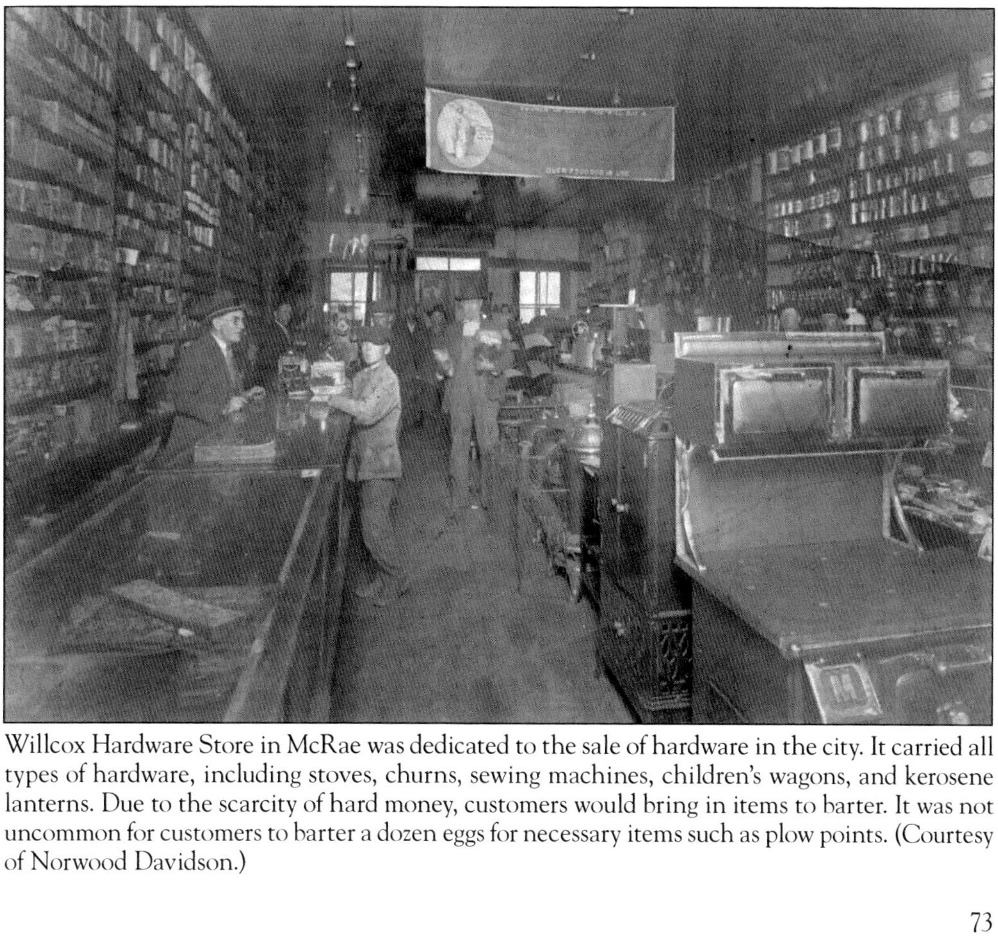

Willcox Hardware Store in McRae was dedicated to the sale of hardware in the city. It carried all types of hardware, including stoves, churns, sewing machines, children's wagons, and kerosene lanterns. Due to the scarcity of hard money, customers would bring in items to barter. It was not uncommon for customers to barter a dozen eggs for necessary items such as plow points. (Courtesy of Norwood Davidson.)

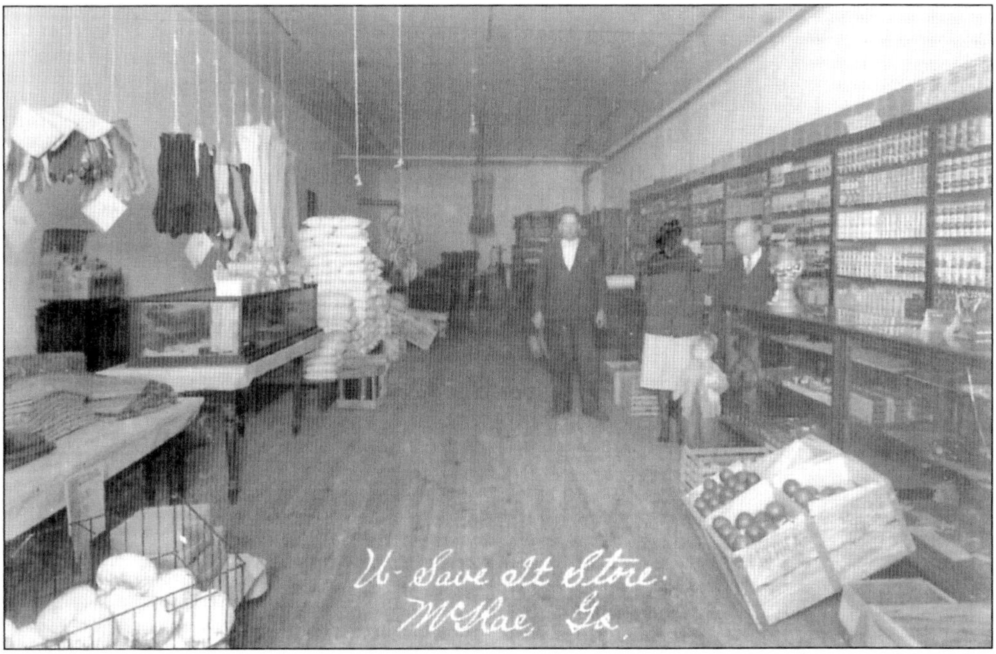


The U-Save-It Store, located on the main street in McRae, was owned and operated by John Kennedy Stallings (right). His wife, Elizabeth, stands in front of him, but she scratched out her face, as she said it was not a good likeness of her and she did not want anyone to see it. The photograph was taken about 1928. (Courtesy of Karen Scott.)

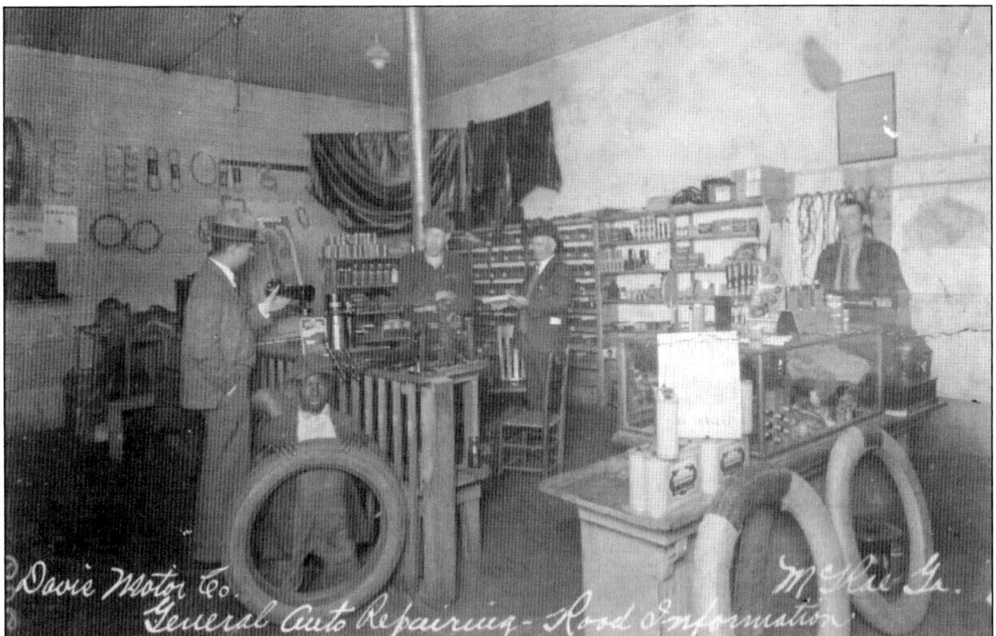


The Davis Motor Company was an early automobile parts store in McRae. This photograph was taken around 1920. The company sold automobile parts and accessories, and it also provided general mechanical repairs to early automobiles and, as the caption reveals, "Road Information" as well. (Courtesy of Rita Williams.)

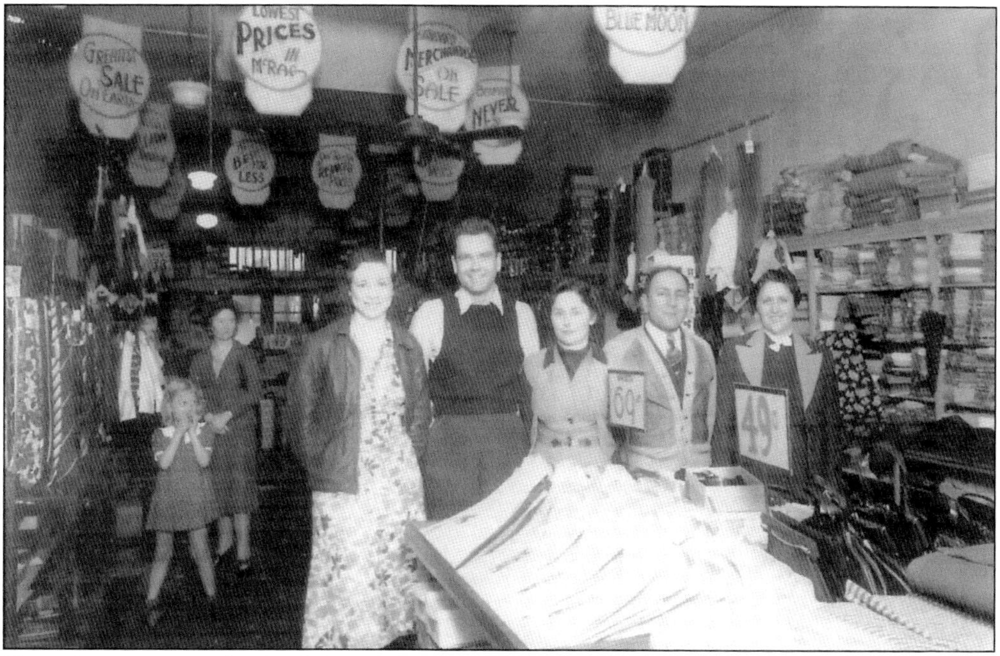


Harry Berman owned a local department store, Berman's. He is shown here (second from the right), along with James Campbell (second from the left) and Campbell's wife, Maggie (far left). Berman's was a popular department store in the 1950s and 1960s. James Campbell was a longtime employee and ran the store after Berman died. (Courtesy of Norwood Davidson.)

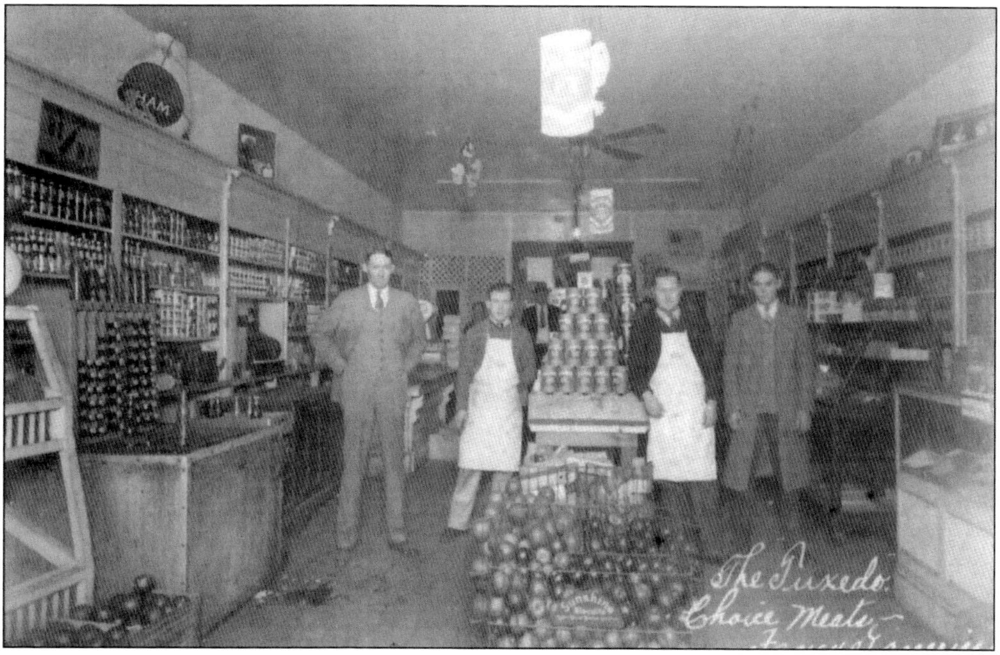


Tuxedo Choice Meats, a local butcher shop specializing in choice meats, was owned by Ed Holland and located on the main street in McRae. Holland is shown in the suit on the left. His son E.T. Holland is on the far right. The gentleman in the dark suit and hat in the background is James W. Pope Sr., owner of Pope's Grocery in McRae. (Courtesy of Norwood Davidson.)

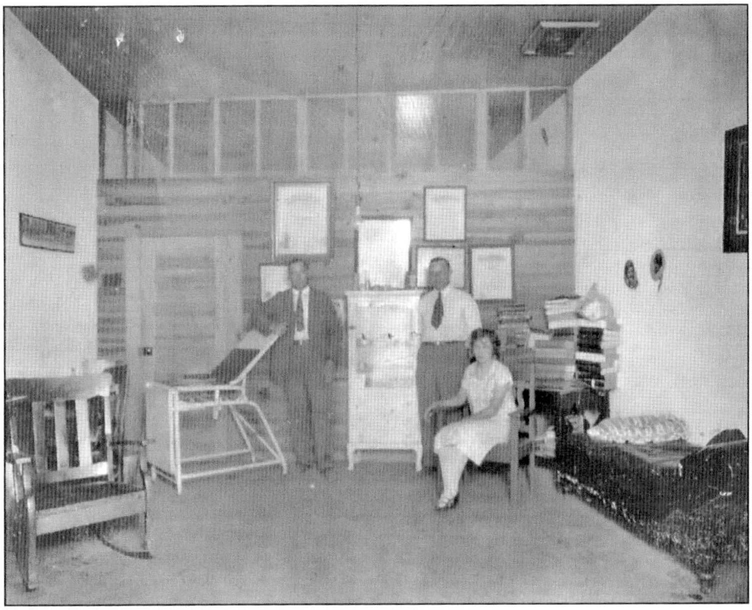

Dr. Thomas J.M. "Dr. Tom" McMillan (left), Dr. Daniel W.F "Dr. Tuck" Maloy, and Maloy's wife, Clara Bullington Maloy, were photographed in their medical office in Milan, Georgia. Both men were graduates of Emory University Medical School and brothers-in-law. (Courtesy of Rita Williams.)

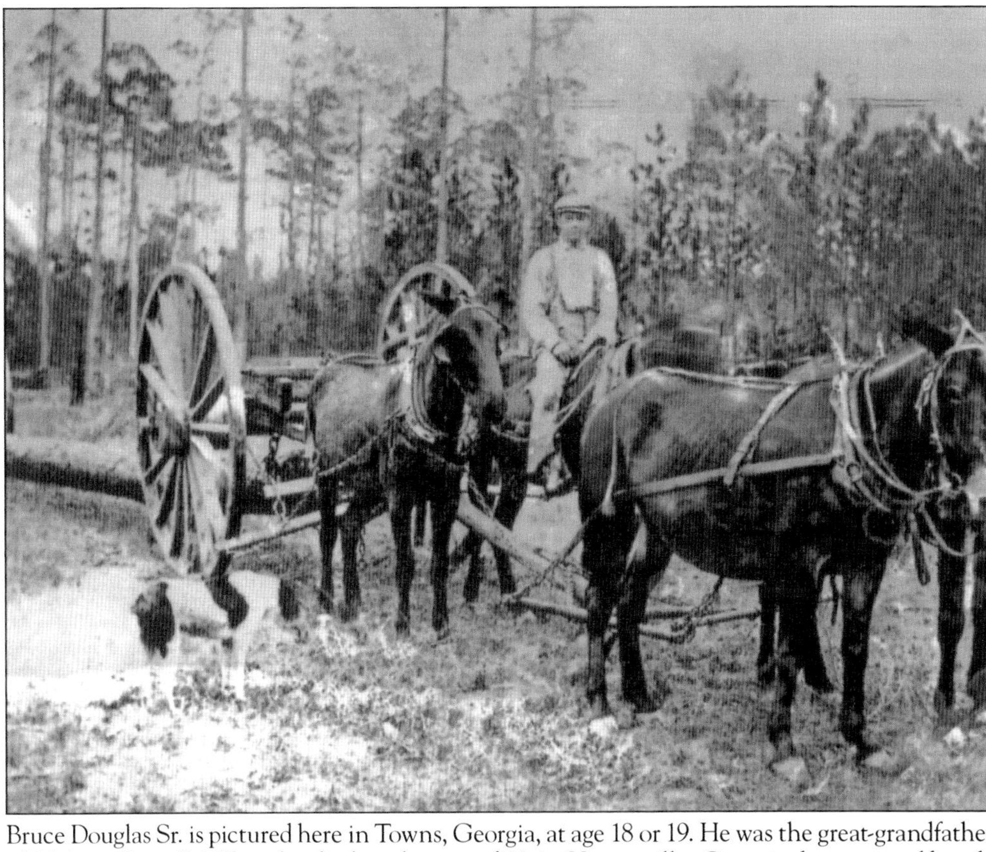

Bruce Douglas Sr. is pictured here in Towns, Georgia, at age 18 or 19. He was the great-grandfather of Melissa Carroll. When he died at the age of 92 in Homerville, Georgia, he was a self-made millionaire. (Courtesy of Melissa McGinty Carroll.)

Henrietta Rebecca Sikes Mann was the wife of Dr. Frank Rambo Mann Sr. Henrietta was the daughter of Simeon Sikes and Elizabeth Bone. She was born in 1860 and died in 1907. She and her husband are buried in the Blockhouse Baptist Church cemetery in Jacksonville, Georgia. (Courtesy of Janet Smith Fields.)

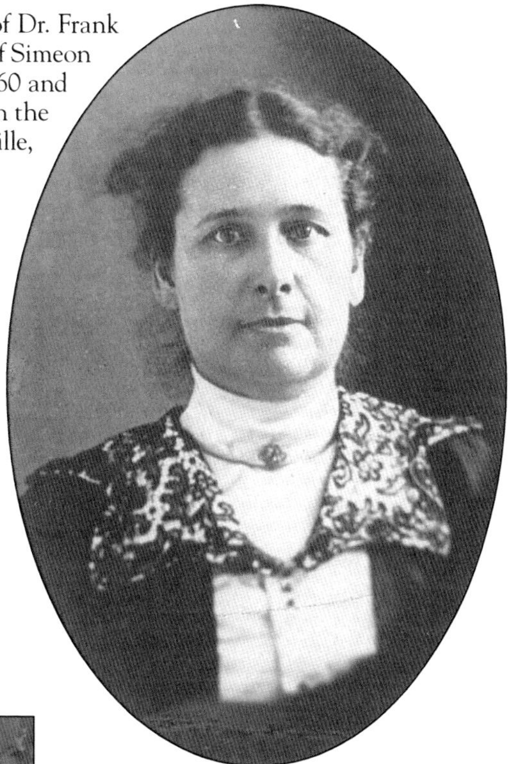

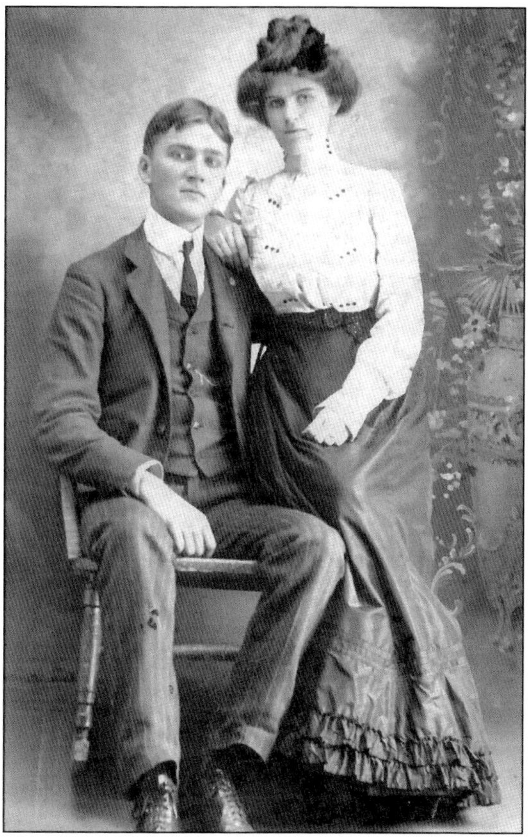

Chester Arthur Ryals and Clyde DeLoach pose in this wedding photograph taken July 26, 1901. Ryals established Ryals Drug Store in McRae in 1899. It is the oldest continuous business in McRae, having been passed to his son Chester A. Ryals Jr. The drugstore was purchased by Mickey Nelson in 1971, who owned it until 2013, when it was sold to Hugh Yawn. (Courtesy of LoAnn Montgomery Ryals.)

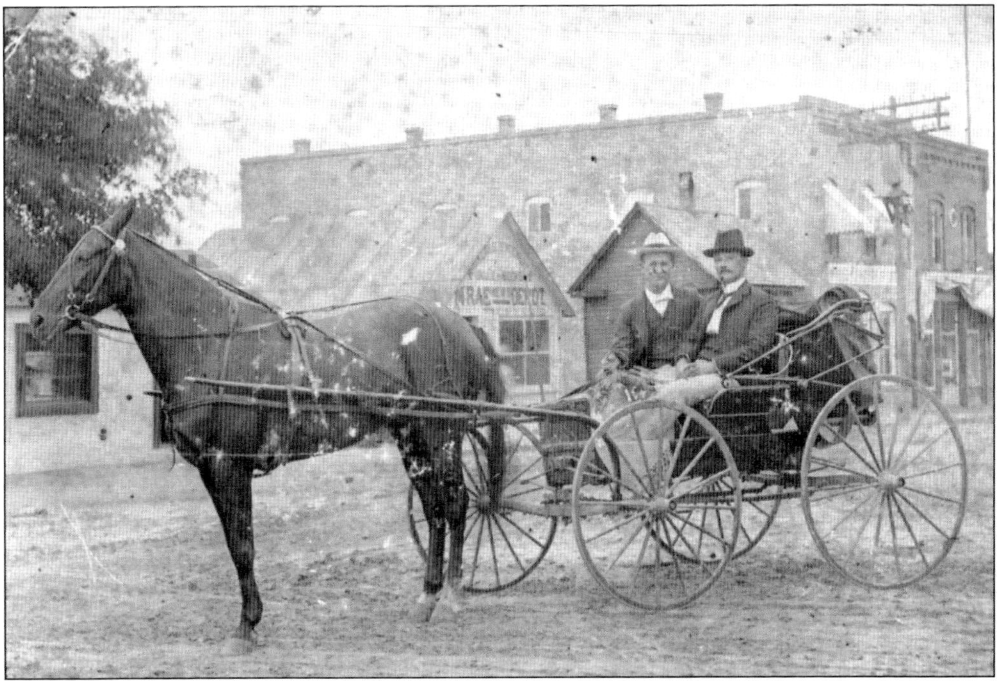

This street scene in McRae shows John Thaddeous McLean, with the black hat, in his horse-drawn buggy. It is dated prior to 1904, the year McLean died. In the background is the McRae News Depot, located on the main street. (Courtesy of Norwood Davidson.)

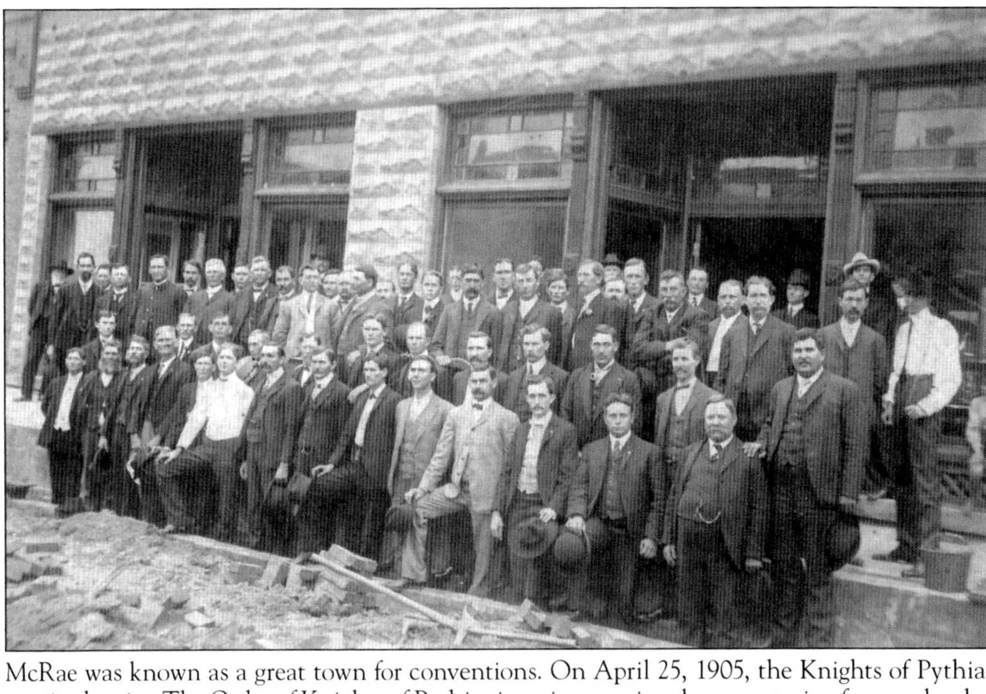

McRae was known as a great town for conventions. On April 25, 1905, the Knights of Pythias met in the city. The Order of Knights of Pythias is an international, nonsectarian fraternal order, established in Washington, DC, in 1864 by Justus H. Rathbone, the first fraternal order to be chartered by an act of Congress. (Courtesy of the *Pioneer* and the Telfair Museum of History.)

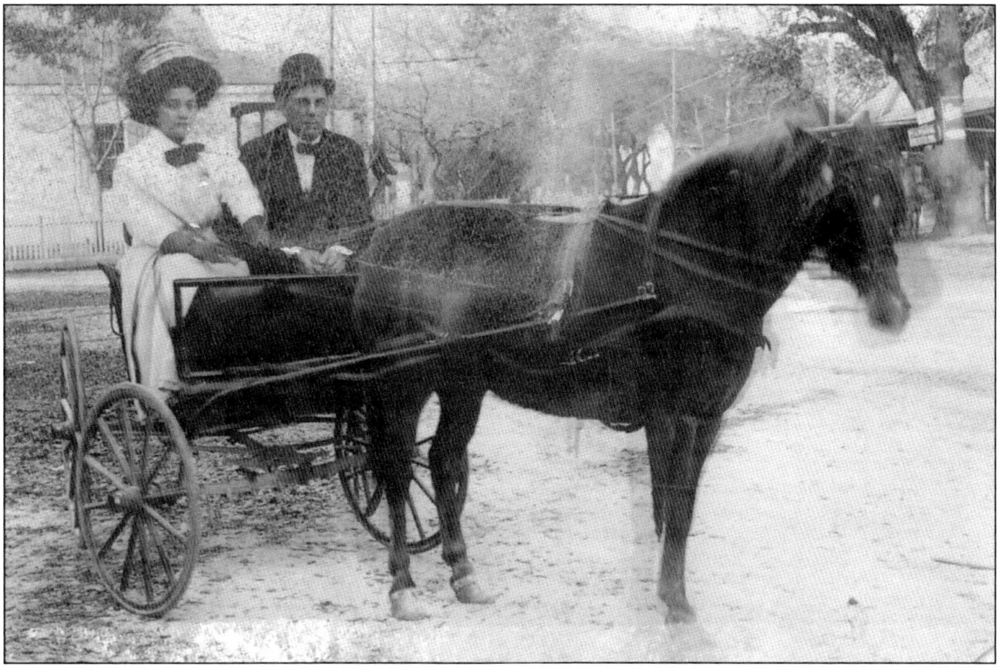

Floris Perkins Mann was born in South Carolina, arriving in Telfair County in 1909 as the wife of William Simeon Mann Sr. Immediately, she became active in the community. She was instrumental in having a historical marker placed at the Blockhouse Baptist Church near Jacksonville. Perhaps her greatest contribution was the writing of an early *History of Telfair County*. Mann is shown in this 1900s photograph. (Courtesy of Janet Smith Fields.)

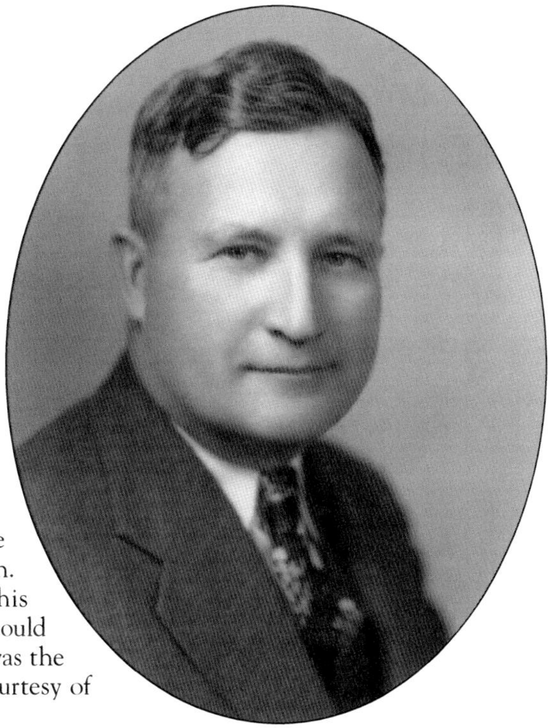

In 1892, Dr. Charles John Maloy was born in Telfair County. After his son's death at the age of four, he devoted much of his time and medical practice to treating children. He was known to take his patients in his car to Macon or Atlanta or wherever he could find help for them. For over 50 years, he was the physician for the Seaboard Railroad. (Courtesy of Ruby Maloy White.)

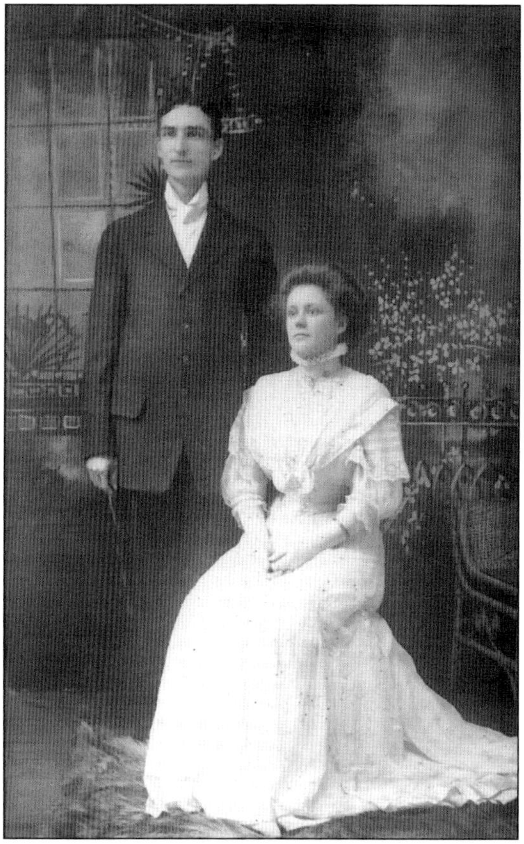

Bud and Edna Ryals are shown on their wedding day in January 1908. Bud owned a very successful feed business in McRae and also bought and sold cotton. (Courtesy of LoAnn Montgomery Ryals.)

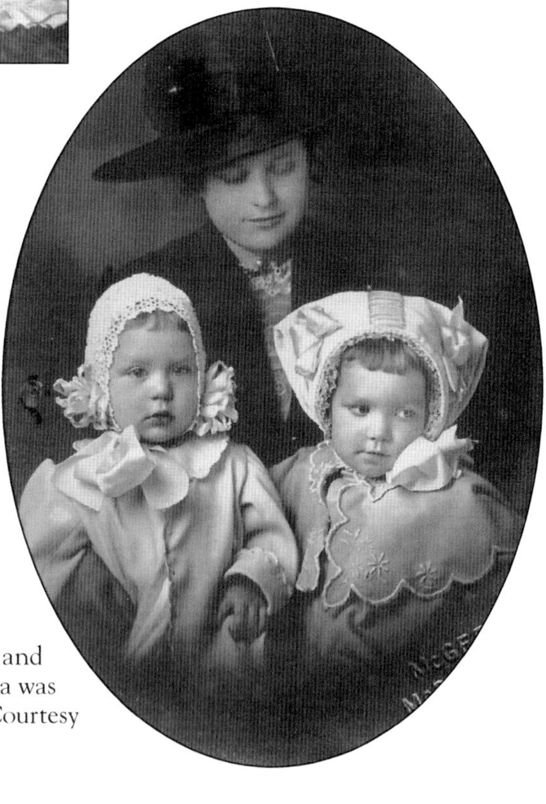

Edna Ryals's children, E.C. Ryals Jr. (left) and Edith Ryals are shown with their mom. Edna was the grandmother of E.C. "Lee" Ryals III. (Courtesy of LoAnn Montgomery Ryals.)

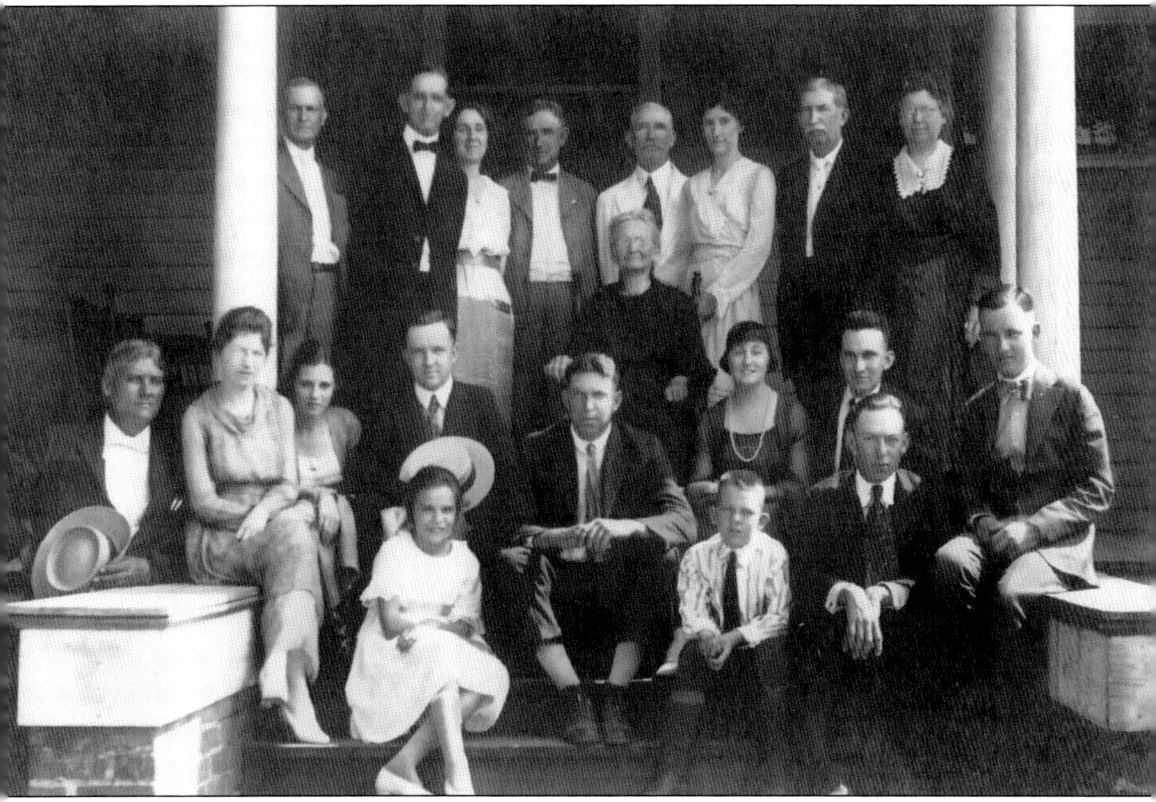

Susannah McRae was the wife of Daniel McRae. McRae, Georgia, is located on what was once his property. Pictured here in 1919 are, from left to right, (first row) Effie Pritchett, Charles Pritchett, D.M. McRae, and Marion B. Folsom (on buttress); (second row) Max L. McRae, Mildred McRae, Thelma Pritchett, Leon Folsom, Sidney B. McRae, Elizabeth Pritchett, and William Pritchett; (third row) Susannah Green McRae; (fourth row) Hy E. Pritchett, Oscar F. McRae, Effie McRae Pritchett, Charlie McRae, E. Farquhar McRae, Fannie McRae, A.S.J. McRae, and Minnie Lee McRae. (Courtesy of the McRae United Methodist Church History Committee.)

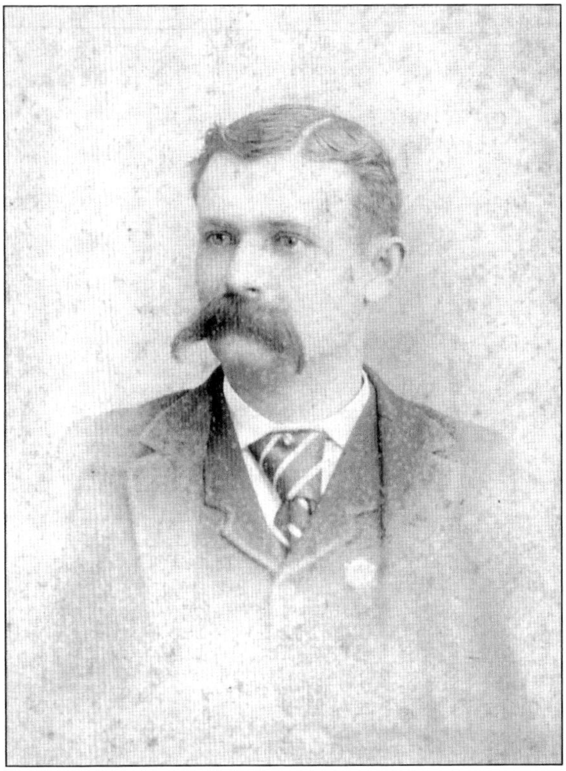

Dr. Benning Moore Kennon was a prominent physician and druggist in McRae. He and his wife, Dollie, moved to McRae in 1890. They were faithful and loyal members of the McRae Methodist Church. He owned Kennon's Drug Store, as well as a large farm near McRae. Almost all members of his family were talented musicians, playing piano, organ, cello, and trumpet. (Courtesy of the Telfair Museum of History.)

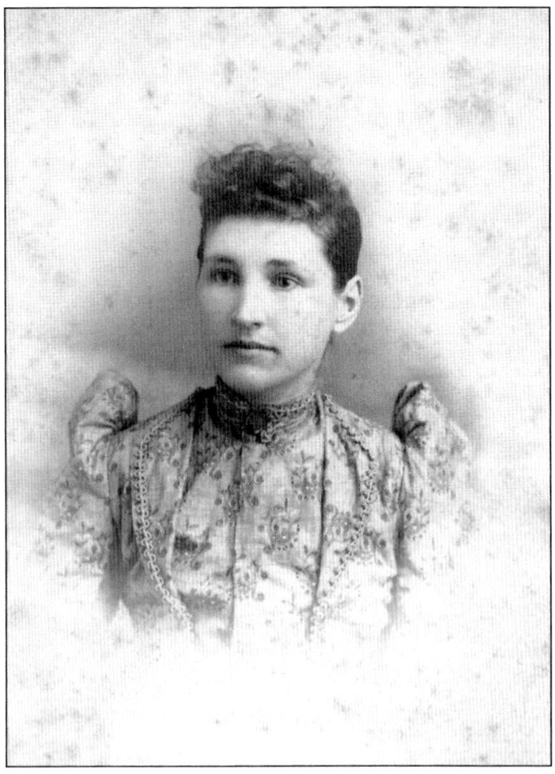

Known affectionately as "Miss Allie," Dollie Kennon moved to McRae in 1890 after marrying Dr. B.M. Kennon in 1885. She was a teacher by profession, having taught in both junior and senior high schools for 24 years. She lived to be 104 years old and died on November 16, 1972. Pictured here is Dollie at about 23 years of age. (Courtesy of the Telfair Museum of History.)

Sarah Elizabeth "Sallie" Maloy was born in 1882 and died in 1953. According to her daughter Ruby, she loved to sew, crochet, and play the piano. She attended South Georgia College in McRae and later worked at the telephone company in nearby Helena. (Courtesy of Ruby Maloy White.)

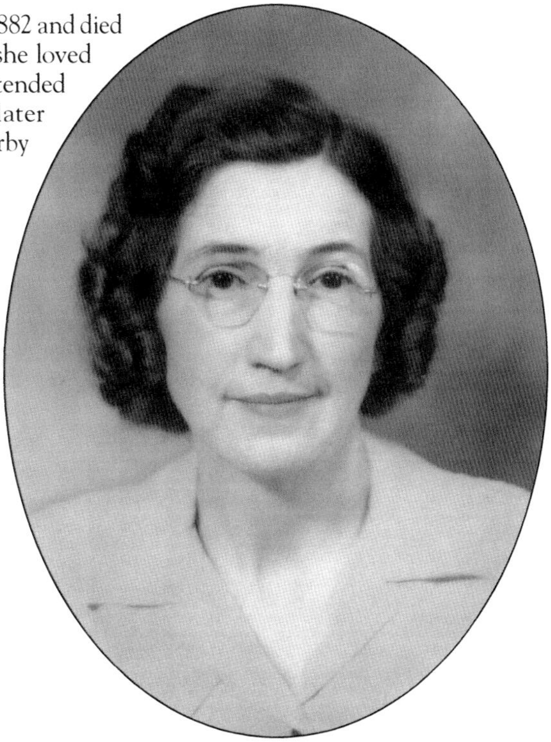

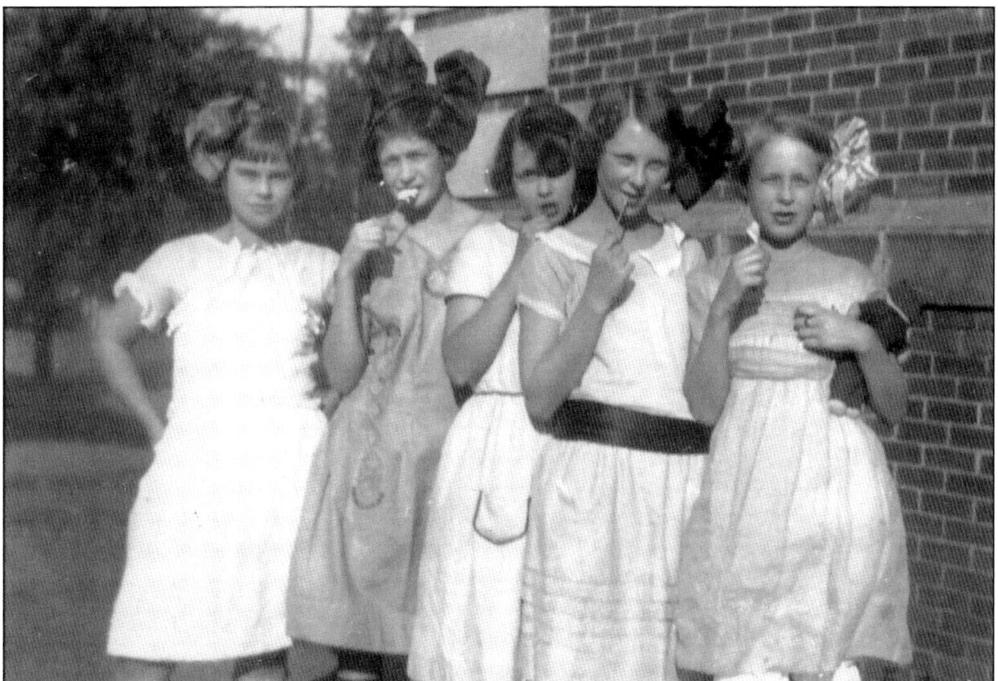

The girls are made up for a Kid's Day at South Georgia College in McRae in the early 1920s. Four of these frolicsome young ladies are unidentified; however, the young lady second from the left is Norma Parker Manley. (Courtesy of Norwood Davidson.)

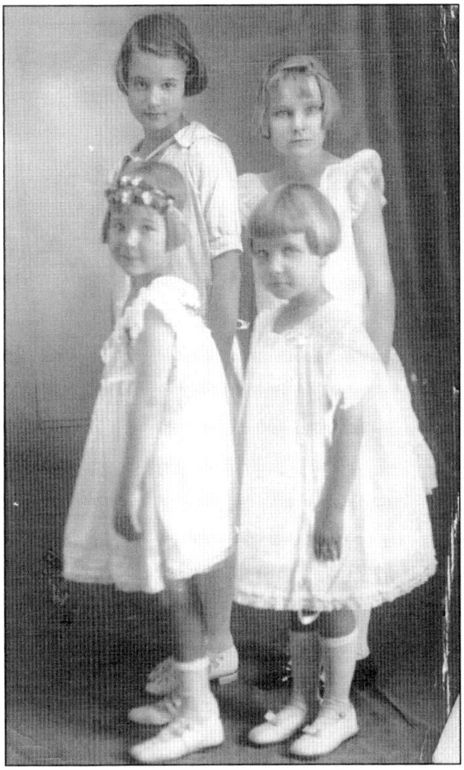

The grandchildren of Frank Rambo Mann Sr. and Henrietta Sikes Mann are striking in their white dresses. Pictured here around 1923, the granddaughters are, from left to right, (top) Janet Mann Hungerford and Evelyn Burch Mabry; (bottom) Mary Doby Mann Smith and Marjorie Mann Luckey. (Courtesy of Janet Smith Fields.)

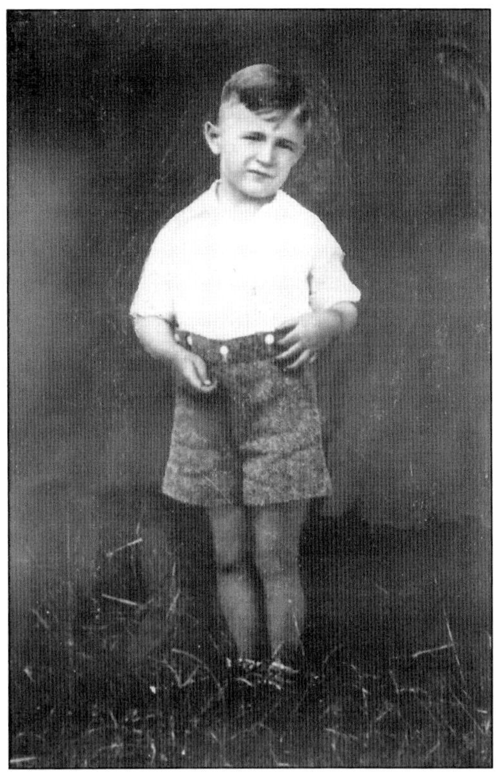

Kenneth Weeks Maloy (1928–1933), who died of leukemia, was the younger brother of Ruby White. He is four years old in this photograph. Ruby remembers that her mother and father took Kenneth by train to Johns Hopkins Hospital in Baltimore, Maryland. After being diagnosed with leukemia, he lived only around four months after that visit. (Courtesy of Ruby Maloy White.)

This photograph of D.J. Burch was made in 1931. Little did he envision growing up that he would be a part of World War II, which would take him away from home for four long years. (Courtesy of Marjorie Lord Burch.)

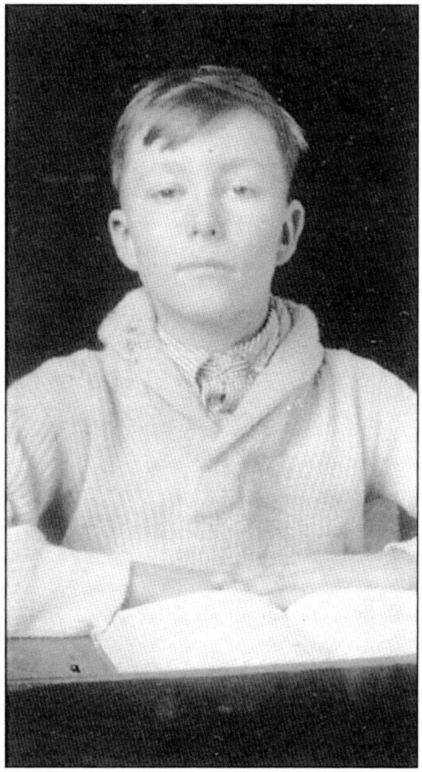

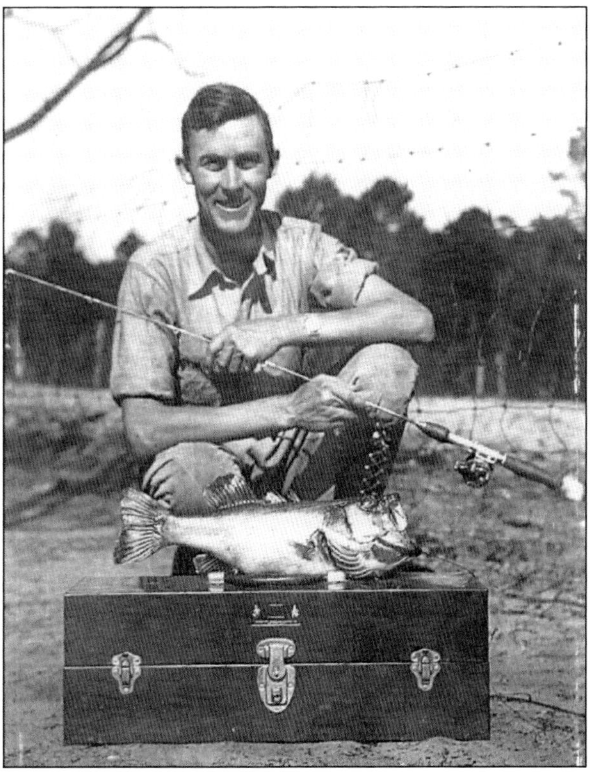

In 1932, George W. Perry caught the world-record bass in Montgomery Lake, an offshoot of the Ocmulgee River, in Telfair County. Perry won the Field and Stream Big Fish Contest in 1932 and 1934. Although the fish in this photograph is not the record-holding bass, a replica of the fish caught by Perry can be seen in the Telfair Museum of History. (Courtesy of the Telfair Museum of History.)

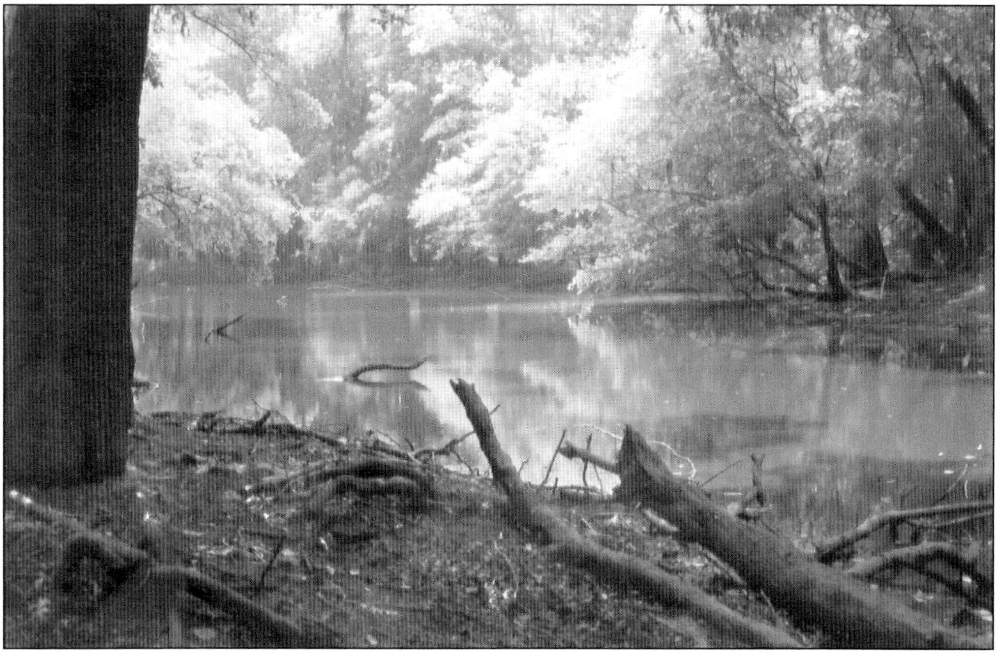

Montgomery Lake comes out of the Ocmulgee River about five miles south of Jacksonville and about 15 miles from Lumber City. The fish Perry caught weighed 22 pounds and four ounces. When asked what he did with the fish, Perry replied that he ate it—it fed his family for three days. (Courtesy of Bill Babb and the Telfair Museum of History.)

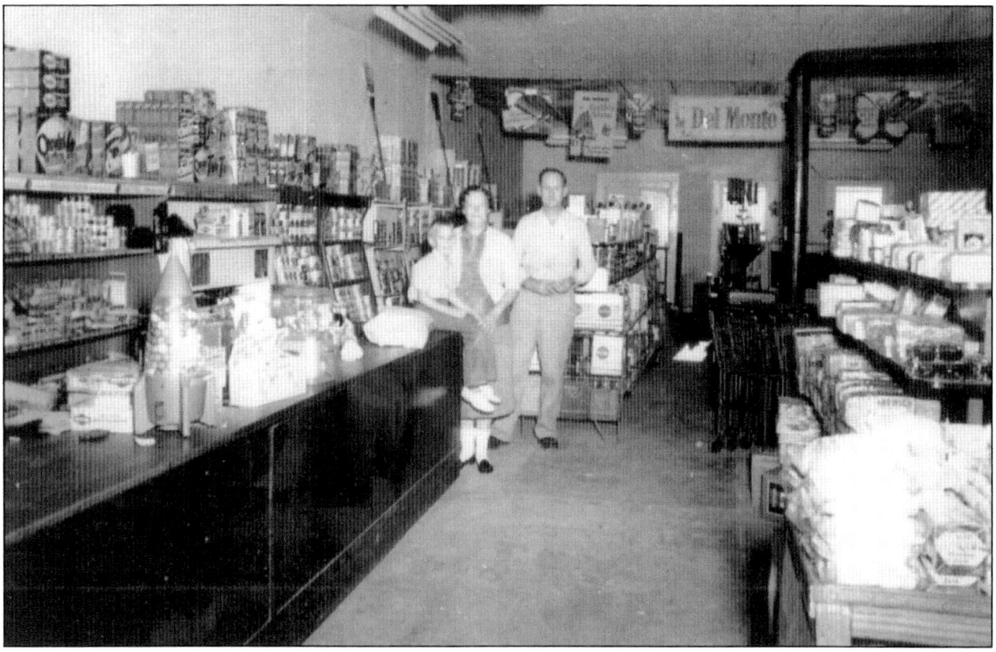


When George W. Perry caught the monstrous bass in 1932, he carried it to J.J. Hall Grocery Store in Helena to be weighed. The store was later purchased by Bill Fowler, who operated it in 1988 when this photograph was taken. The store is empty now, but the building is still standing. (Courtesy of the Telfair Museum of History.)

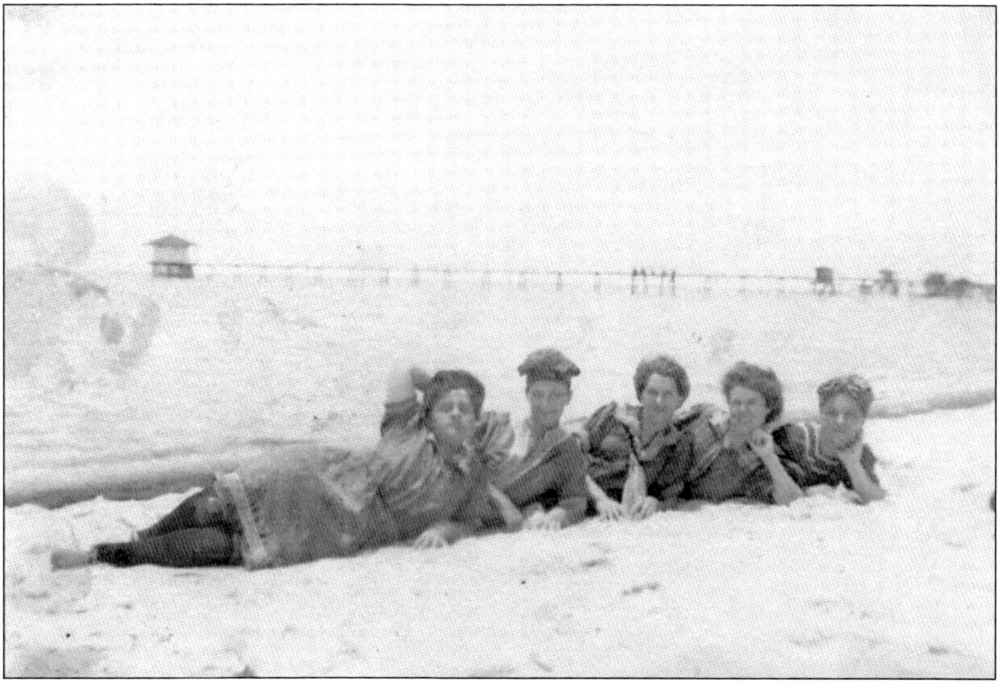

In a photograph taken at Tybee Island, Georgia, around 1900, Floris Perkins Mann (far left), wife of William Simeon Mann Sr., takes in the sun with some friends. (Courtesy of Janet Smith Fields.)

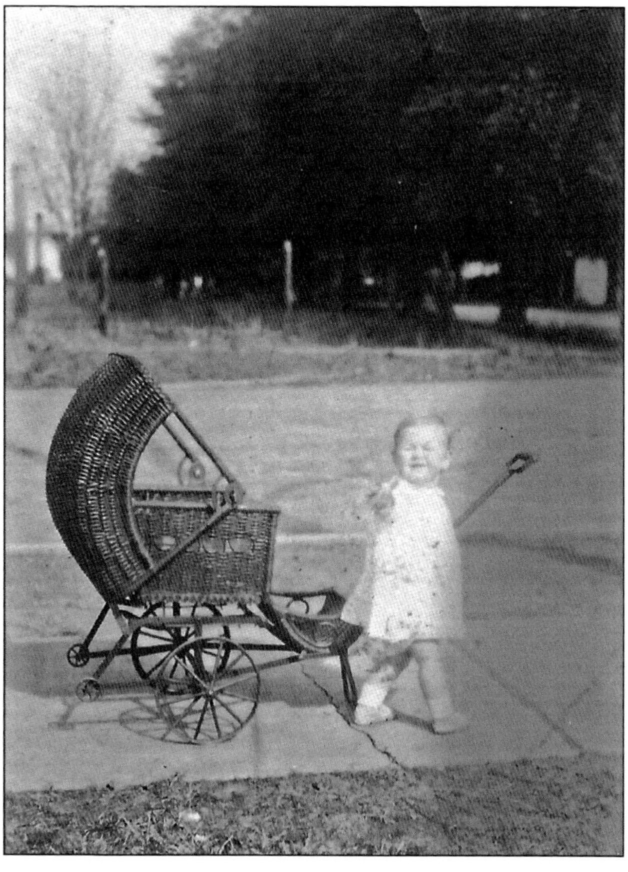

Jan Douglas is pictured here by her stroller in front of her grandparents' home (V.S. and Orpha Parker) at 301 Huckabee Street in 1932. Parker came to McRae as the depot agent in 1915. When he and his wife moved to McRae, there were only two houses large enough for their family of nine. The family lived at this home on Huckabee Street until 1997. (Courtesy of Melissa McGinty Carroll.)

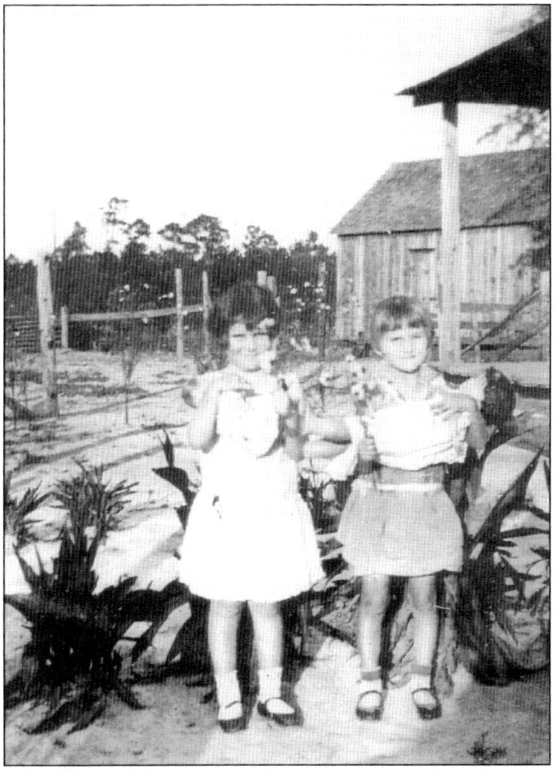

Audrey Powell (left) and Lois Ashley grew up on a farm in the Workmore community. As with all little girls at the time, they found their pleasure playing with dolls. The two are cousins of Ruby (Gay) Dyal. (Courtesy of the Telfair Museum of History.)

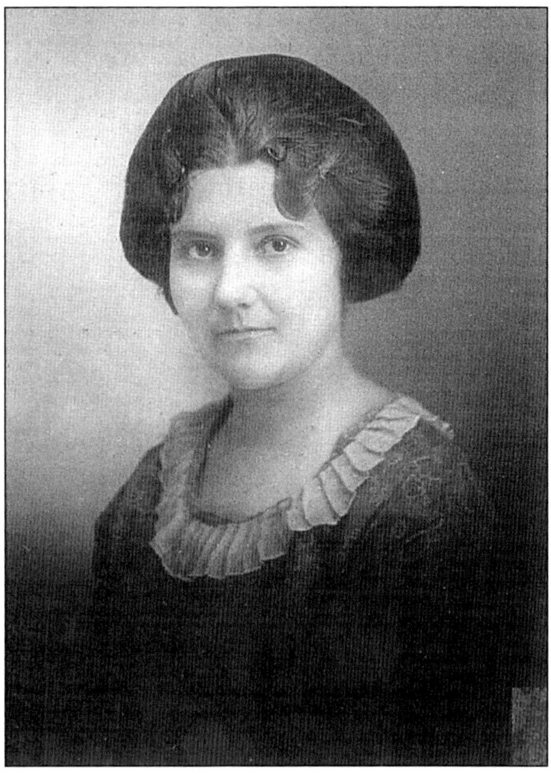

With her hairstyle and clothing dated to the 1920s or earlier, Leila Green Ashley Gay posed for this photograph in 1920. No one seems to know any details of her life, but her photograph is an interesting one. (Courtesy of the Telfair County Library.)

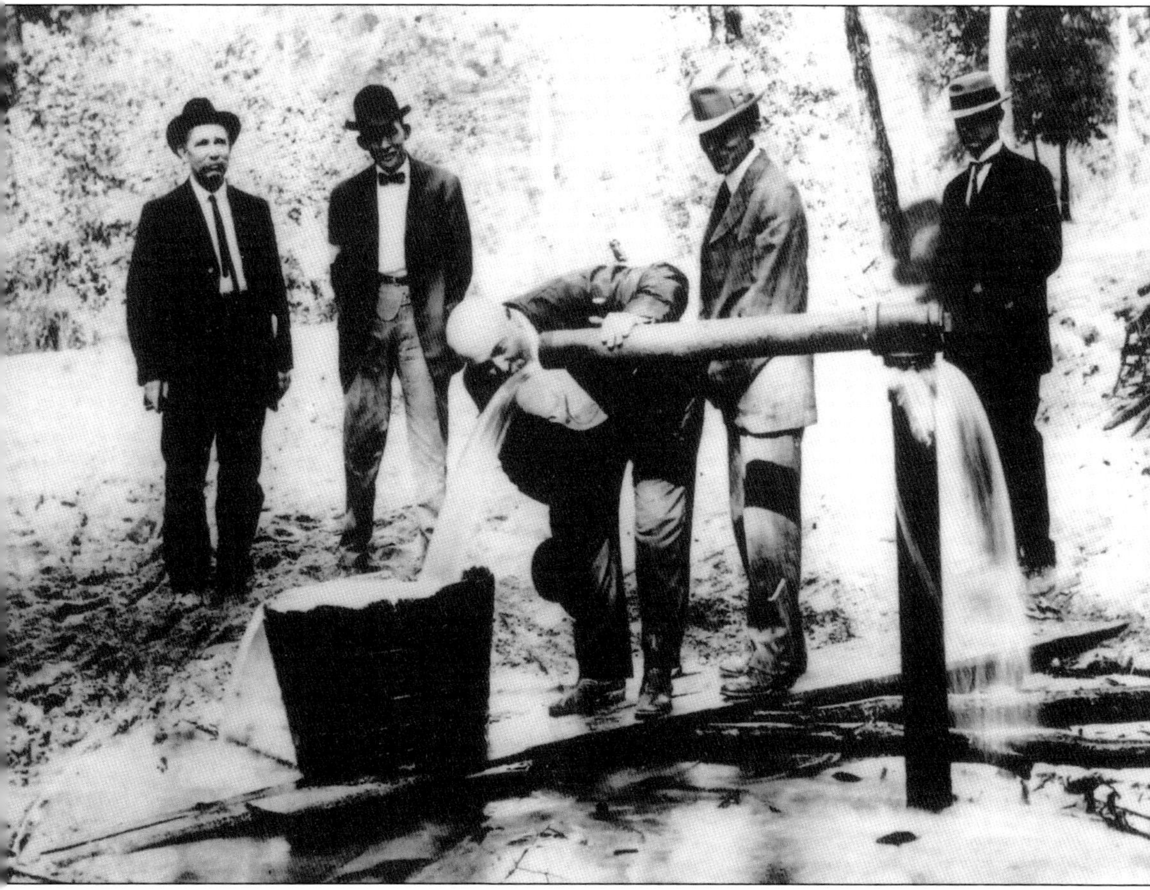

Dr. Frank Rambo Mann Sr. is shown drinking water from an artesian well in Scotland, Georgia. To the right is Dr. Frank Rambo Mann Jr. Both were longtime physicians in Telfair County. William Simeon Mann Sr. is to the extreme right of Dr. Mann Sr. (Courtesy of Janet Smith Fields.)

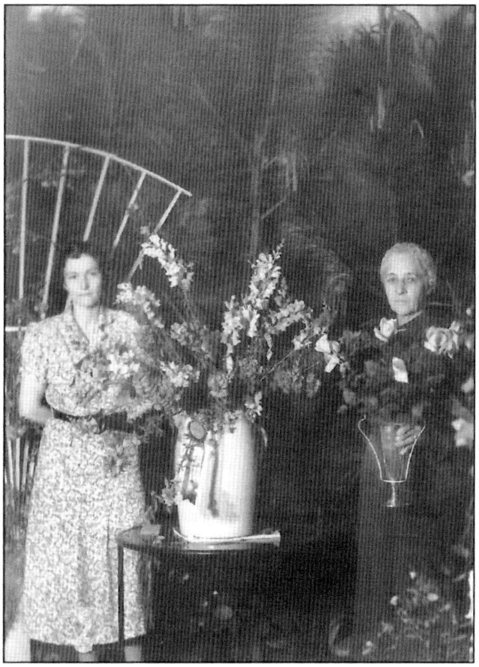

The Lyonia Garden Club was organized in 1932 by 20 ladies of the community and a Methodist minister, Rev. J. Lytle Jones, pastor of the McRae Methodist Church. The club was named after the plant *Lyonia ligustrina*. The club planted the courtyard at the McRae United Methodist Church in 1936. Annie Hunt and Ruby Born show their arrangement at a Lyonia Garden Club flower show about 1940. (Courtesy of The Telfair County Library.)

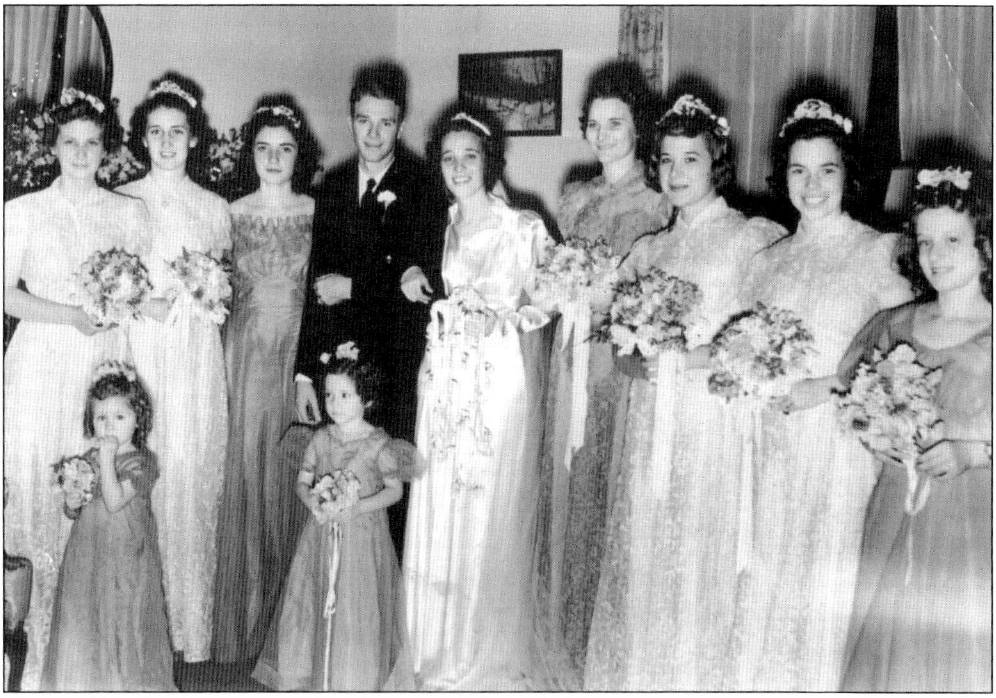

The wedding of Marjorie Lord and D.J. Burch was held on June 1, 1947, at the Dexter Baptist Church in Dexter, Georgia. Participants included Russell Lord (bride's brother), Margaret Williams (bride's college roommate), Delacey Lord (bride's brother), Frances Scoggins (D.J.'s cousin), Imogene Lord (bride's sister), Robert Hugh Calhoun, Jeanette Lord (bride's aunt), Marshall Lord (brother of the bride), Eleanor Smith (soloist), and Minton Lord (bride's uncle). (Courtesy of Marjorie Lord Burch.)

William Simeon Mann Sr. speaks at a political rally for Herman Talmadge. W.S. Mann was a legal representative for both Gene and Herman Talmadge. Mann represented Herman Talmadge in the historic "Three Governors Controversy." (Courtesy of Janet Smith Fields.)

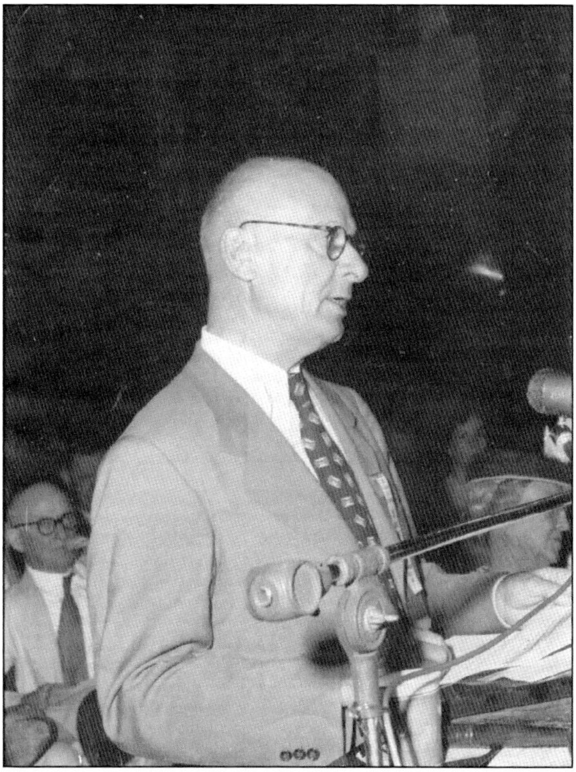

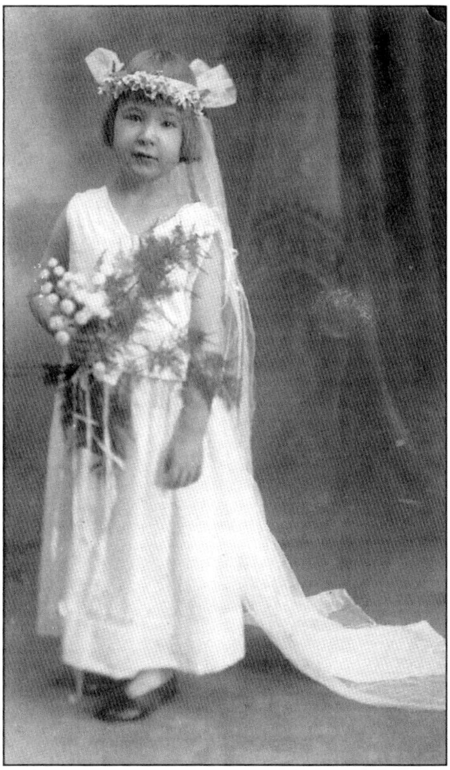

Mary Mann Smith was the daughter of William Simeon Mann Sr. and Floris Perkins Mann. She was affectionately called "Doll" all of her life. This photograph was taken when she was about four years old. (Courtesy of Janet Smith Fields.)

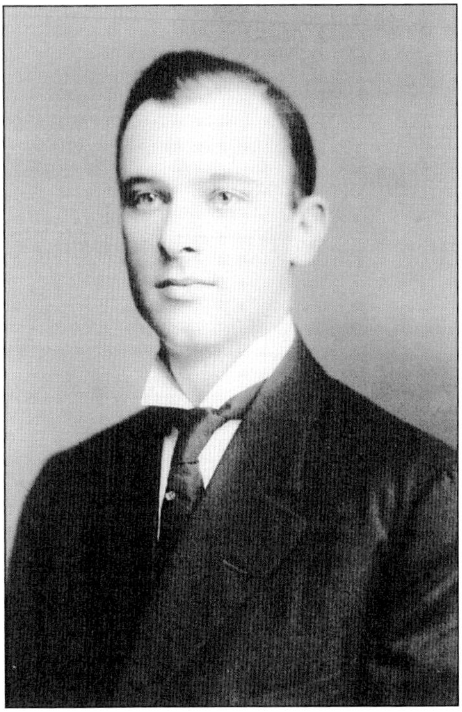

William Simeon Mann Sr., son of Frank Rambo Mann Sr. and Henrietta Sikes Mann, is pictured here. He was a prominent attorney in Telfair County and earned his law degree in 1908 from the University of Georgia. He was mayor of McRae and a Georgia state senator, where he was instrumental in the creation of Wheeler County. Colonel Mann also served as president of the Merchants and Citizens Bank. (Courtesy of Janet Smith Fields.)

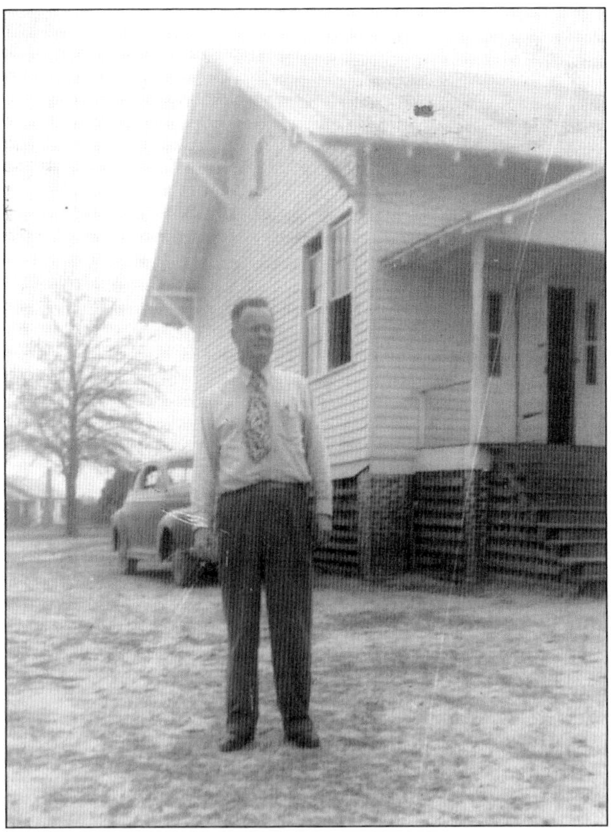

V.M. Thornton, principal of Workmore High and Elementary School, is shown at the old schoolhouse, which has been torn down. The photograph was taken in the 1940s. (Courtesy of Sarah Jones Bowen.)

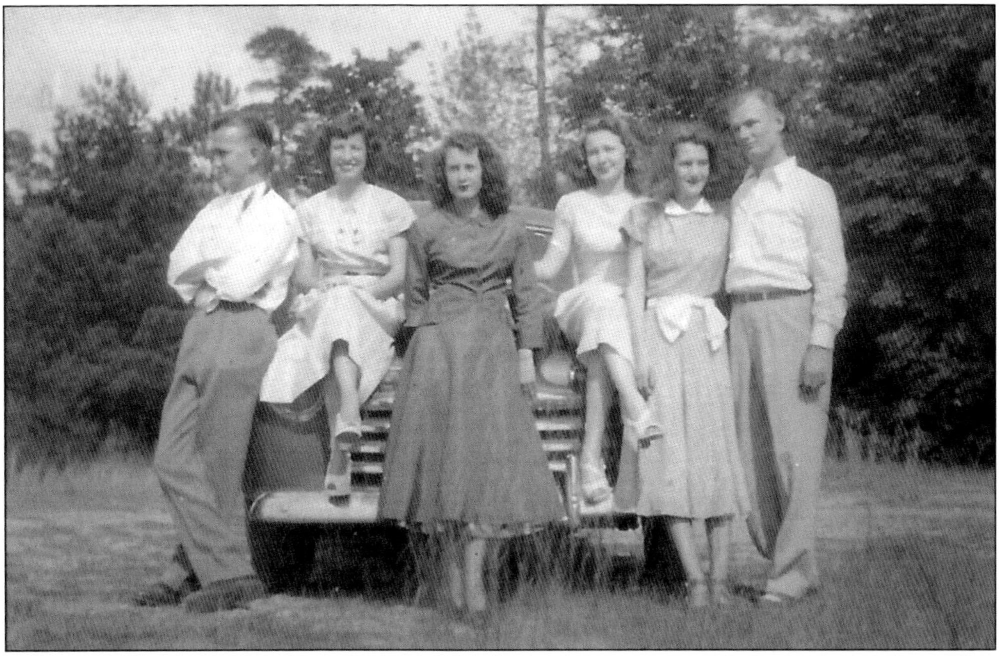

Around Easter 1947, these friends posed for a photograph together. They are, from left to right, Henry Coleman, Betty Fuller, Joyce Johnson, Betty Rawlins, Jan Douglas, and Jack McGinty. Joyce later represented Telfair County in the Georgia Turpentine Queen Contest on Jekyll Island the same year that the state purchased the island. In order to attend the contest, the friends went by boat, then school bus, to the other side of Jekyll. The driver jokingly announced to the group that anyone who was for M.E. Thompson should stay on the bus. Everybody got off the bus. (Courtesy of Melissa McGinty Carroll.)

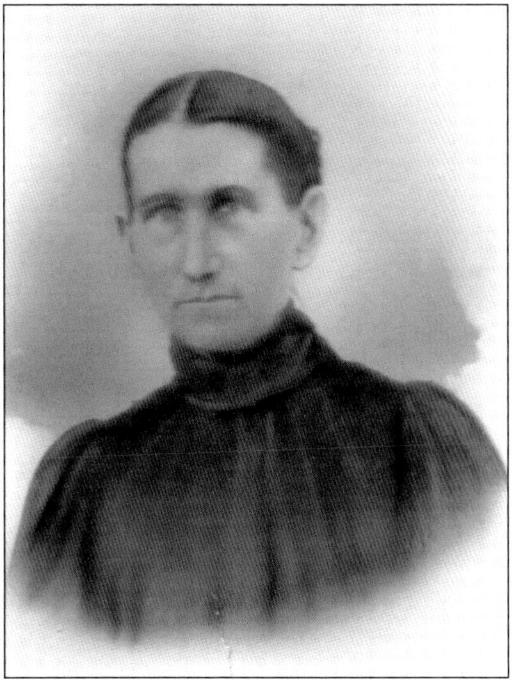

Ruby White's grandmother was Mary Emily Seigler Weeks (1855–1926), pictured here. According to Ruby, she was a stern woman who bore eight children. She loved to do needlework, which included tatting and quilting. (Courtesy of Ruby Maloy White.)

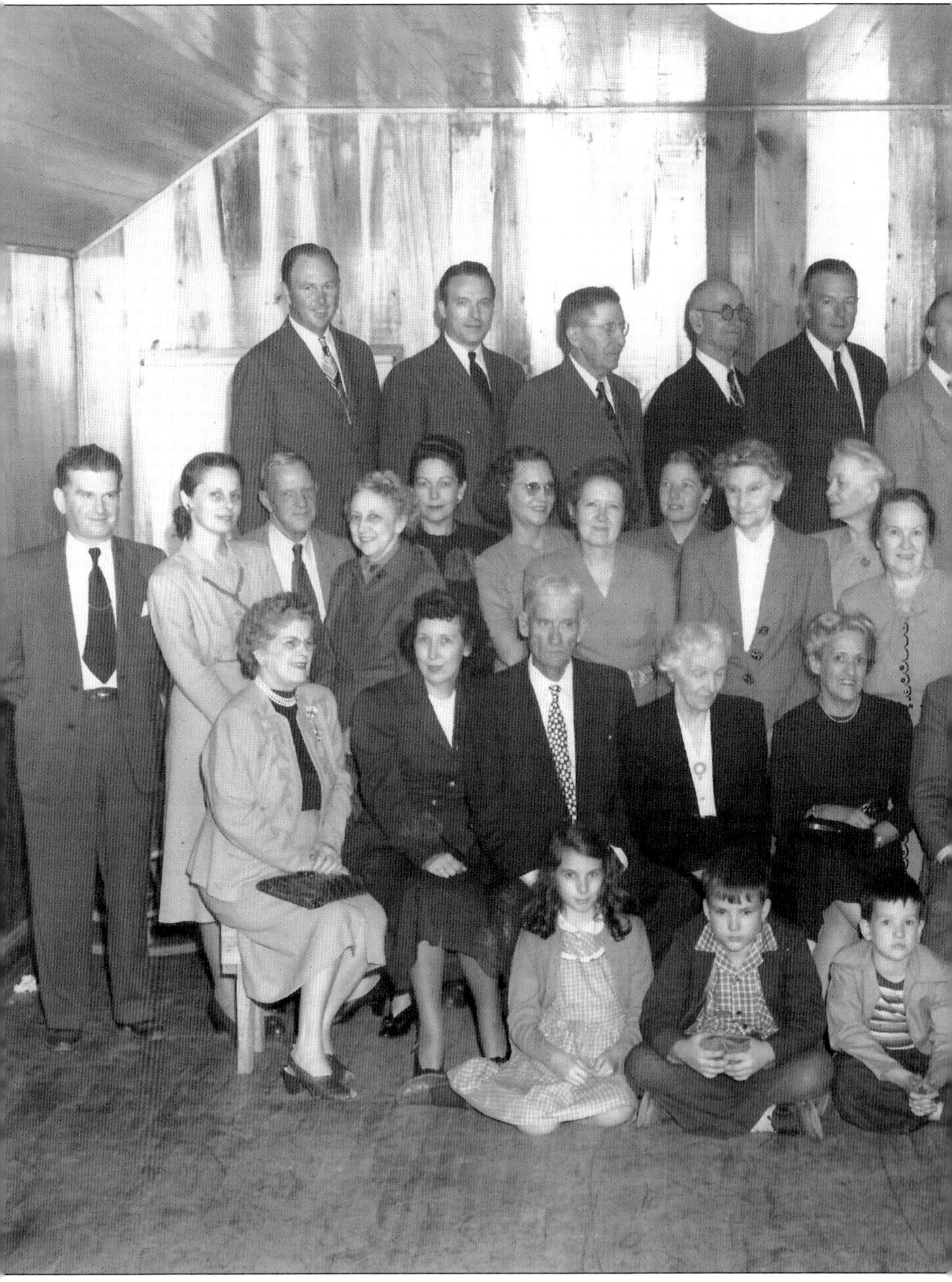

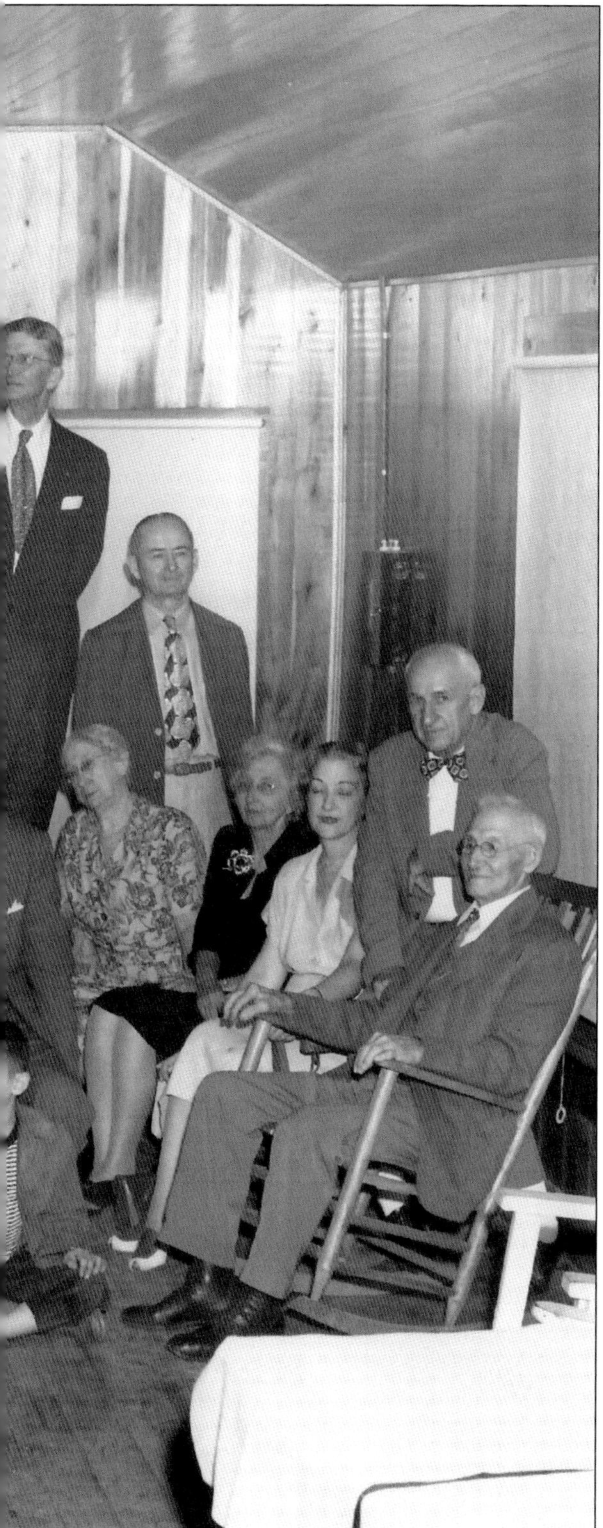

Some of Telfair County's leading citizens posed for this 1940s photograph. In this image are, from left to right, (first row) four unidentified children; (second row) Mrs. Mary Ryals, Sallie McRae, Max L. McRae, Mrs. Marlon McRae, Captain and Mrs. Bebie, Mrs. A.J. Ellis, Mrs. Frances Smith, Mrs. Leon Folsom, Jonathon S. Stamps Sr., and Charlie Griffith; (third row) Dr. Bill McRae, Louise McRae, unidentified, Eva Drew, Lucy Thackston, Martha Folsom, Christine Folsom, Evelyn Thrasher, Fannie McRae, Mrs. Bertie Stamps, Mrs. Stewart Evans, Mitz McRae, and Stuart Evans; (fourth row) Tig Thrasher, Findlay McRae, Col. George Harris, Col. W.B. Smith, Parker McRae, Leon Folsom, and Dr. "Ches" Ryals. (Courtesy of Chris McRae.)

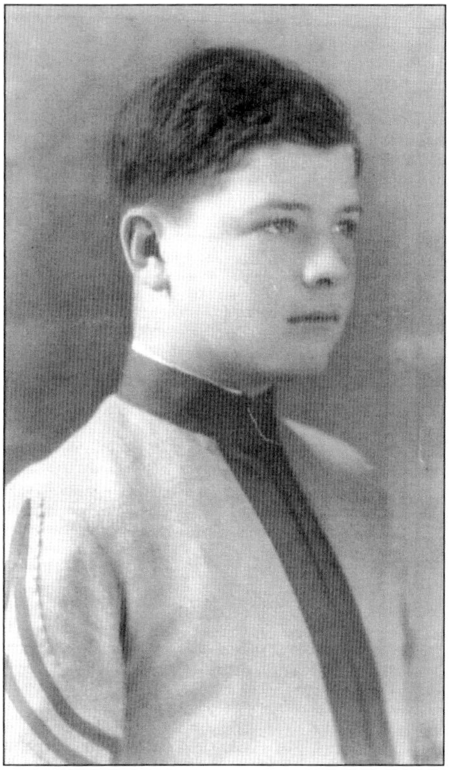

William Mann Jr. attended Riverside Military Academy in Gainesville, Georgia. Upon graduation, he attended the University of Georgia, where he studied law. He married Emily Flanders from Scotland, Georgia. They had two daughters, Kay Mann Rogers and Jane Mann Davidson. Mann practiced law with his father, W.S. Mann Sr. (Courtesy of Janet Smith Fields.)

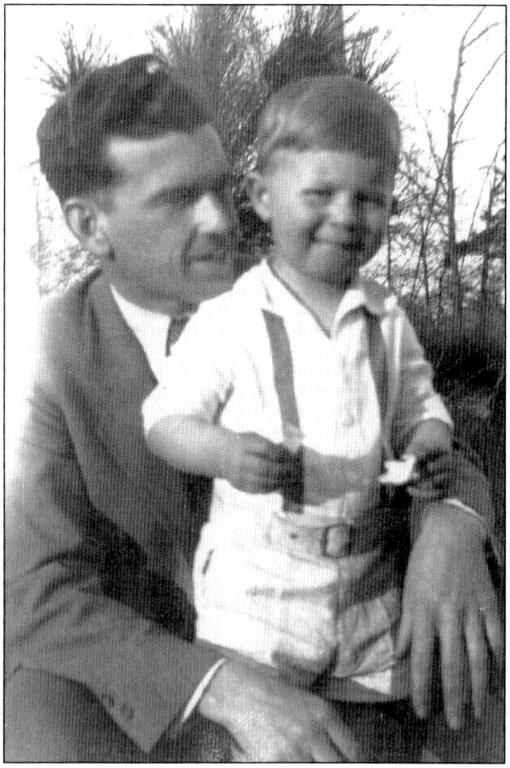

Dr. Bill McRae, pictured here in the 1940s, was the founder and owner of McRae's Pharmacy in McRae. His son Billy also became a pharmacist and later owned and operated McRae's Pharmacy. The McRae family was a family of pharmacists. Dr. Bill's two brothers also owned their own pharmacies, one in Douglas, Georgia, and the other in Dublin, Georgia. (Courtesy of Chris McRae.)

Taken in 1944, this photograph features Delores "Dee" McGinty, sister of Jack McGinty, and Mac McRae Stout. Mac's mother was Mildred McRae Stout, sister of D.M. McRae, whose family gave land for the town of McRae. Dee's father owned McGinty's Restaurant for many years. Her mother owned McGinty Florist. Her brother Jack was a certified public accountant in McRae until his death in 1973. He suffered a heart attack while jogging. (Courtesy of Melissa McGinty Carroll.)

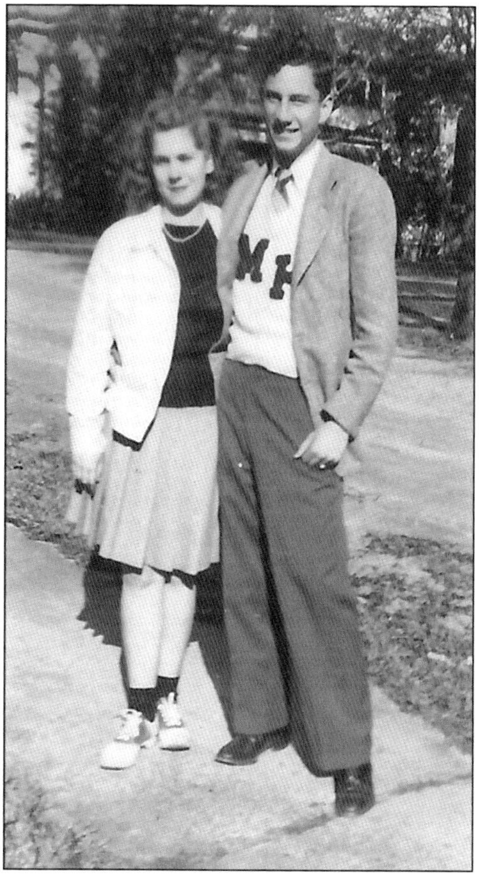

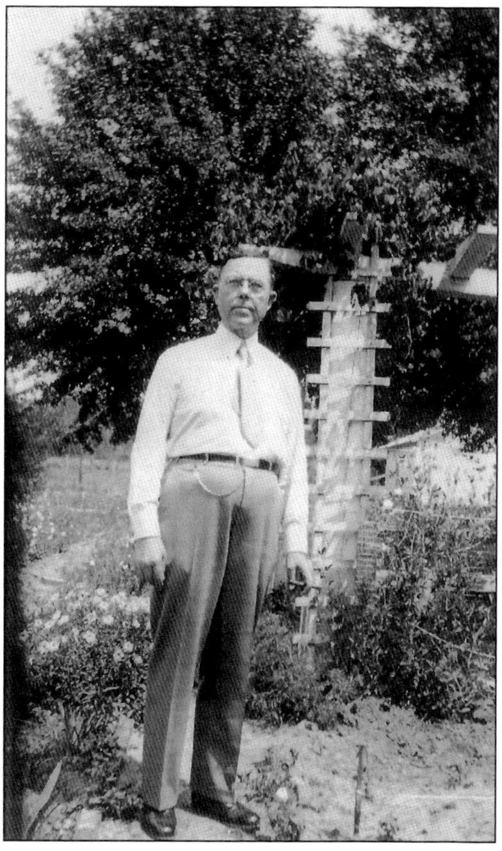

Dr. Wade Hampton Born (1876–1962) was a family physician in McRae. He attended the University of Georgia and the Atlanta College of Physicians and Surgeons, now Emory University Medical School. According to an article in the *Daily Notes* of Canonsburg, Pennsylvania, dated 1926, Dr. Born had the largest dewberry farm in the United States. Some claimed it was the largest in the world. He had 40 acres under cultivation, bringing in $1,000 an acre. (Courtesy of Ruby Maloy White.)

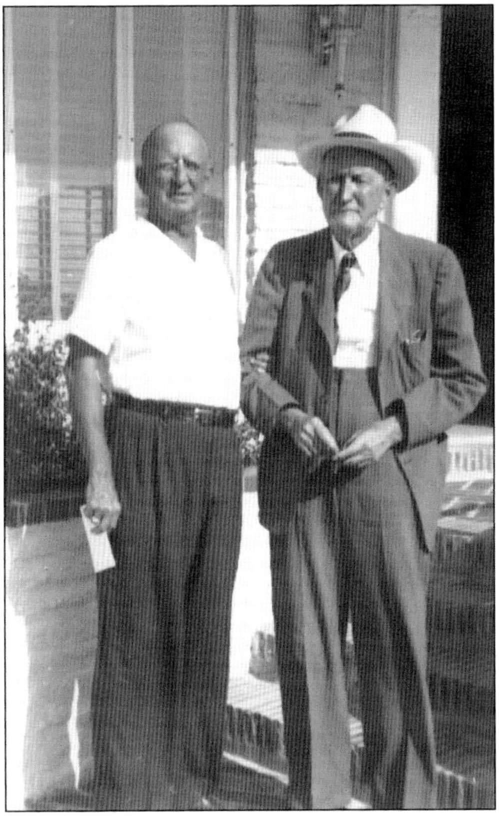

William Daniel Horton (right), well known in McRae-Helena, worked for the railroad but later purchased a sawmill. In 1901, Horton sold his interest in the sawmill and purchased the telephone exchange. Horton later became the owner and publisher of the *Telfair Enterprise*. He served on the city council and as commissioner of roads and revenue. (Courtesy of LoAnn Montgomery Ryals.)

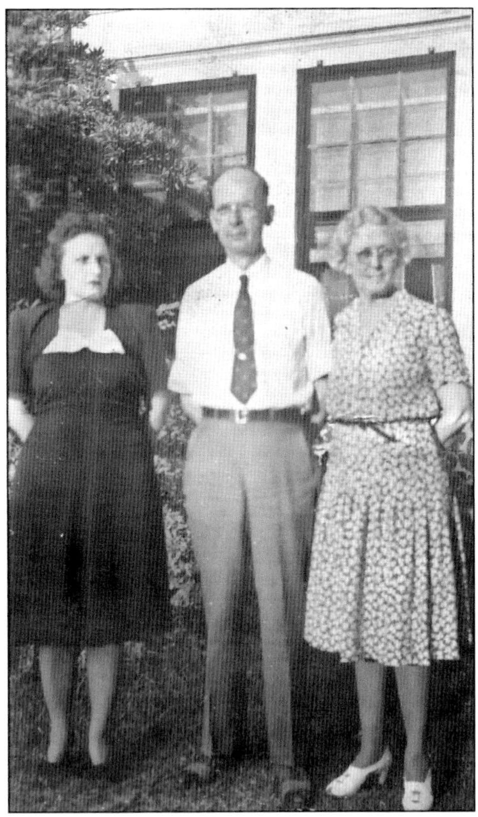

W.L. Bowen and Susie Horton Bowen are shown with their daughter-in-law Helen Walker Bowen (left) in this June 18, 1944, photograph. (Courtesy of Sarah Jones Bowen.)

Sarah Jones and unidentified friend are shown outside Workmore High and Elementary School. The school was located midway between McRae and Jacksonville. It originally housed students in kindergarten through 11th grade and later housed only the elementary grades. The school closed in the 1990s. (Courtesy of Sarah Jones Bowen.)

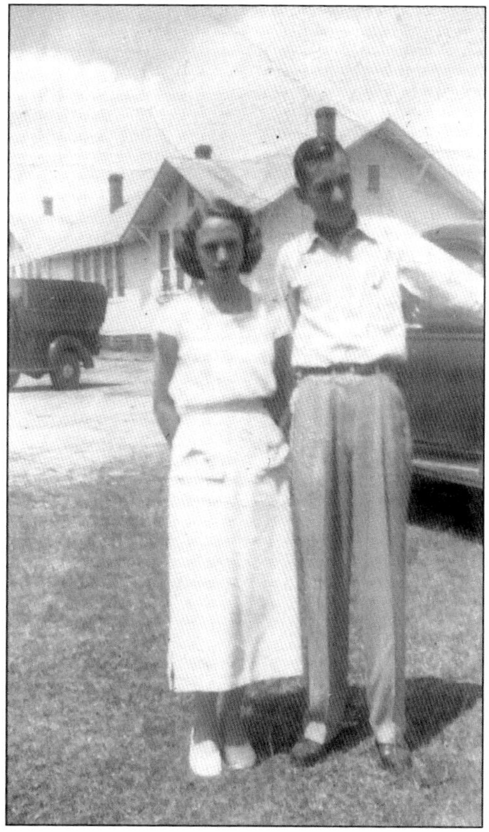

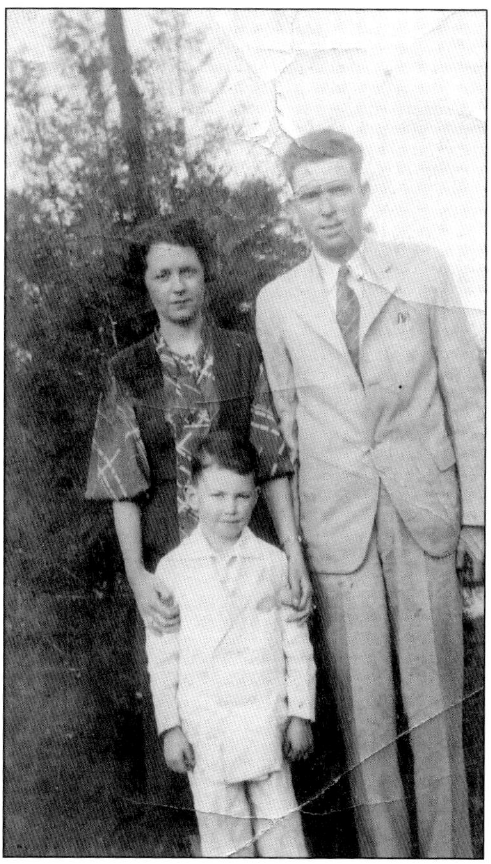

Wade Harbin Sr. was born on a farm near McRae. He attended South Georgia College in McRae, where he excelled in the high jump and was the school champion. His wife, Myrtle, and son Wade Jr. are shown in this early-1940s photograph. Myrtle and Wade Sr. both loved to sing and did so on many occasions. Wade worked for the post office and was a city councilman. (Courtesy of Danny Harbin.)

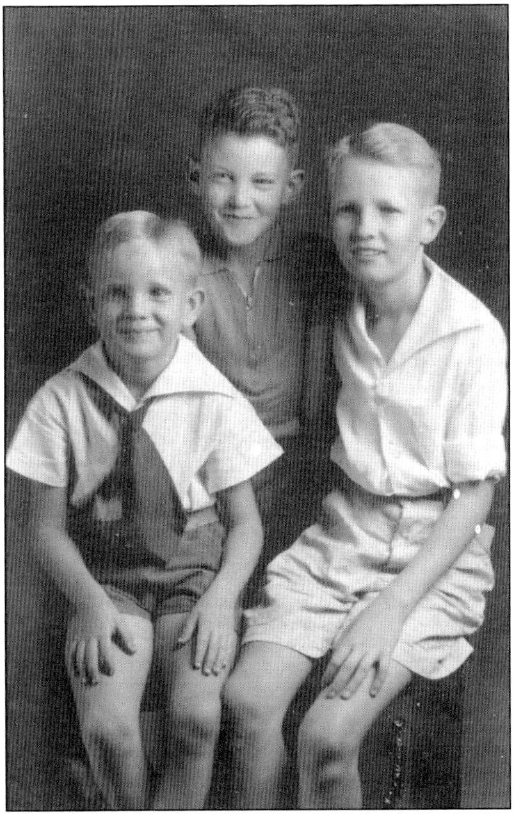

Pictured here in the 1930s are, from left to right, Jerry Harbin, Wade Harbin Sr., and Buddy Harbin. These boys were well-known brothers in McRae and Telfair County. All three had beautiful singing voices. They lent their talents in churches, the community, and wherever there was a call for songs of praise. (Courtesy of Norwood Davidson.)

The graduating class of 1940 at the McRae-Helena High School is resplendent in their caps and gowns. Albert Butler (top row, far left) was the president of the class. Ralph McGill, noted journalist, was the commencement speaker. (Courtesy of H.B. Barnes.)

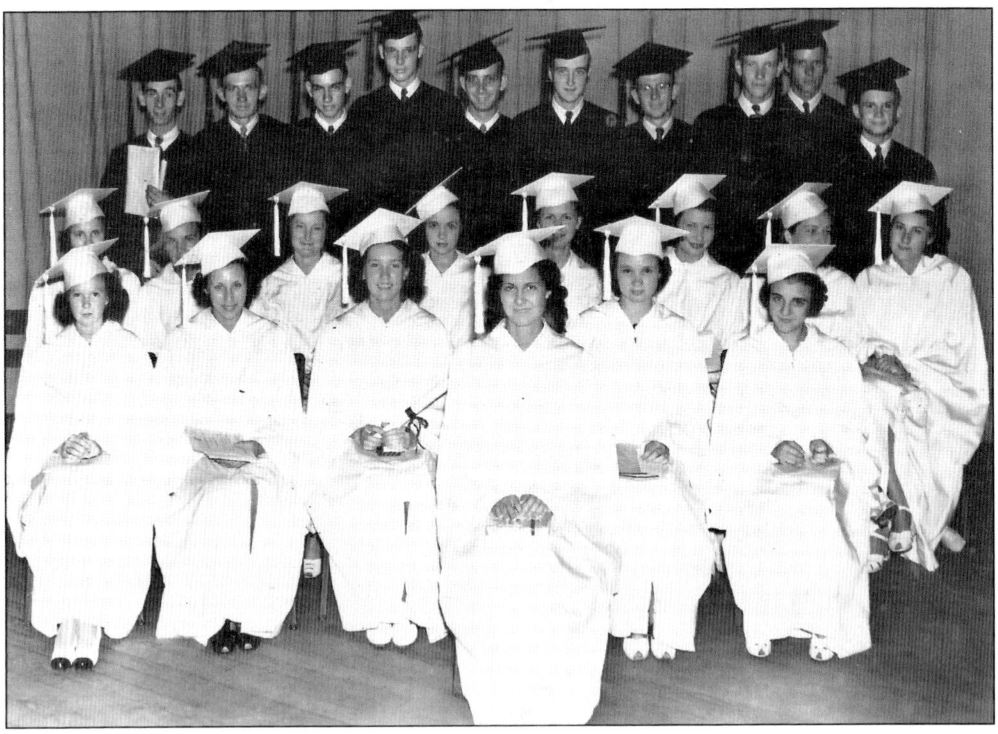

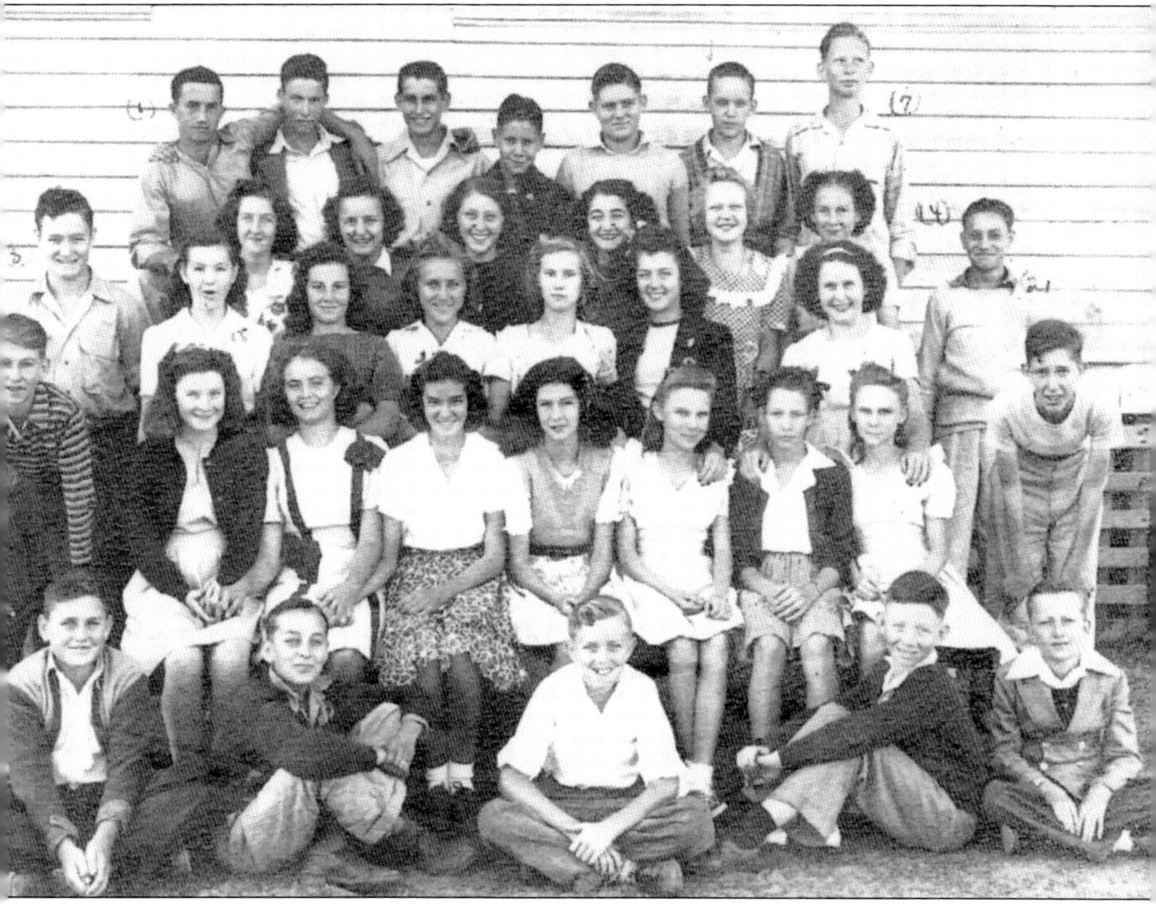

Workmore High School's class of 1949 is shown in this photograph. They were beginning their sophomore year. Pictured here from left to right are (first row) Fred Jones, Maurice Rawlins, Alvin Floyd, Dave Walker, and Walter White; (second row) James L. Graham, Blondell Lake, Laverne Rawlins, Lena Mae Tucker, Doris Scott, Madaline Sellers, Collette Walker, Madgeline Sellers, and Osborn Smith; (third row) Edwin Hulett, Dorothy Gore, Geraldine "Dumpy" Cartwright, Adell Powell, Rose Ann Rogers, Celestine Spires, Emily Alligood, and Calvin Swain; (fourth row) Janelle "Judy" Reynolds, Runette Williams, unidentified, Mary Frances Willis, unidentified, and Geraldine Patterson; (fifth row) J.L. Bowen, Clifford Graham, John L. Walden, Wendell Thornton, Jack Jones, Walter Batchelor, and Clarence Padgett. (Courtesy of Sarah Jones Bowen.)

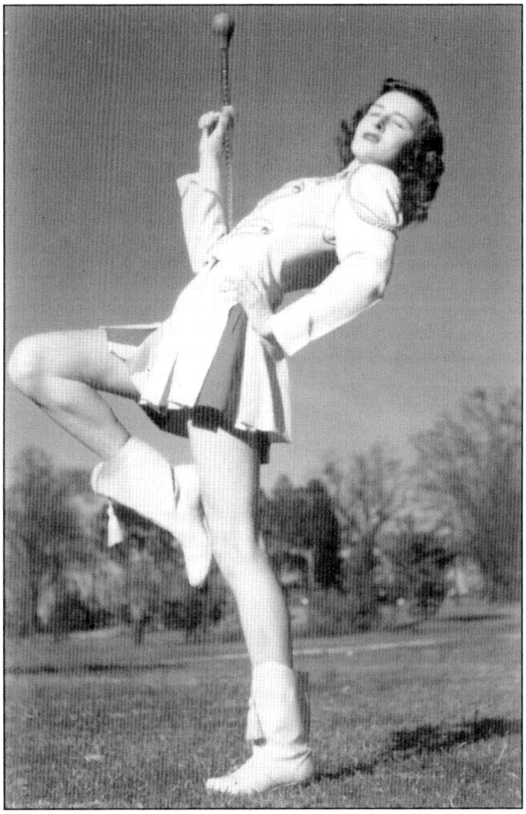

Janiece McRae was a majorette in the University of Georgia Redcoat Marching Band. She was the wife of Dr. Billy McRae, who owned and operated McRae's Pharmacy. Janiece was very active in the Telfair Art Association and sang in the McRae Methodist Church choir, to which she added her beautiful, rich soprano voice. (Courtesy of Chris McRae.)

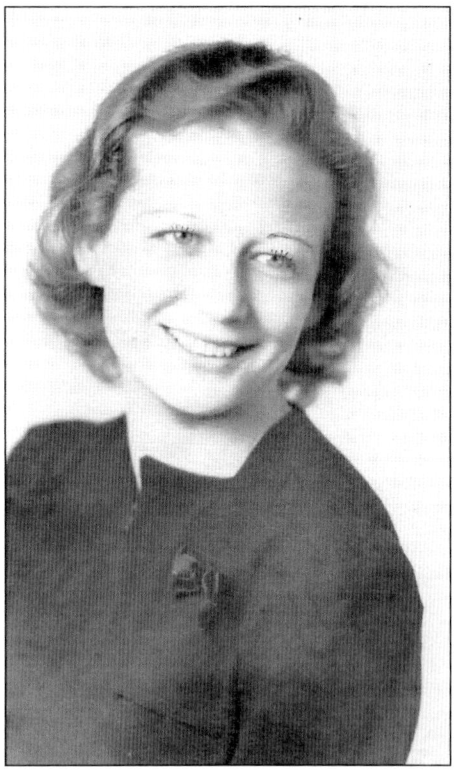

Although Nancy Montgomery was born in California, she was a true daughter of Telfair County and McRae. She moved to McRae in 1942 and became a real estate developer. She was responsible for the construction of the first apartment complex in McRae, Villa East Apartments. During her lifetime, she contracted to build over 50 houses in the community. She is the mother of LoAnn Ryals. (Courtesy of LoAnn Montgomery Ryals.)

Ruby White was a senior at Wesleyan College in Macon when this photograph was taken in 1942. Ruby majored in chemistry and minored in music, hoping to follow in the footsteps of her father and attend medical school. Plans changed when she married Rufus King "R.K." White in 1960. They had two children, Kenneth and Sarah. R.K. (1892–1952) had two children, King and Ed, from a previous marriage. (Courtesy of Ruby Maloy White.)

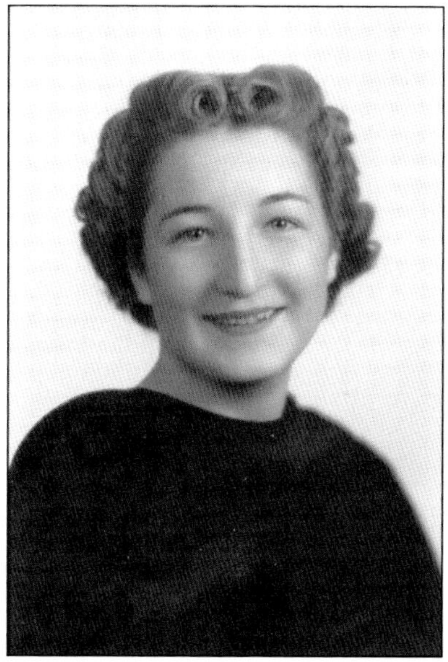

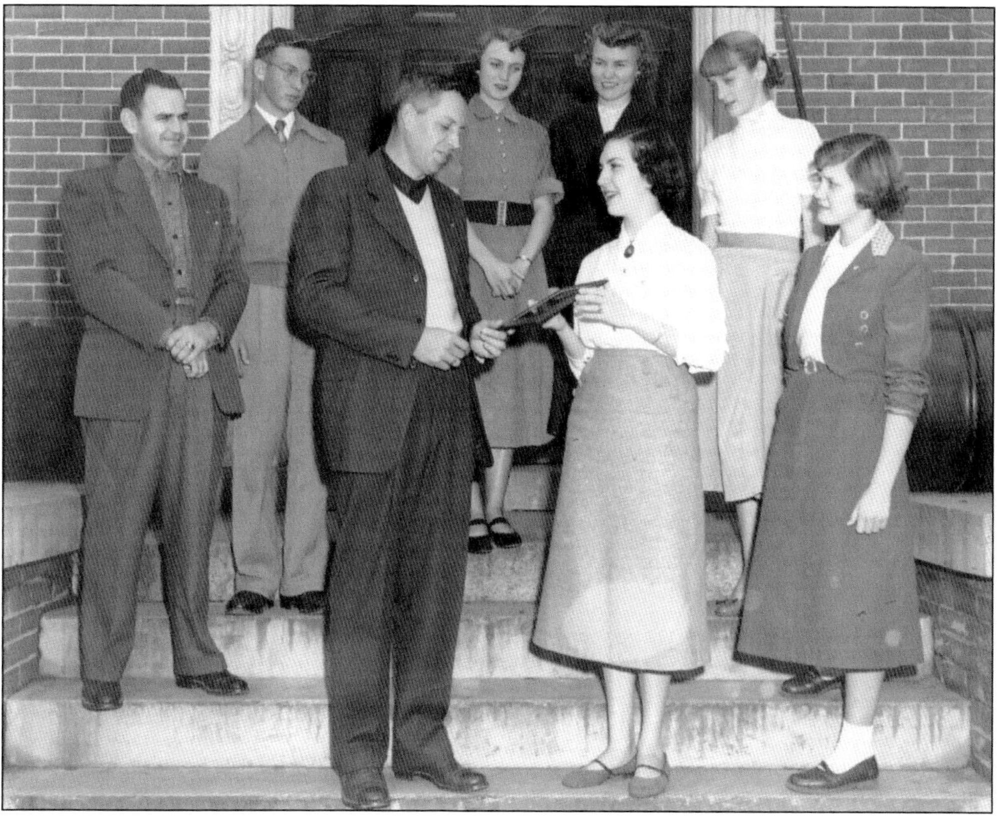

Walter Dyal, Telfair County commissioner, is shown presenting a plaque to Nancy Barnes, 4-H Club president, sometime around 1949 or 1950. Looking on are, from left to right, D.Q. Harris (Telfair County extension agent), an unidentified student, Sarah Jones (who later married Edwin Bowen), Meryle Wade (extension agent), an unidentified student, and Kathryn Jones. (Courtesy of Sarah Jones Bowen.)

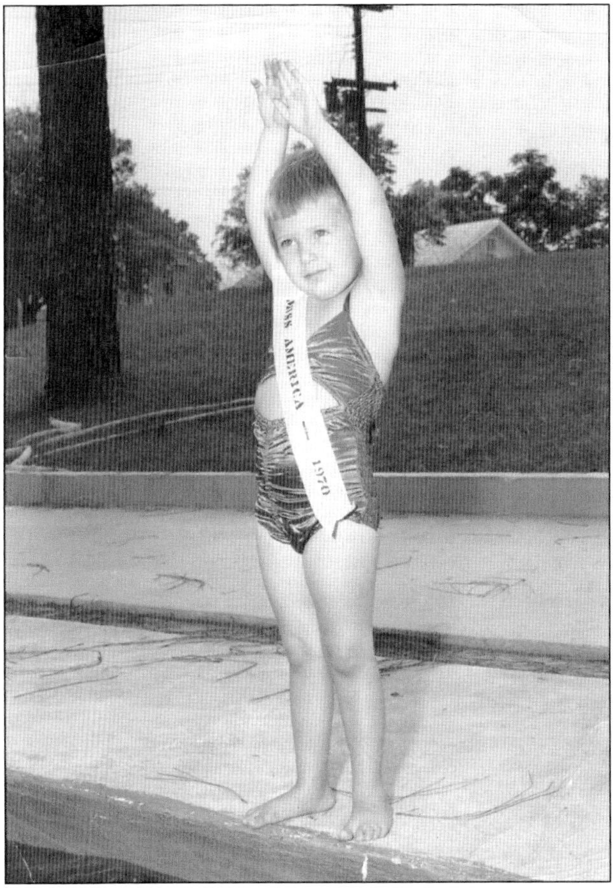


Janet Fields Smith, daughter of Lt. Col. and Mrs. C.O. Smith, was a participant and winner in a water carnival staged by the McRae-Helena PTA around 1952. The old pool was located near the old Gene Theater in McRae. (Courtesy of Janet Smith Fields.)

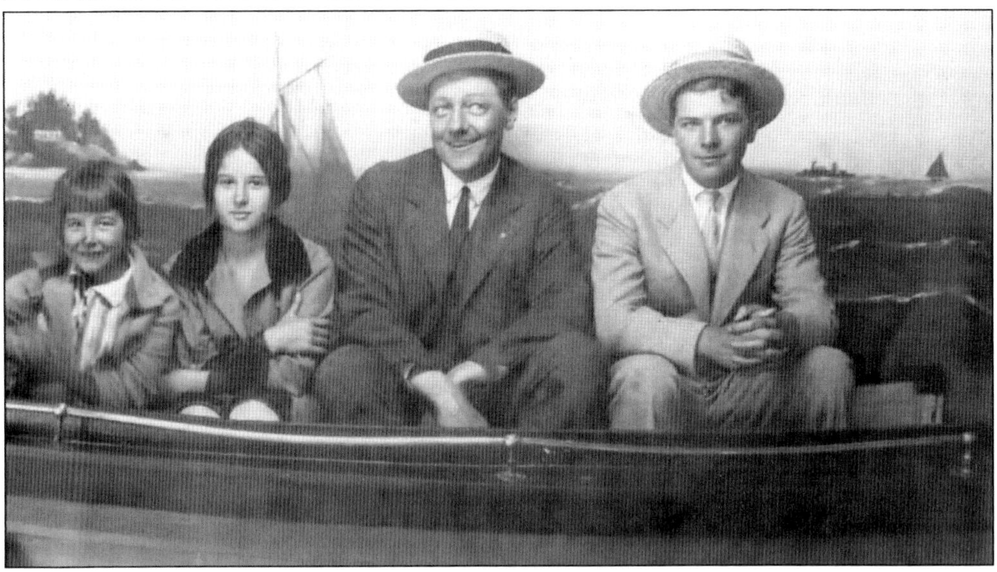

From left to right, Mary Mann Smith, Janet Mann Hungerford, William Perkins (uncle of the children), and William Simeon Mann Jr. enjoy a photography session around 1928. All three are children of William Simeon Mann Sr. and Floris Perkins Mann. (Courtesy of Janet Smith Fields.)

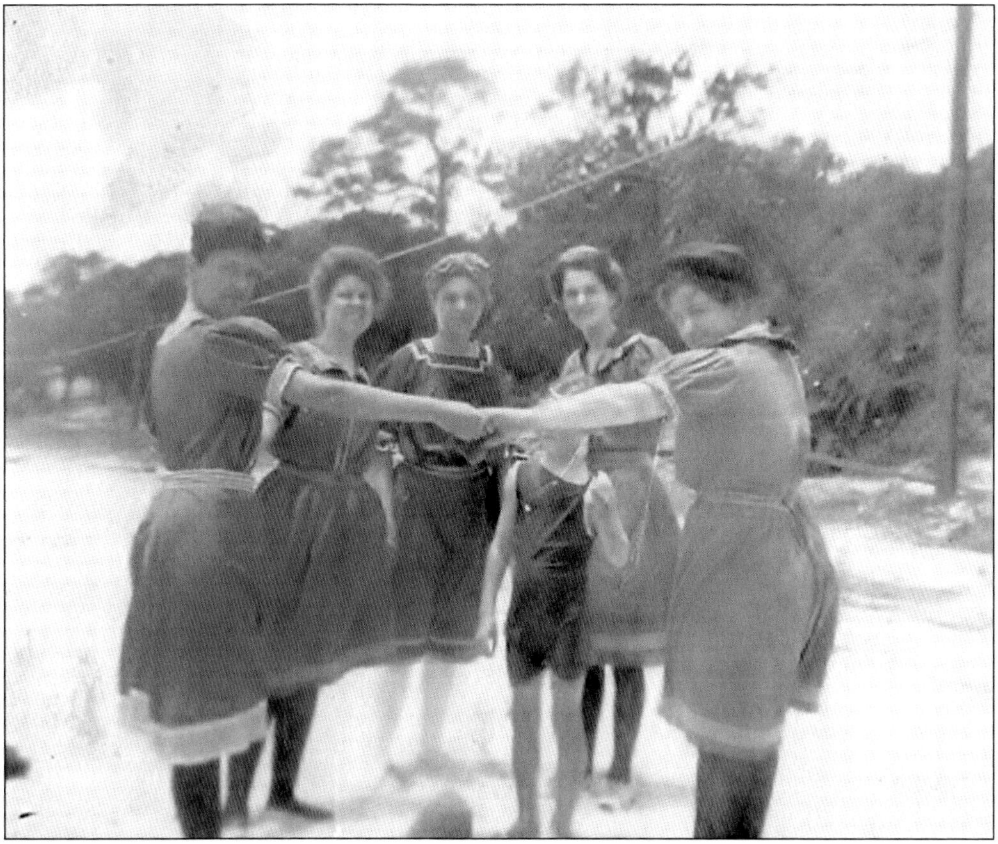

Floris Perkins Mann (far left), wife of William Simeon Mann Sr., and some unidentified women are enjoying the beach at Tybee Island, Georgia, around 1900. (Courtesy of Janet Smith Fields.)

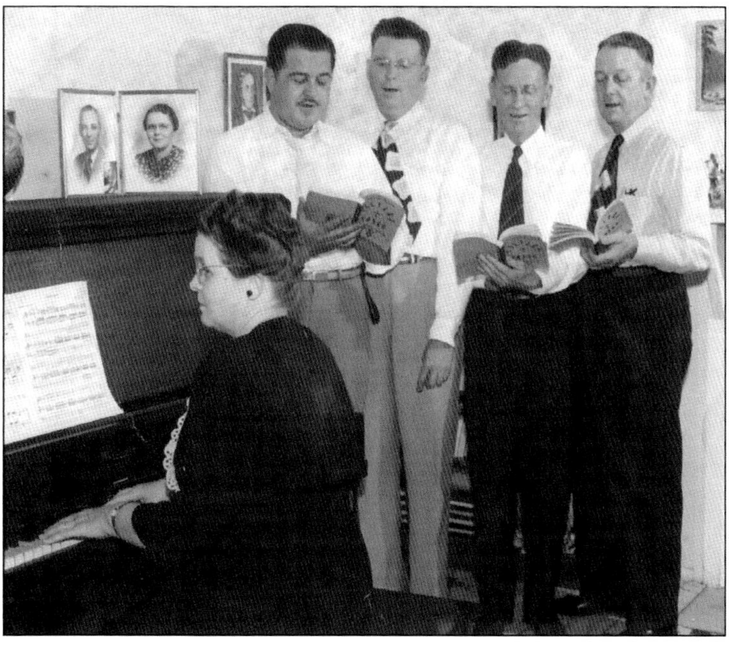

Wade Harbin Sr.'s passion was music, specifically singing. In the 1940s, he brought this passion to fruition by organizing the Harbin Quartet. This popular quartet sang in churches, for funerals, and for civic functions. Members of the quartet included, from left to right, Leroy Clements, Herman Harbin, Wade Harbin Sr., and John Daniels. Pennie Hardin was their accompanist. (Courtesy of Danny Harbin.)

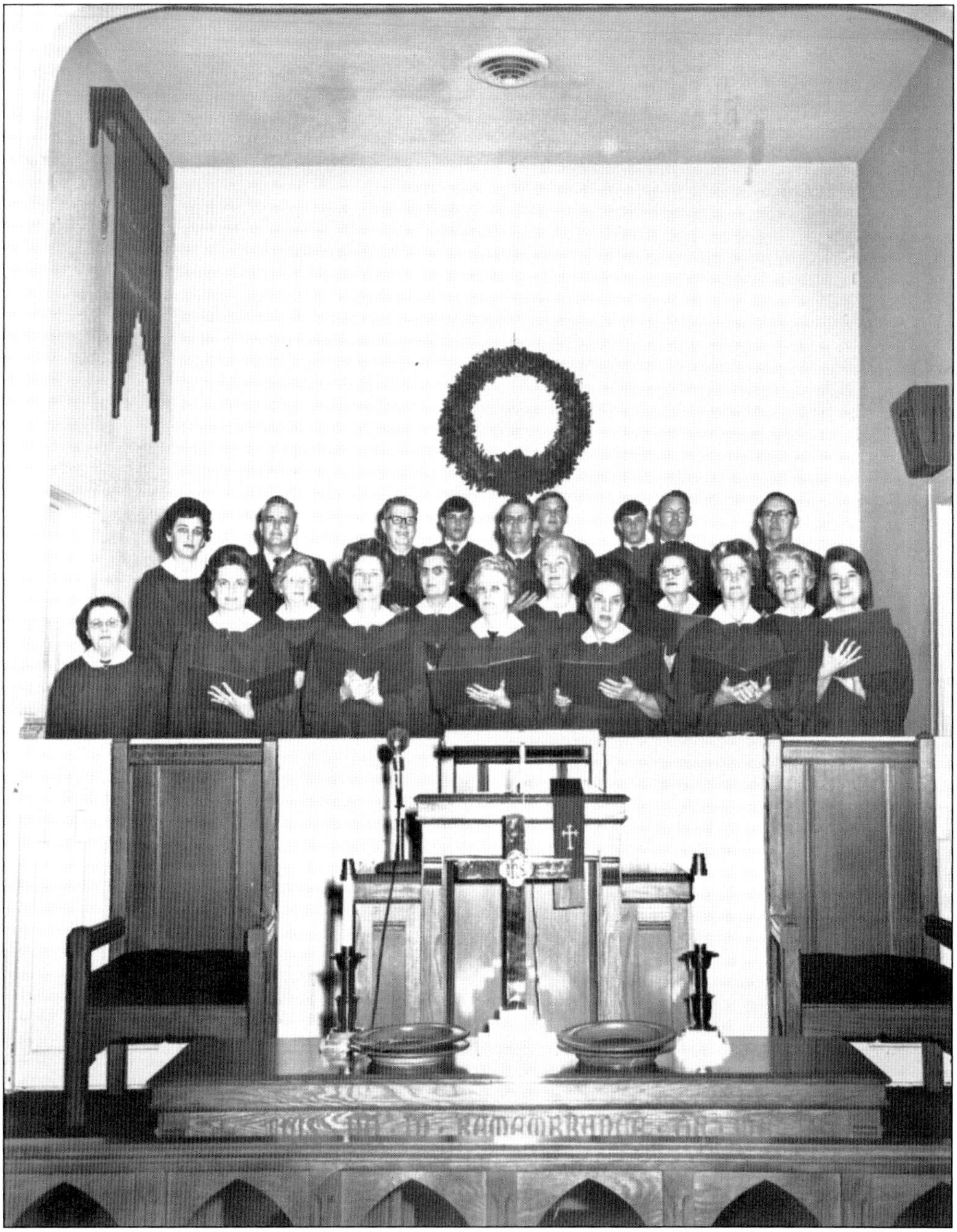

The McRae Methodist Church choir is shown in this 1960s photograph. All are now deceased except Anne Smith and the Hawkins brothers in the third row. The choir members are, from left to right, (first row) Pennie Hardin, Vivian Billing, Janiece McRae, Myrtle Harbin, Nellie Claire Smith, Sarah Dopson, and Jewell Geiger; (second row) Mildred Stout, Frank McRae, Anna Belle Bradfield, and Elizabeth Tankersley; (third row) Anne Smith, Jeff Smith, Wade Harbin Sr., Jack Hawkins, Buddy Harbin, Fred Hawkins, James Hawkins, Wade Harbin Jr., and Bill Bowen. (Courtesy of Chris McRae.)

Marion B. Folsom, born in McRae, Georgia, was the chief architect of the Social Security Act of 1935, appointed by Pres. Franklin D. Roosevelt. Folsom was named secretary of health, education, and welfare in 1955 by Pres. Dwight D. Eisenhower. He was prominently associated with Eastman Kodak throughout his life, and he is buried in Arlington Cemetery. (Courtesy of the Telfair County Library.)

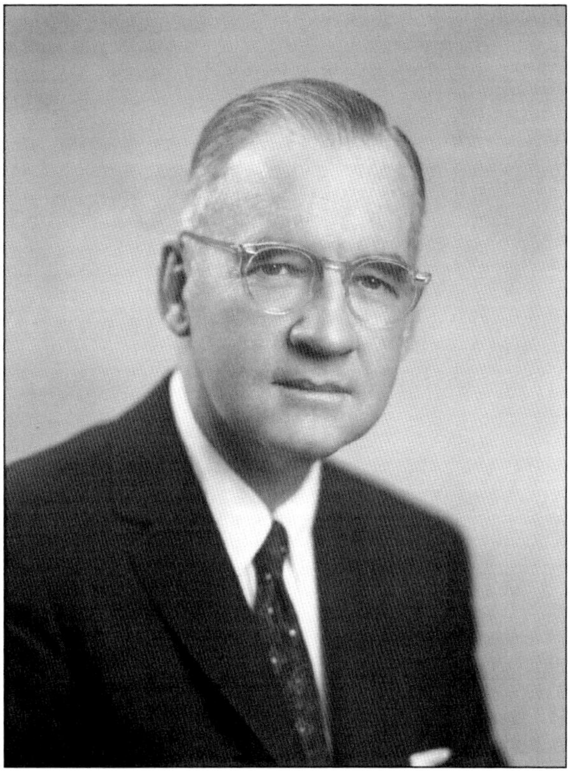

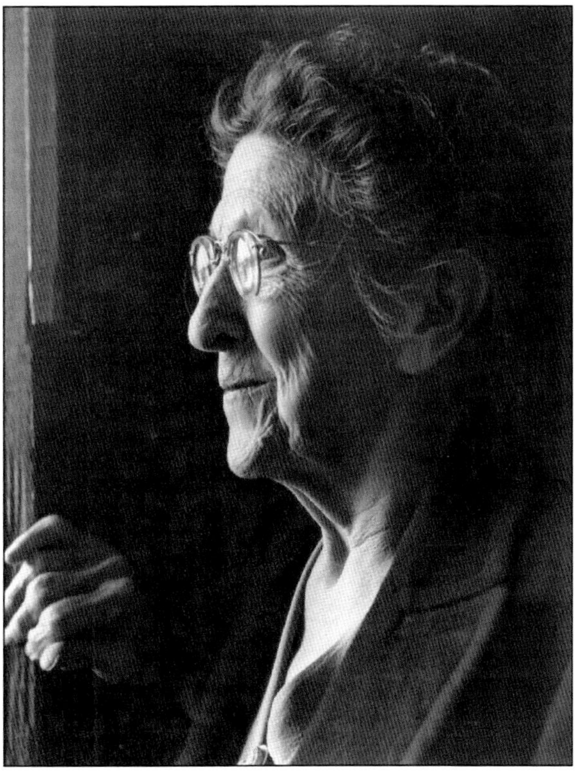

Lila Windsor taught both former senator Herman Talmadge and Marion B. Folsom. In 1958, Windsor was awarded the Golden Key Award for her outstanding contribution to education. She was nominated by Secretary Folsom. The award was presented to her in St. Louis, Missouri, to which she arrived by taking her first airplane ride at age 82. (Courtesy of the Telfair County Library.)

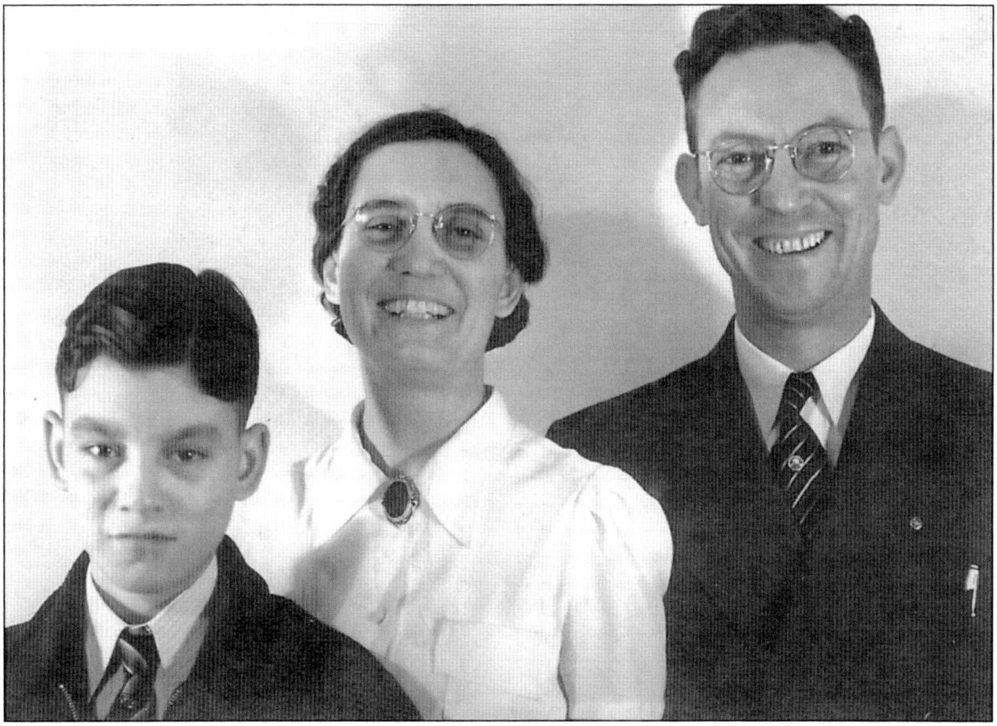

Daniel Murphy McRae (right), grandson of Daniel M. McRae in whose honor McRae, Georgia, was named, was employed by Merchants and Citizens Bank. He served in almost every bank position. D.M.'s wife, Frank (center), also worked in the bank, where she remained until her retirement in 1973. D.M. and Frank were the parents of Murphy McRae (left). (Courtesy of Mary Margaret McRae Batcha and Jane McRae.)

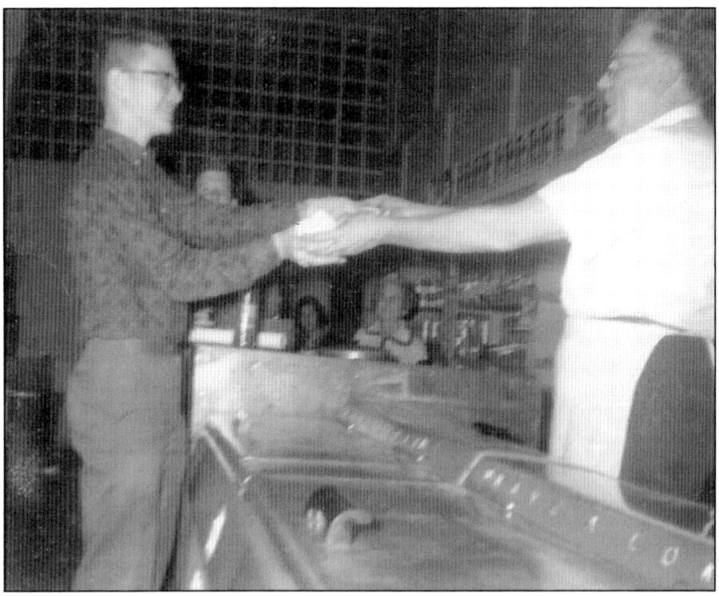

Life was good in the 1950s and 1960s, when a person could buy a hamburger for 10¢. Wade Harbin Sr. (right) waits on customer Dan McRae in his Harbin Hamburger Store in 1953. Known as the Dixie Grill, it was a popular hangout for teenagers, famous for its good food. The Dixie Grill could be considered McRae's first fast-food restaurant. (Courtesy of Danny Harbin.)

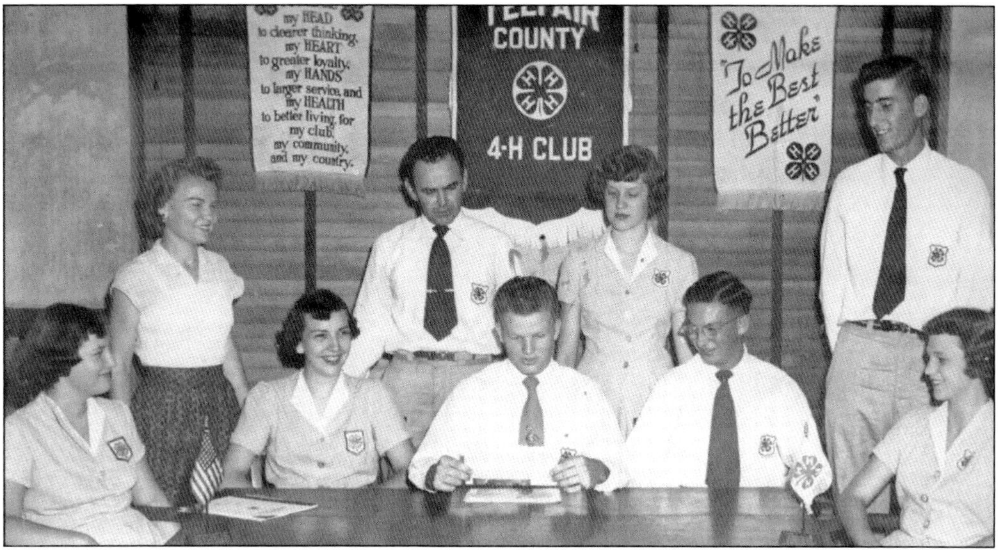


The Telfair County 4-H Club Council is meeting in this 1954 photograph. Notice the distinctive uniforms. From left to right are (first row) Eleanor Best (secretary), Nancy Barnes (girls' vice president), George Spires (president), Edison Thomas (boys' vice-president), and Sarah Jones (song leader); (second row) Merle Wade (home demonstration agent), D.Q. Harris Jr. (county agent), Kathryn Jones (reporter), and Joel Ussery (treasurer). (Courtesy of Eunice Calhoun Harris.)

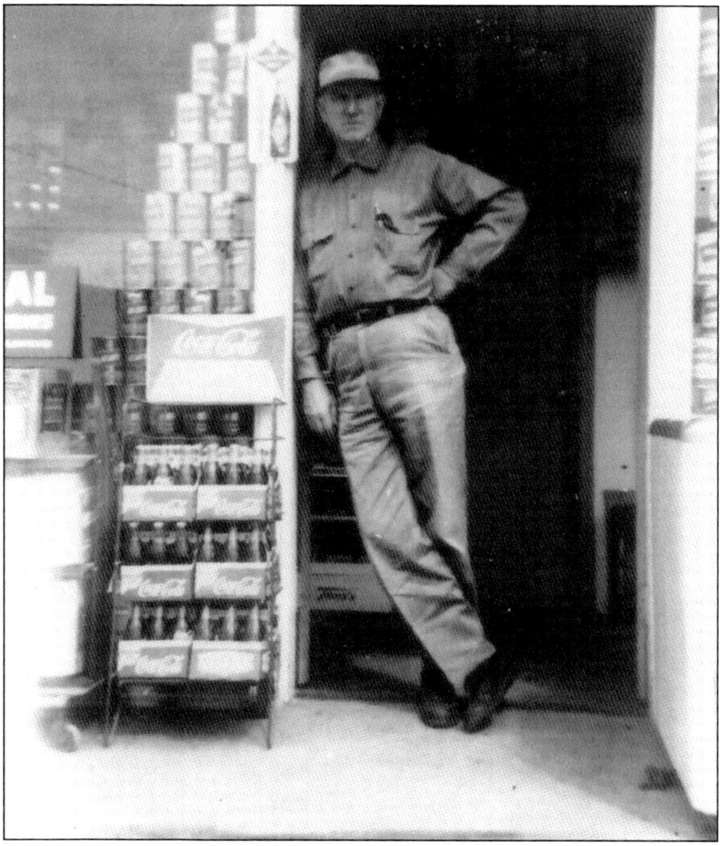

T.L. Faircloth is shown in the doorway of his McRae service station in the 1950s. Faircloth was a well-known businessman in the area. He was a member of the McRae Methodist Church and the father of Zell Stanley. (Courtesy of Chris McRae.)

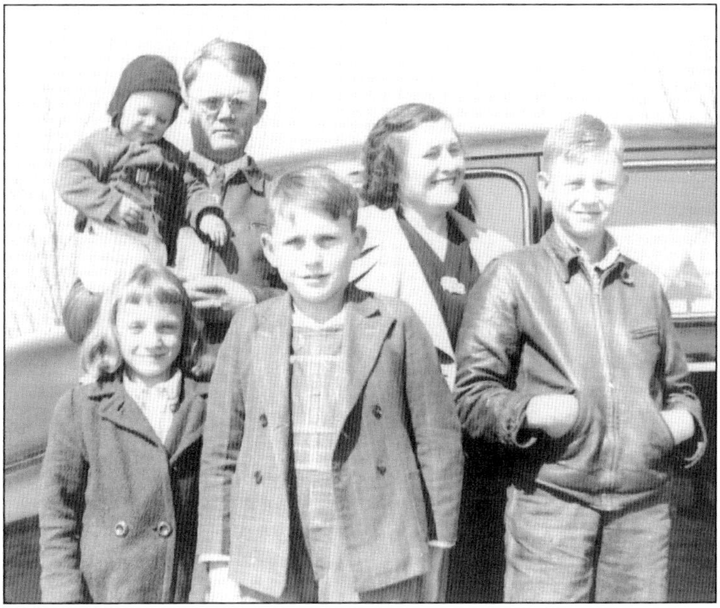

This is the Sidney Bird Jones family, shown around 1943. From left to right are (first row) Sarah Jones (later married to Edwin Bowen), Fred Jones, and Maloy Jones; (second row) Sidney Bird, holding his son Danny, and Audrey Maloy Jones, Sidney's wife. (Courtesy of Sarah Jones Bowen.)

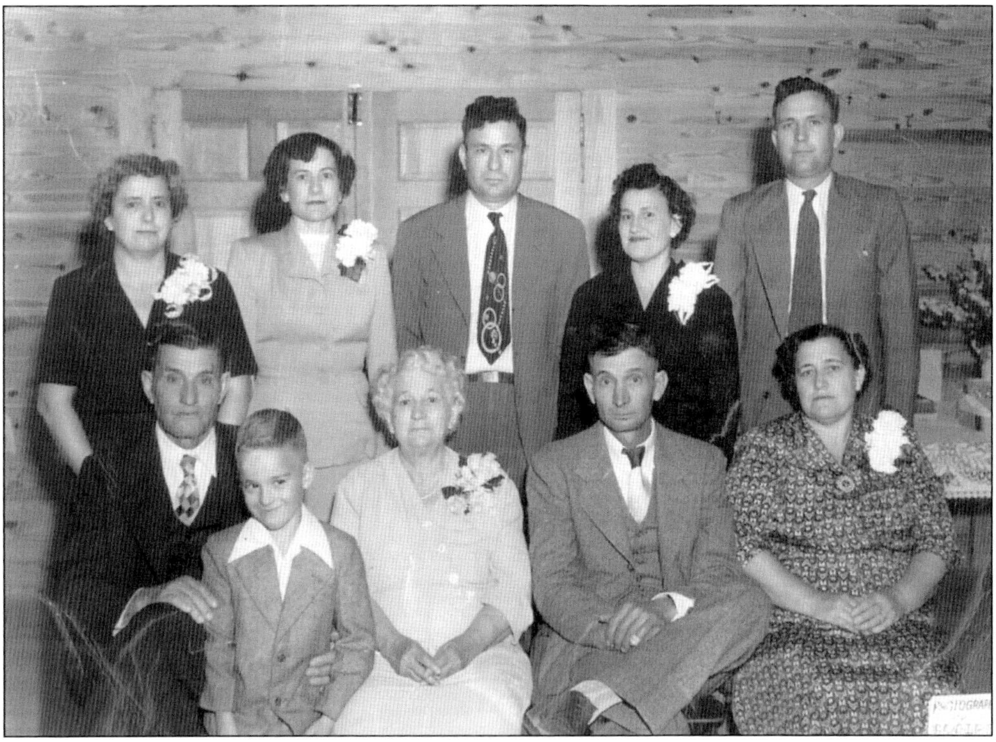

Shown around 1946 at a 50th wedding anniversary celebration is the Daniel H. Maloy family of the Sharon community of Telfair County. Pictured from left to right are (first row) Dan Maloy, Wayne Maloy, Fannie Williams Maloy, Jim Maloy, and Audrey M. Jones; (second row) Eliza M. Johnson, Beatrice M. Heath, Dan "Tuck" Maloy, Dorothy M. Ray, and Jack Maloy. (Courtesy of Sarah Jones Bowen.)

Married June 1, 1947, Marjorie and D.J. Burch moved to McRae in 1948. D.J. was the owner of the McRae Burial Vault Company for many years. He died in 1997. Marjorie served as director of the McRae Duplicate Bridge Club for 26 years. (Courtesy of Marjorie Lord Burch.)

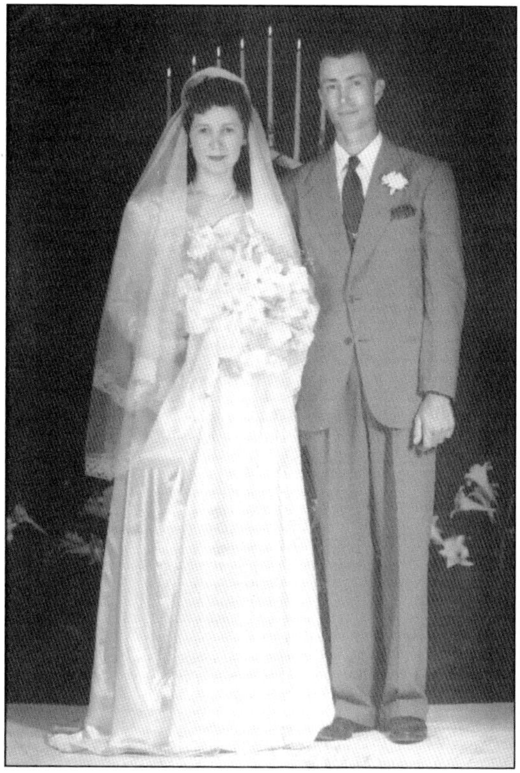

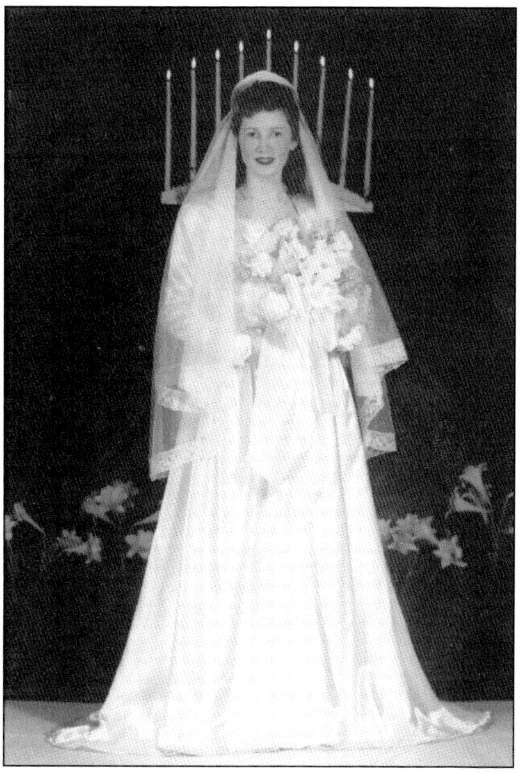

Marjorie Burch's wedding dress has had quite a history. Working as a first-year teacher at Montrose Elementary School in Montrose, Georgia, she made $100 a month. Marjorie remembers spending a month's wages for her lovely wedding dress. She said she bought the dress at Davison's Department Store in Macon for her wedding on June 1, 1947. Since her wedding, several others in her family have also worn the dress, including her sister-in-law Trudie Lord and Marjorie's youngest daughter, Ellen, who wore it as a bride in 1983. (Courtesy of Marjorie Lord Burch.)

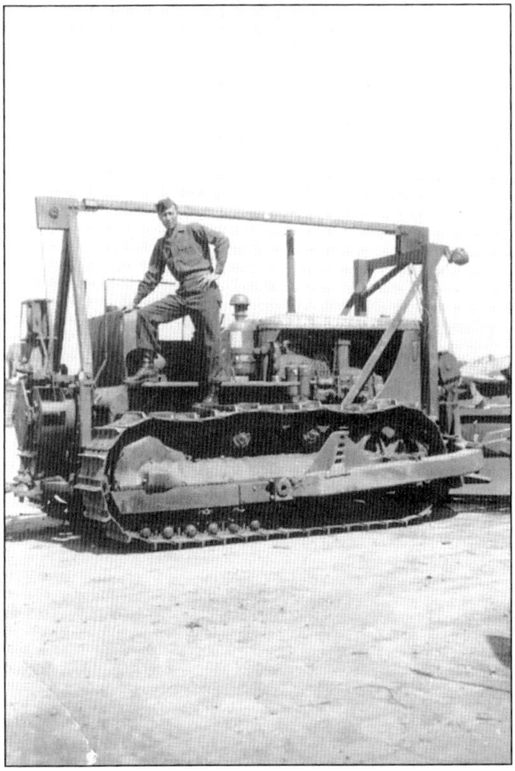

D.J. Burch is shown in 1945 standing on an Army tank in Germany. He belonged to the 832nd Battalion, which built many of the airstrips for Allied planes during World War II. (Courtesy of Marjorie Lord Burch.)

This is a photograph of Cpl. D.J. Burch (left) and fellow soldier Pfc. George Lacefield, made in England in 1943. Burch served in World War II for four years. According to his widow, Marjorie Burch, he left as a fun-loving young boy and returned a much different, more introspective man after his war experience. (Courtesy of Marjorie Lord Burch.)

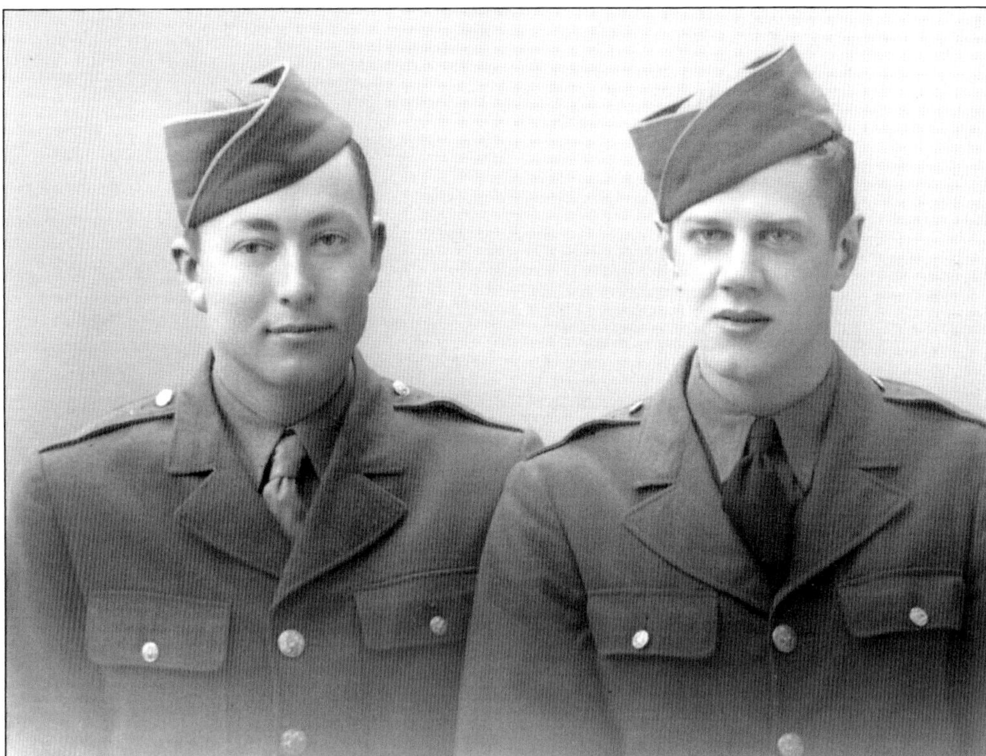

Jack McGinty, an accountant in McRae for many years, is wearing his World War II uniform. During the Battle of the Bulge, he lost all of his toes due to frostbite. After his discharge from the Army, he studied at the University of Georgia, where he served as treasurer of Pi Kappa Alpha fraternity and was nicknamed "Pinch Penny McGinty." In 1953, after passing the certified public accountant exam, he opened his own firm in McRae. (Courtesy of Melissa McGinty Carroll.)

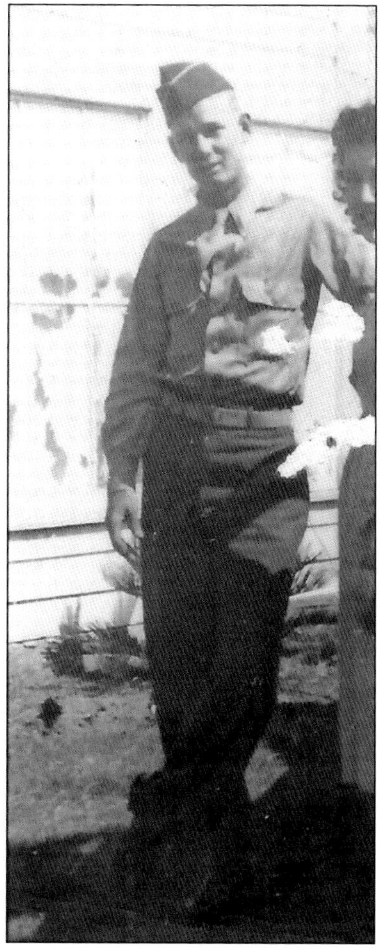

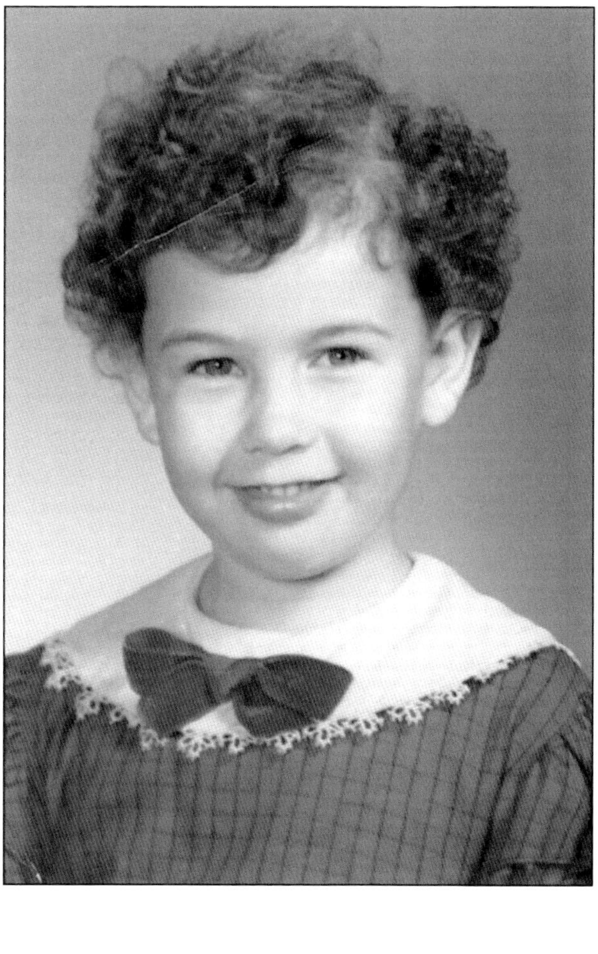

This is a first-grade photograph of Connie Burch LaFavor, dated 1959–1960. She attended grammar school in the building behind the only structure left (now called the Old South Georgia College building) of the college, which closed in 1928. (Courtesy of Marjorie Lord Burch.)

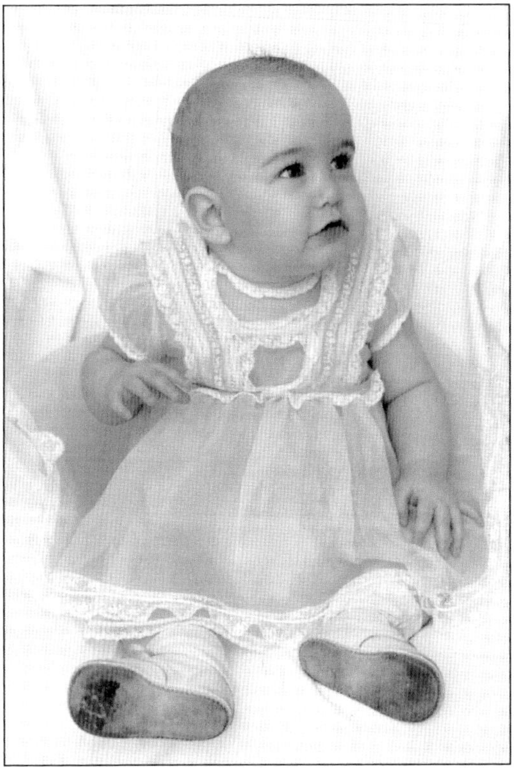

This precious baby is Connie Burch LaFavor, born on October 22, 1953. Her mother, Marjorie Burch, said she purchased the little blue dress from Davison's in Macon. The dress was used in photographs made of Marjorie's other two daughters when they were around the age of eight months. (Courtesy of Marjorie Lord Burch.)

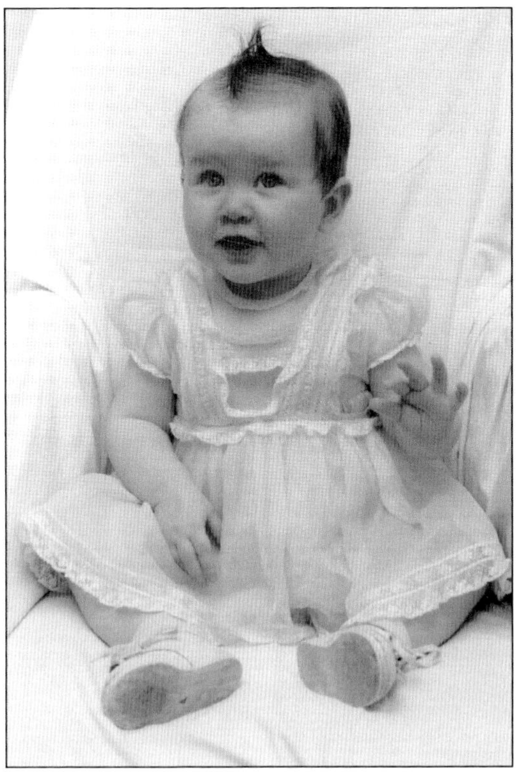

Another delightful baby in the same family is Christy Burch Stapleton, born on February 17, 1959. The same lovely little dress had been packed away for six years until the occasion of this baby's birth, and age, brought it out again. (Courtesy of Marjorie Lord Burch.)

The third and last daughter of Marjorie and D.J. Burch, Ellen Burch Burgess, made her entrance into the world on April 10, 1962. She, too, wore the same dress, which had been carefully kept for another three years until she was also photographed in it. (Courtesy of Marjorie Lord Burch.)

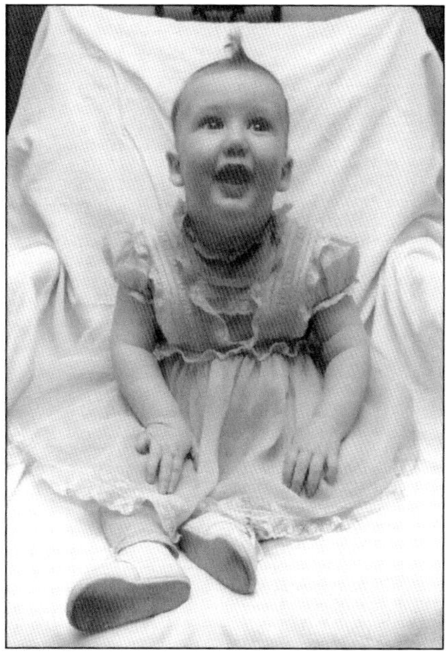

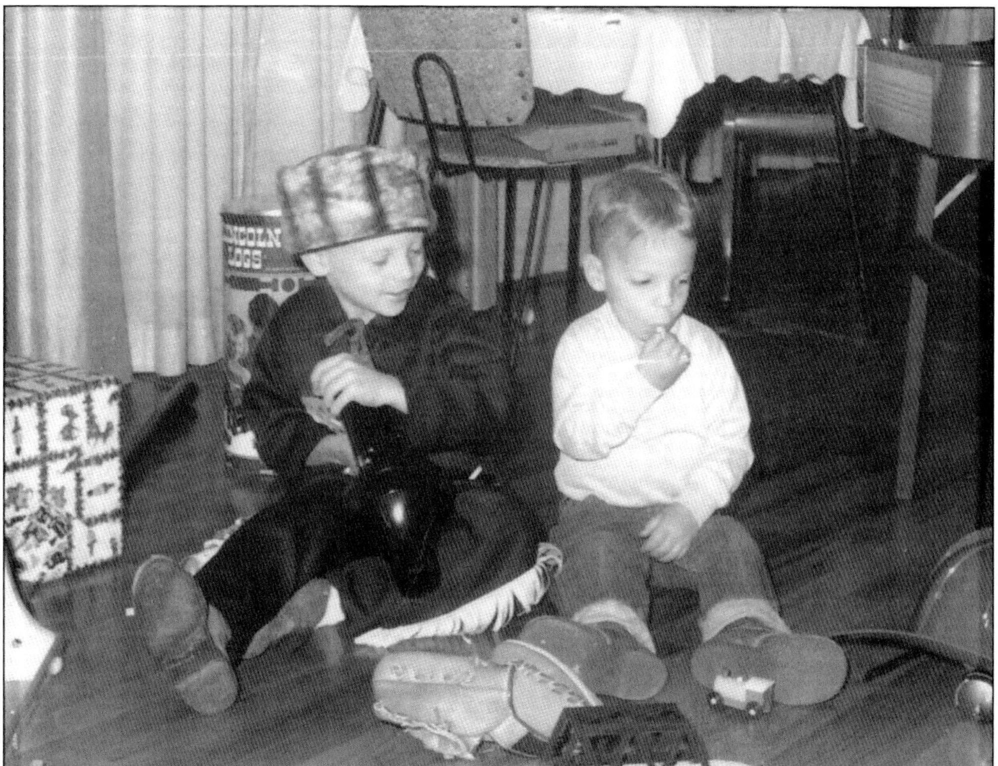


Santa had already come to the Bowen residence by the time this c. 1965 photograph was taken. Edwin (left) and Gary Bowen, sons of Edwin and Sarah Jones Bowen, are enjoying their Lincoln logs, baseball mitt, and what appears to be a train track laid out on the floor. (Courtesy of Sarah Jones Bowen.)

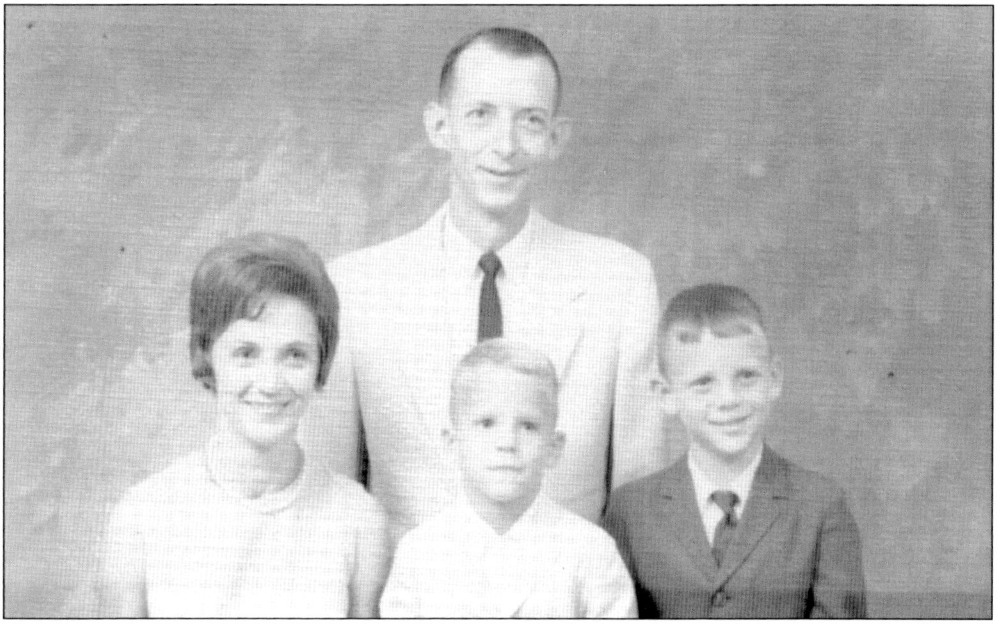

Edwin and Sarah Jones Bowen were publishers of the *Telfair Enterprise* for many years. They are shown with their two sons, Gary Bowen and Ed Bowen Jr., around 1967. (Courtesy of Sarah Jones Bowen.)

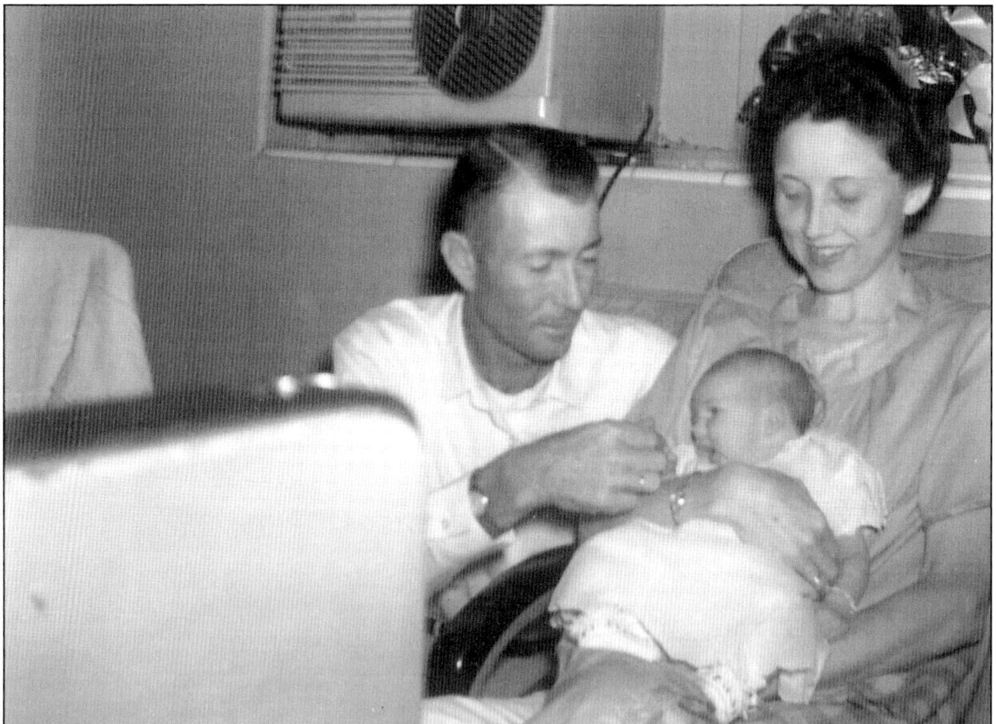

Happiness is written on the faces of D.J. and Marjorie Burch as they welcome their first-born daughter, Connie, into their family in 1953. This photograph was taken in the old Telfair County Hospital. (Courtesy of Marjorie Lord Burch.)

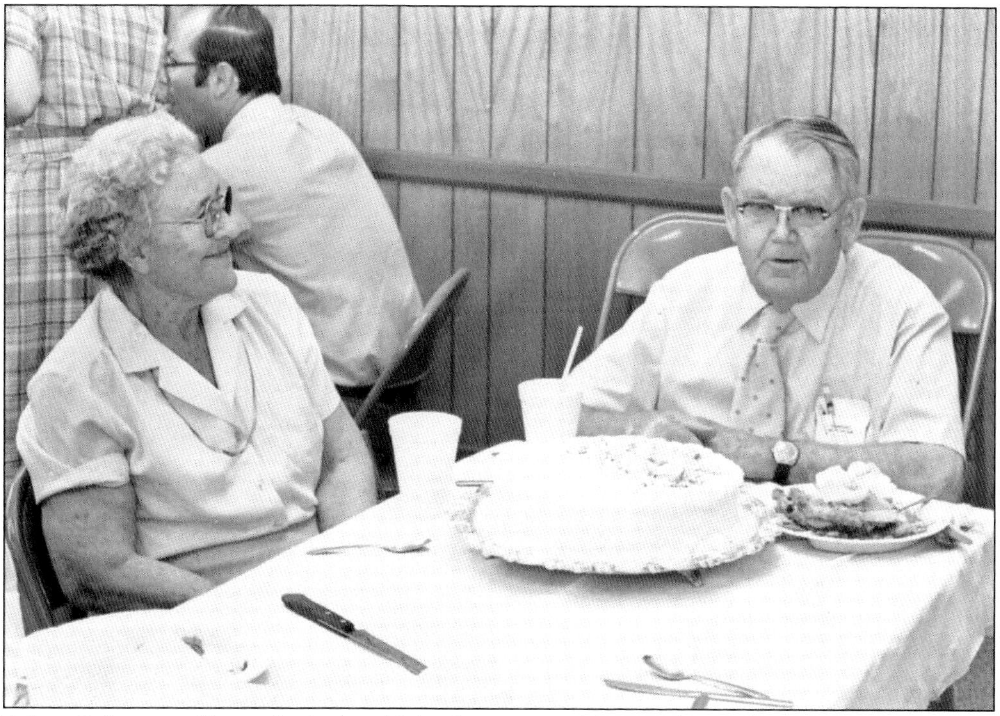

Sidney B. Jones and his wife, Audrey Maloy Jones, are celebrating his 80th birthday in September 1962. (Courtesy of Sarah Jones Bowen.)

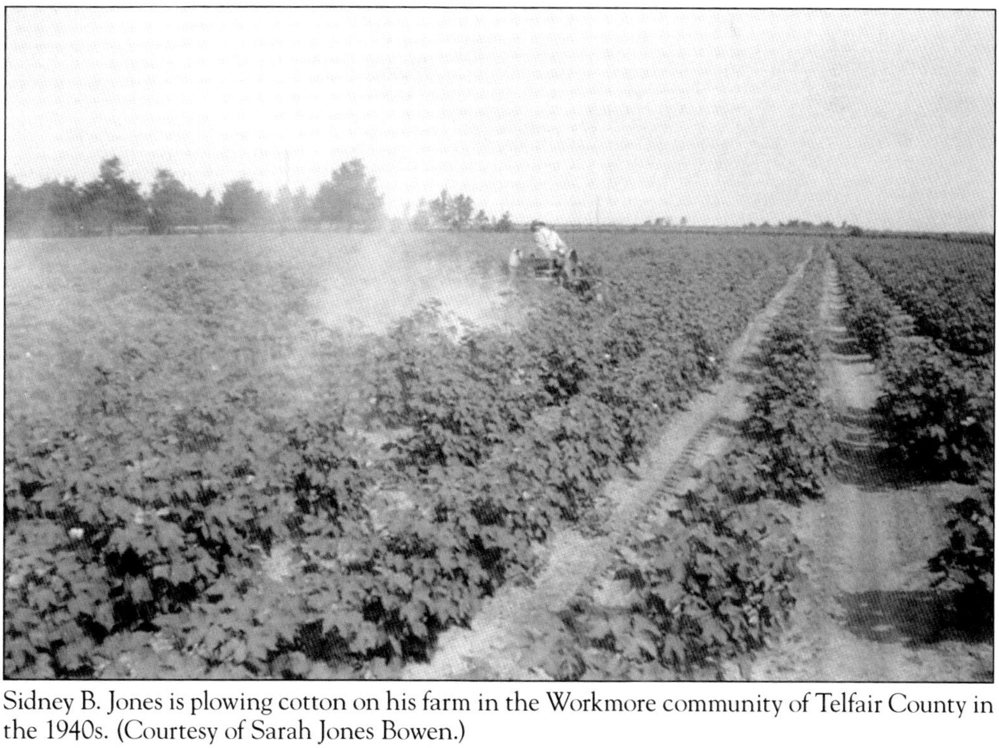

Sidney B. Jones is plowing cotton on his farm in the Workmore community of Telfair County in the 1940s. (Courtesy of Sarah Jones Bowen.)

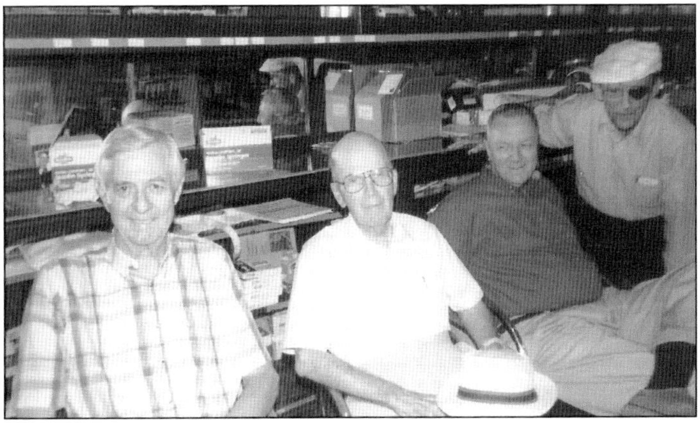

Outstanding businessmen gather at Ryals Drug Store in McRae. Pictured here from left to right are Jack Walker (former sheriff of Telfair County), Chester Ryals (owner of Ryals Drug Store), Lec Ryals (local businessman), and Bob Smith (co-owner of Telfair Loan Company). (Courtesy of Dr. Mickey Nelson.)

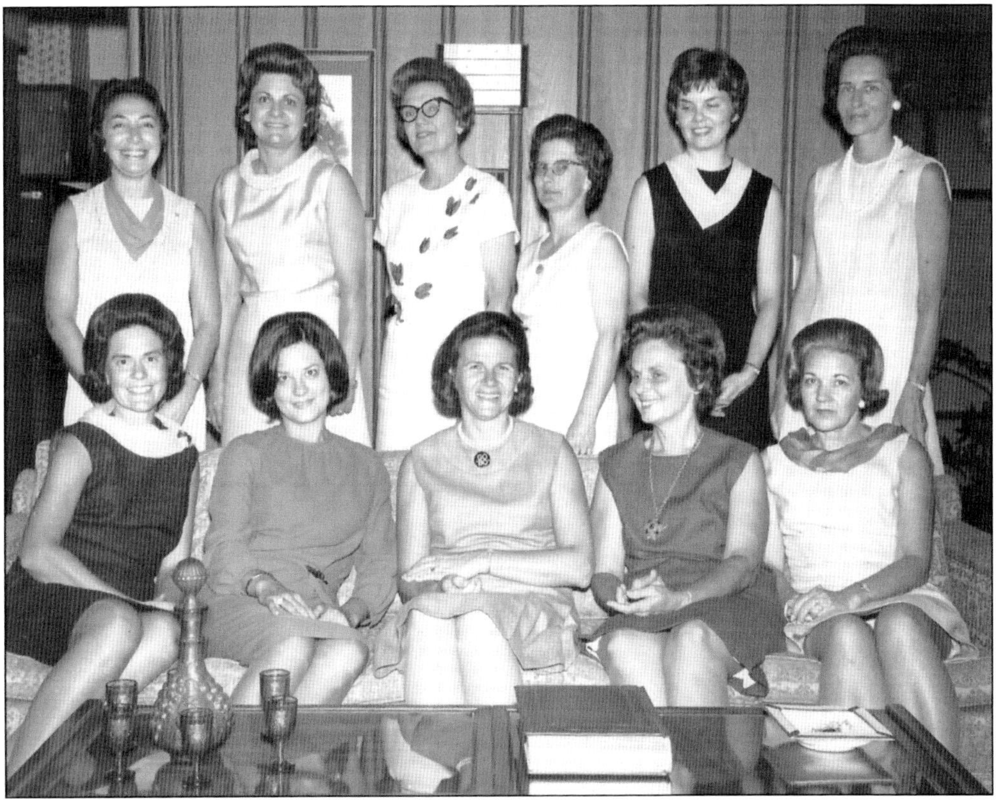

McRae voters were encouraged to back Howard "Bo" Callaway for governor of Georgia in 1966. Callaway had to petition in order to be placed on the ballot, and he eventually lost the gubernatorial race to Lester Maddox; however, Callaway received support from groups such as the Women for Bo Callaway. The members pictured here are, from left to right, (first row) Ruth Mizell, Beverly Warnock, Beth Callaway (Bo's wife), Louise McRae, and Bobbie Smith; (second row) Lee Ague (Callaway campaign worker), Sue Bell, Margaret Callahan, Lutrelle Fussell, Jane Walker, and Janiece McRae. All who were Telfair residents are now deceased except for Beverly Warnock, Bobbie Smith, and Jane Walker. The photograph was taken in the home of Dr. Bill and Louise McRae. (Courtesy of Chris McRae.)

Dr. Billy McRae Jr. followed in the footsteps of his father, Dr. Bill McRae Sr., as owner and operator of McRae's Pharmacy. In 1964, Dr. McRae Jr. moved the location of the pharmacy from the corner of Oak Street and Second Avenue to a larger store building farther south on Oak Street. (Courtesy of Dr. Mickey Nelson.)

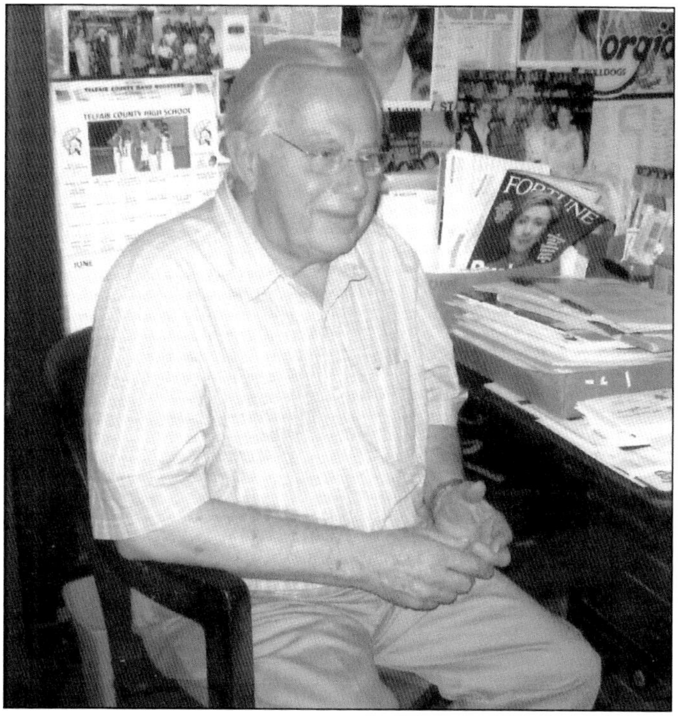

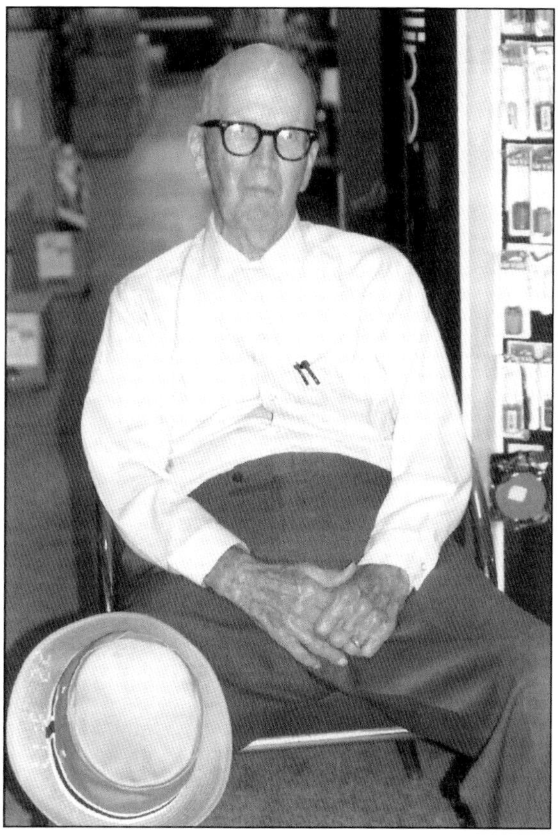

After graduating from the University of Georgia, Chester A. Ryals Jr. worked for his father in the insurance business. He remained in this business until he sold it to Henry Walker in 1977. Chester was a director of the First Federal Savings and Loan Association, becoming president in 1975, and a director of Merchants and Citizens Bank. He was a charter member of the McRae Rotary Club, which was created in 1941. During the 1930s, he was superintendent of Little Ocmulgee State Park construction by the CCC camp of McRae. (Courtesy of Dr. Mickey Nelson.)

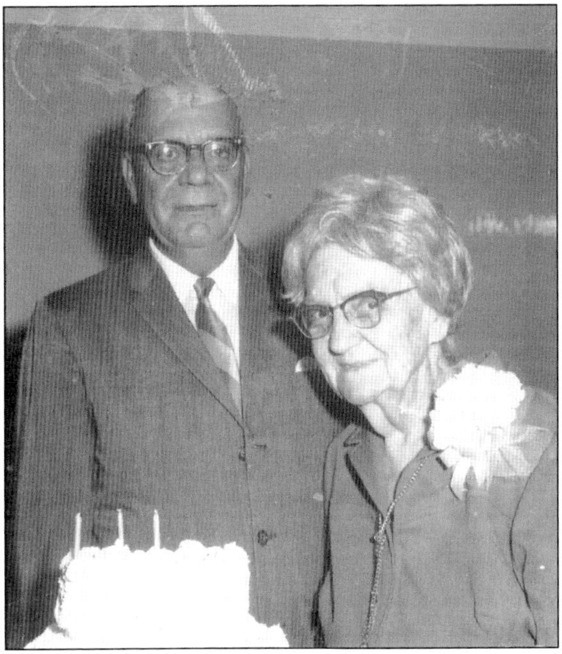

Bessie Oliver retired to McRae after serving as a Methodist missionary to Korea and Japan from 1912 to 1957. When she left the mission field, Oliver came to McRae and lived with her sister Mrs. Minnie Lee Johnson. Oliver is shown with Rev. J.W. Herndon, pastor of the McRae United Methodist Church, as she celebrated her birthday. (Courtesy of the McRae United Methodist Church History Committee.)

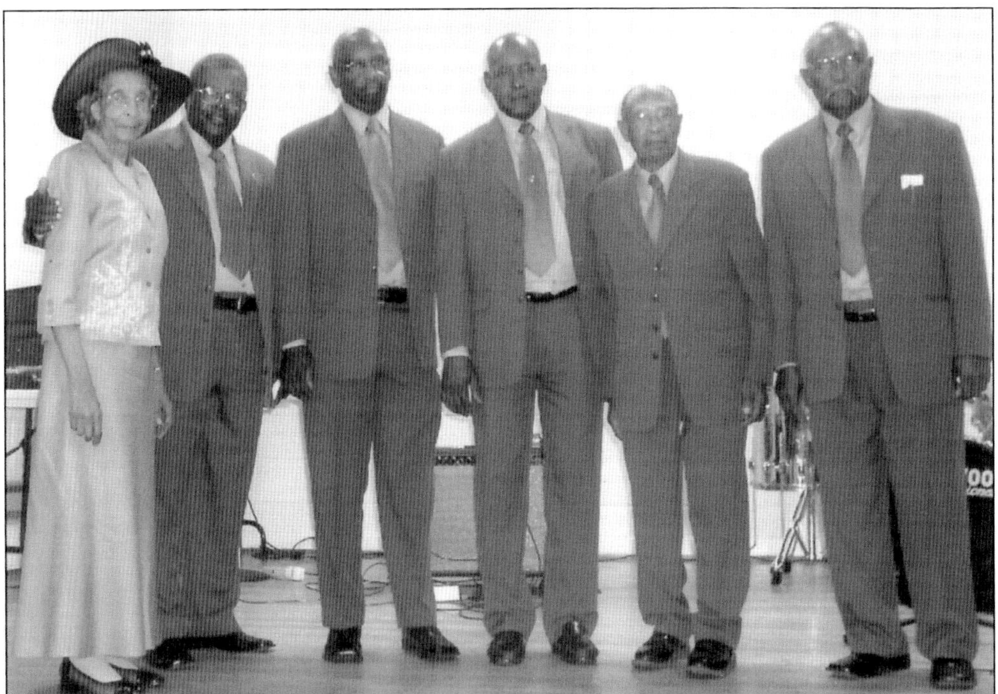

Originally named the Royal Travelers, this group was first introduced at Rock Hill C.M.E. Church in Jacksonville, Georgia. Eventually, the group was renamed the Five Stars of Harmony. The group sang in many area churches and as far away as Pennsylvania, Maryland, and Washington, DC, and they were featured on the local radio station. The Five Stars of Harmony was one of the first groups to perform live on the station, and they continue to do so today. (Courtesy of Ruby Maloy White.)

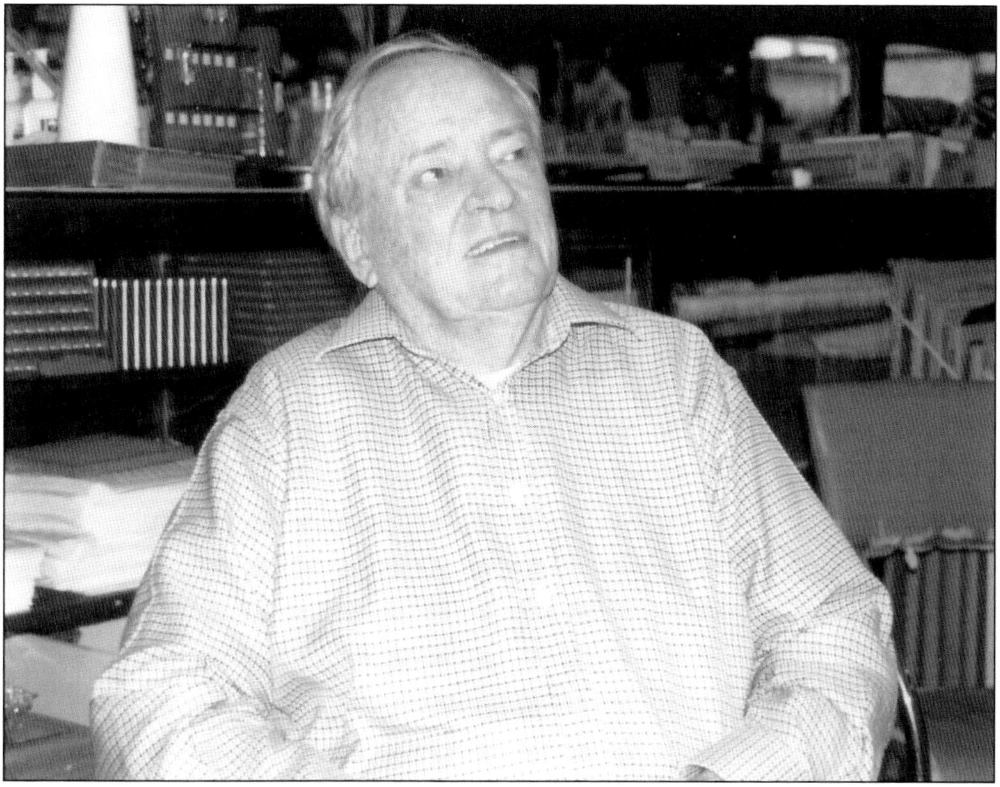

Alex P. Smith (above) and Robert "Bob" Smith (below) were the proprietors of the Alex P. Smith Company in McRae. They were the sons of Alex Smith Sr., who founded the company on the main street in McRae. The company was a loan and insurance company. (Courtesy of Dr. Mickey Nelson.)

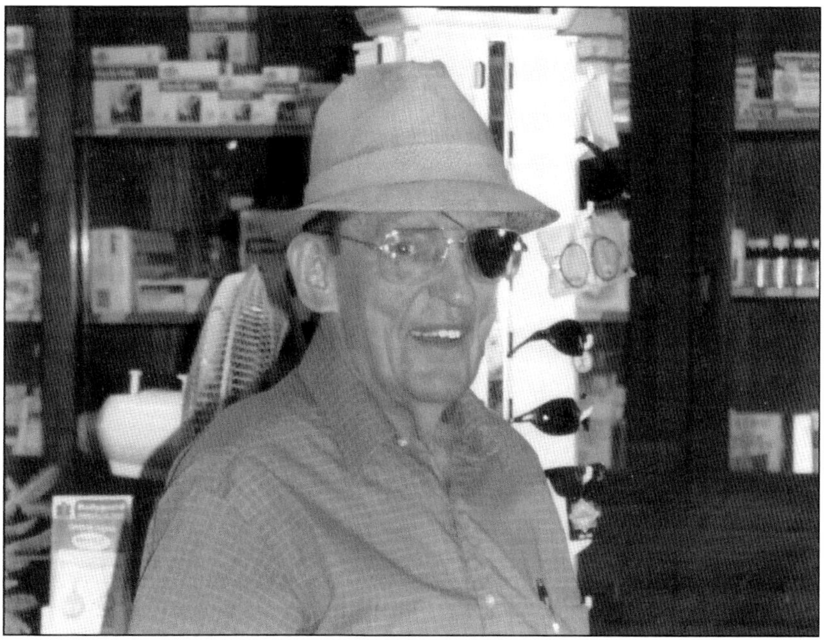

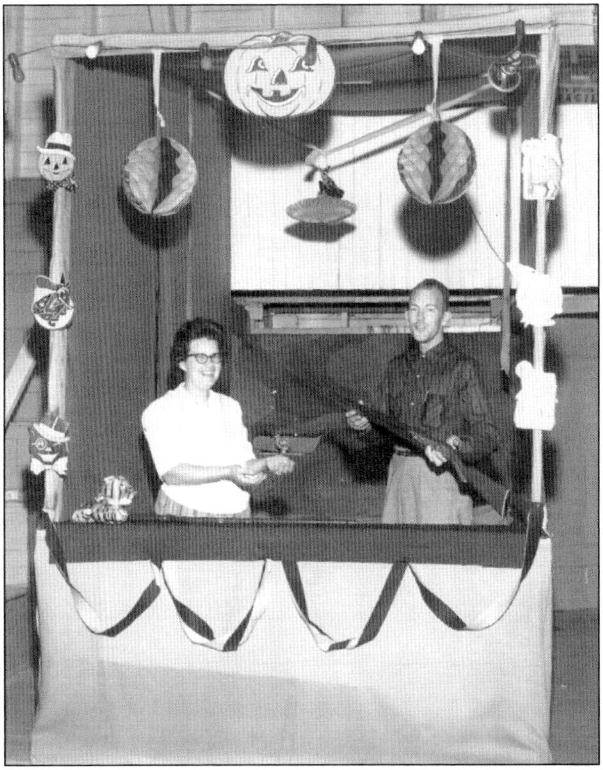

Telfair County is a place where many activities occurred, several of which revolved around the public schools. At these carnivals, parents manned booths, such as the one pictured, for the enjoyment of both parents and students. Marjory and Wade Harbin Jr. encourage those present to test their shooting skills at the shooting range at the McRae-Helena Elementary School carnival in the early 1960s. (Courtesy of Norwood Davidson.)

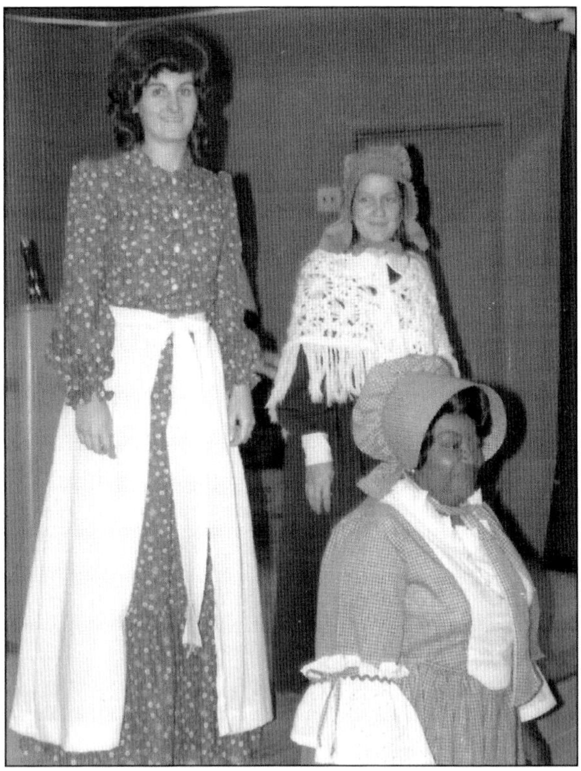

Joining with communities all over the United States, Telfair County celebrated the 200th birthday of the nation. Workmore Elementary School, located in the geographic center of the county, did its part. Faculty and staff dressed in period costumes to celebrate the event. Ella Mae Norwood (right foreground), Sue Harrell (back left), and Janice Strom model their dresses as the school helped celebrate the bicentennial. (Courtesy of Robert Herndon.)

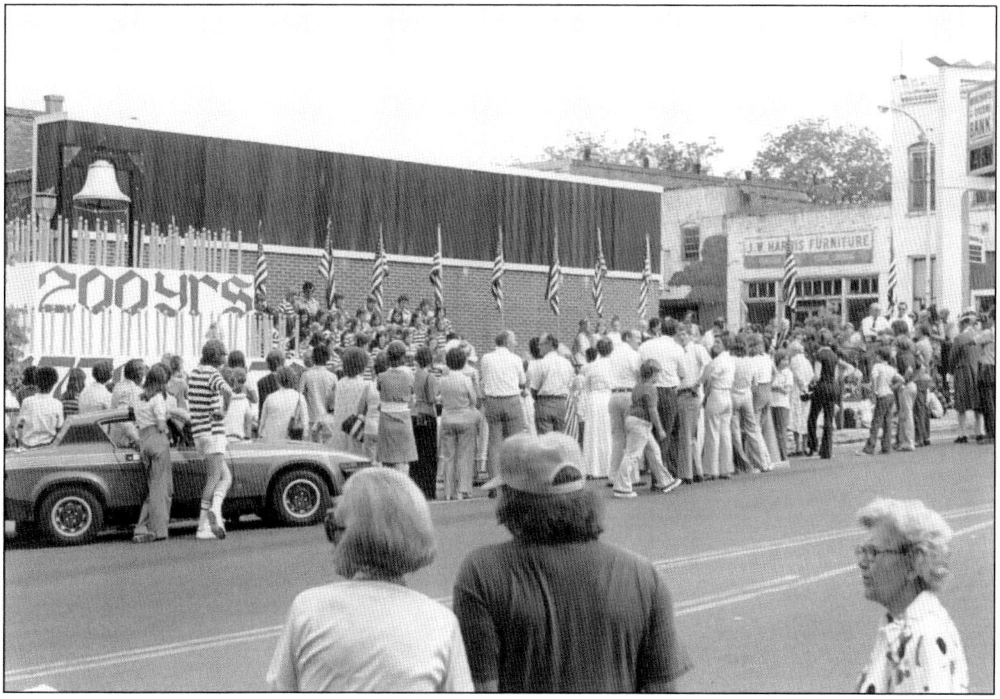


Communities all over the nation celebrated the bicentennial of the United States in 1976, and Telfair County was no exception. The celebration brought all Telfair County together for a big parade held in McRae. It featured floats and bands, and the celebration was enjoyed by all. (Courtesy of Robert Herndon.)

In 1983, noted Southern author and former Telfair County resident Brainard Cheney greets admirers at McRae's Landing in Lumber City to celebrate the river-rafting history of the area. Cheney was born in Fitzgerald but moved to Lumber City when he was six years old. He taught school in Scotland, Georgia, during his early life. He is shown reminiscing with a former student, Emily Flanders Nairn. Cheney wrote the noted Ocmulgee rafting tome *Lightwood*. (Courtesy of Norwood Davidson.)

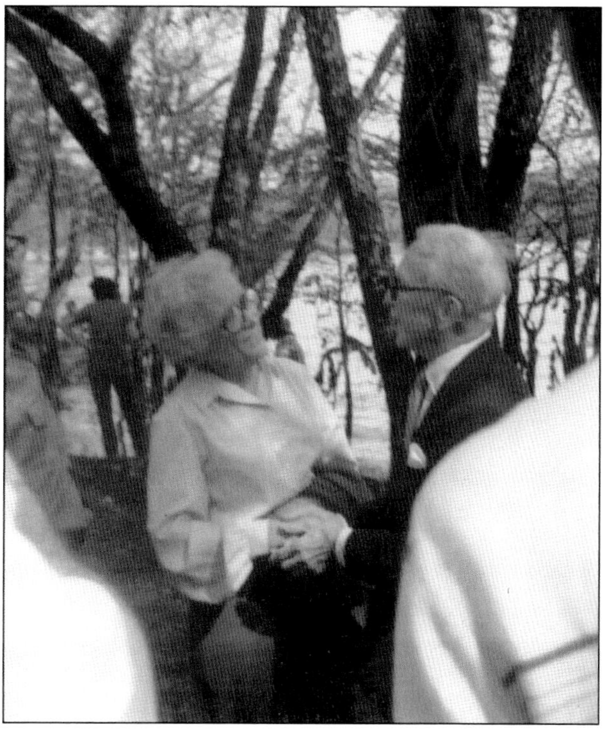

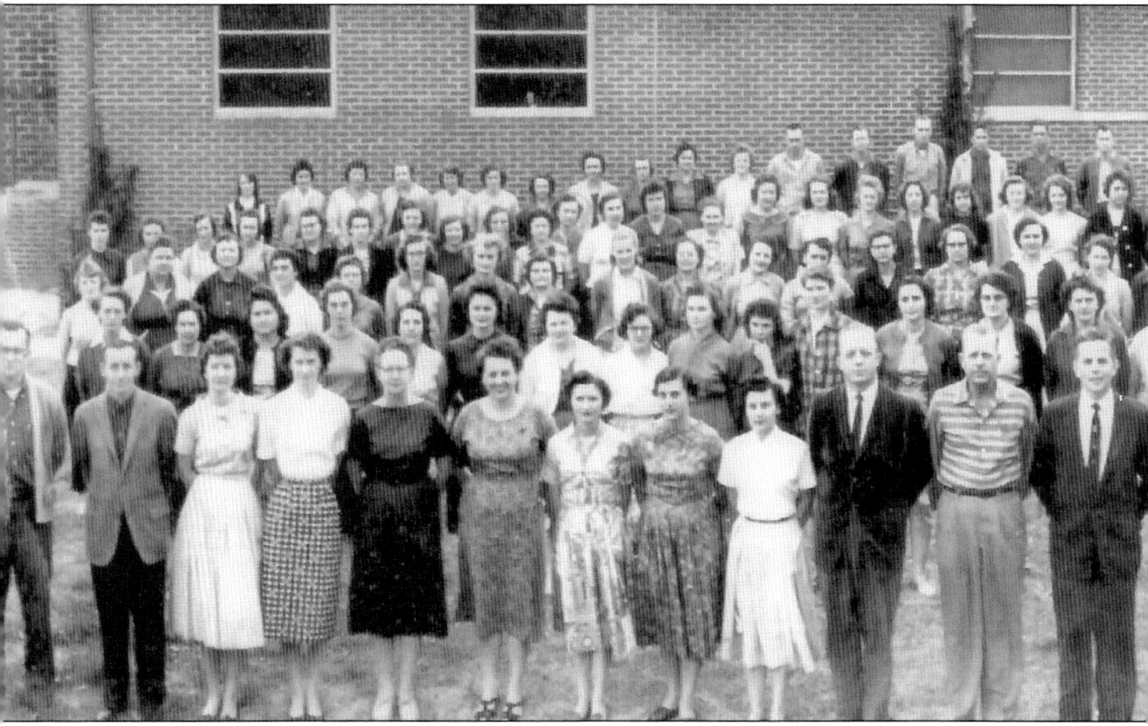

Roydon Wear in McRae, once the largest employer in the county, was located on South Oak Street in McRae. The company was a textile manufacturing company. Dave Billing, in the suit to the left to the man with the striped shirt, was the manager of the plant. Roydon Wear closed

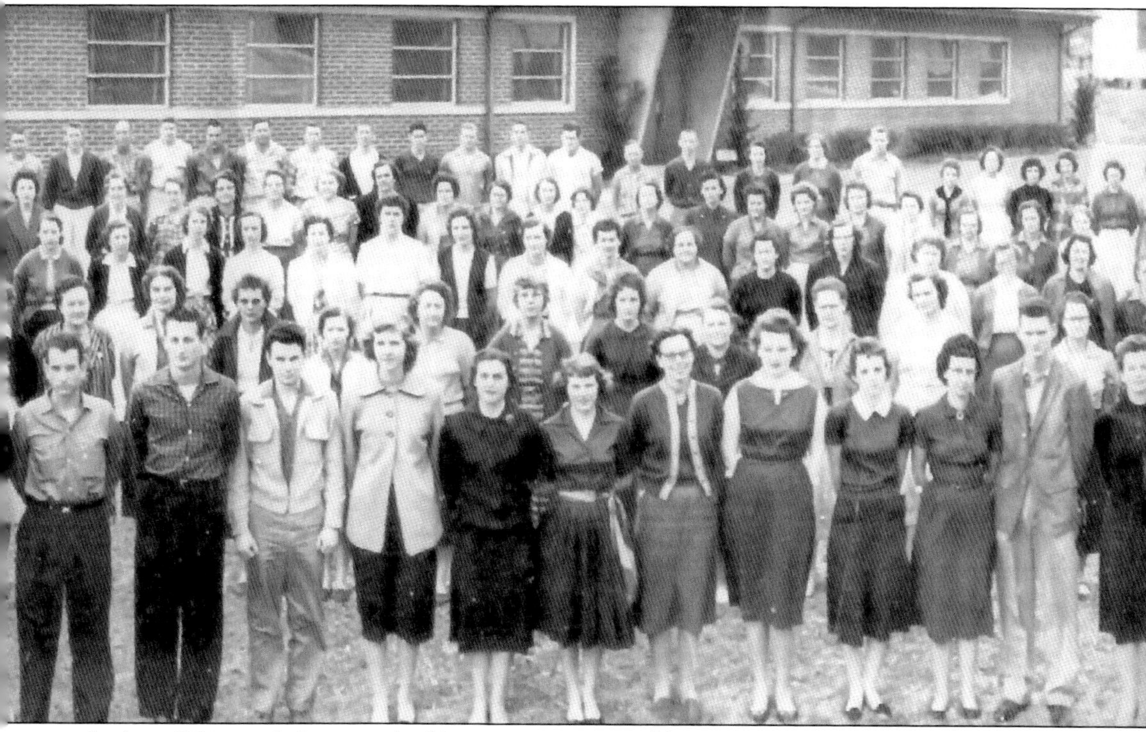

in the late 1990s, and the main building is now occupied by McRae Marketplace Antiques & Flea Market. (Courtesy of Donnie Swanson.)

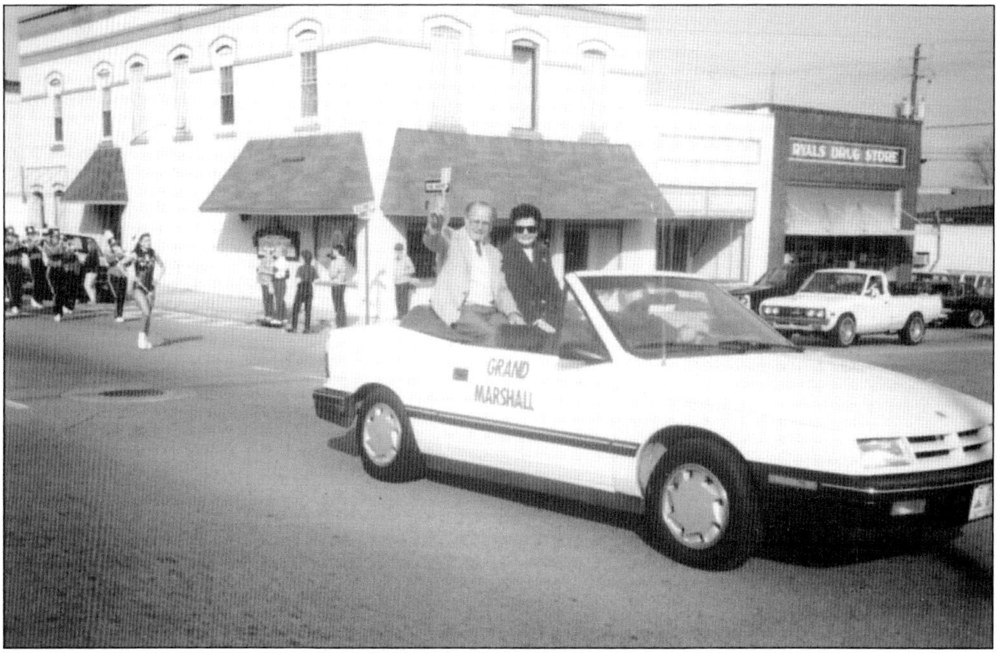


D.Q. Harris and Eunice Harris are riding in the Christmas Parade in 1994. D.Q. was chosen by the Telfair County Chamber of Commerce to lead the parade. (Courtesy of Eunice Calhoun Harris.)

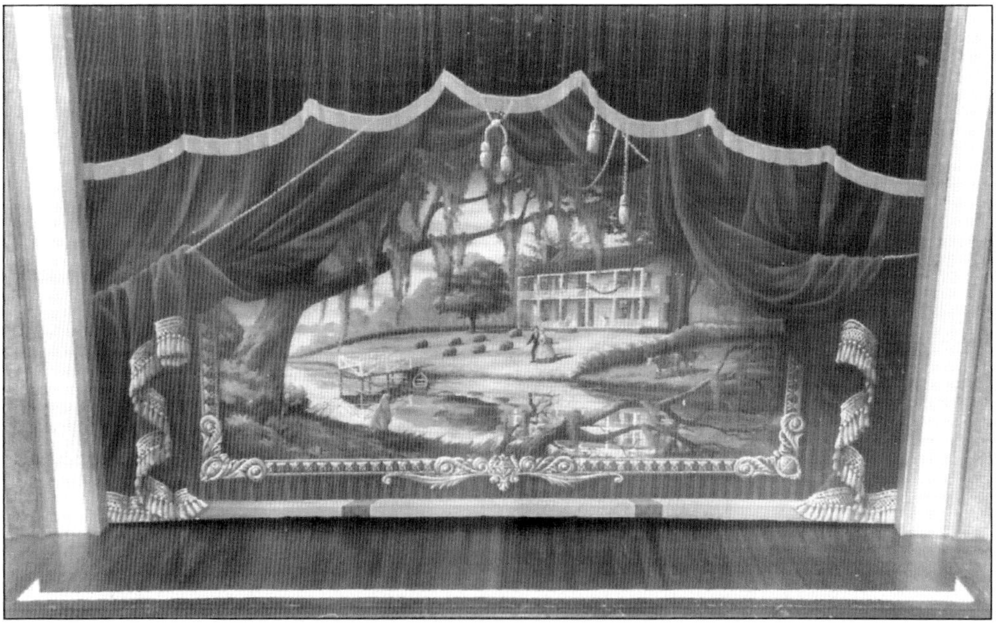

The memorial dedication and unveiling of the new drop curtain in the auditorium of the Old South Georgia College building in McRae occurred on March 2, 1985. The curtain was given to the community by Necia Cotter in memory of her beloved husband, William Edward Cotter. She commissioned Dr. W. Joseph Stell, professor at the University of Georgia, to design and paint the curtain. Though nearly 30 years old, the curtain is still breathtaking in its beauty. McRae mayor Chester Ryals Jr. accepted the gift on behalf of the community. The University of Georgia Show Dawgs closed the evening with a concert. (Courtesy of Jane Walker.)

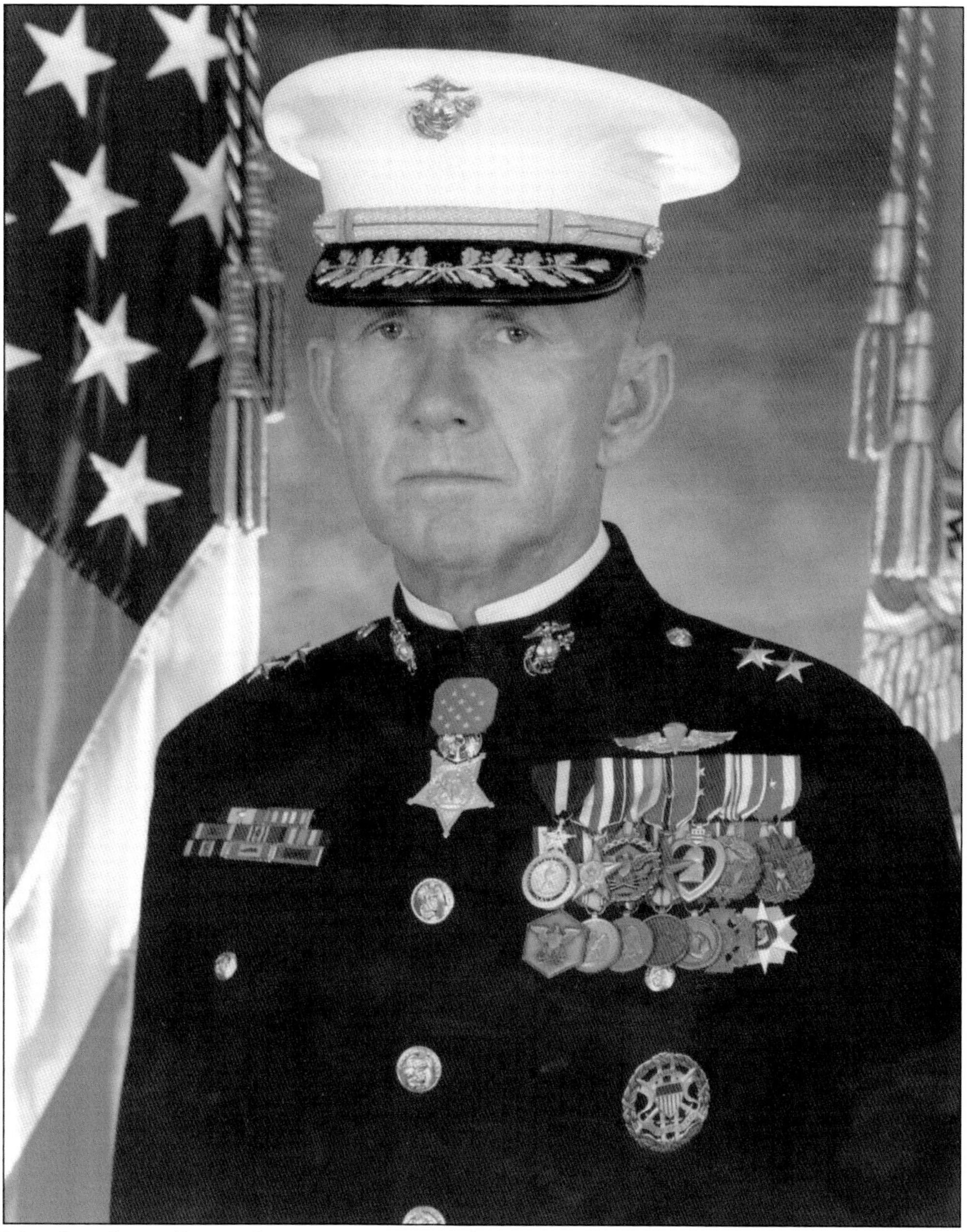

Maj. Gen. James Everett Livingston is a retired US Marine Corps general. He was awarded the United States' highest military decoration, the Medal of Honor, for heroic actions in 1968 during the Vietnam War. Livingston was born in Towns, Georgia, and graduated from Lumber City High School. In the lengthy tribute to Livingston, he was cited "for conspicuous gallantry and intrepidity at the risk of his life above and beyond the call of duty." In retirement, Livingston is serving on the board of trustees of the National World War II Museum. (Courtesy of the Telfair County Library.)

Consistent with our mission to preserve history on a local level, this book was printed in South Carolina on American-made paper and manufactured entirely in the United States. Products carrying the accredited Forest Stewardship Council (FSC) label are printed on 100 percent FSC-certified paper.

MADE IN THE USA